The
Organized
Parent

365 Simple Solutions to Managing Your Home, Your Time, and Your Family's Life

Christina Baglivi Tinglof

Contemporary Books

Chicago   New York   San Francisco   Lisbon   London   Madrid   Mexico City
Milan   New Delhi   San Juan   Seoul   Singapore   Sydney   Toronto

Library of Congress Cataloging-in-Publication Data

Tinglof, Christina Baglivi.
    The organized parent : 365 simple solutions to managing your home, your time, and your family's life / Christina Baglivi Tinglof.
        p.   cm.
    Includes index.
    ISBN 0-07-138099-X
    1. Parents—Life skills guides.   2. Time management.   3. Organization.
4. Home economics.   5. Family—Time management.   I. Title: 365 simple
solutions to managing your home, your time, and your family's life.   II. Title.

HQ755.8 .T568   2002
646.7'0085—dc21   2002073318

Contemporary Books

A Division of The **McGraw·Hill** Companies

3 4 5 6 7 8 9 0   DOC/DOC   1 0 9 8 7 6 5 4 3 2

ISBN 0-07-138099-X

Interior illustrations and back-cover photograph by Kevin Tinglof

McGraw-Hill books are available at special quantity discounts to use as premiums and sales promotions, or for use in corporate training programs. For more information, please write to the Director of Special Sales, Professional Publishing, McGraw-Hill, Two Penn Plaza, New York, NY 10121-2298. Or contact your local bookstore.

This book is printed on acid-free paper.

To Gina Ferrara Bates
A best friend since the third grade.
(You're more organized than you think!)

Contents

Acknowledgments

Although this book was great fun to research and write, it wouldn't have been possible without the help and support of many people. Thanks to my agent Betsy Amster for her helpful guidance and to my editor at Contemporary Books, Judith McCarthy, for believing in this project and making it happen. To my husband, Kevin, for creating the illustrations, often from my obscure directions! And finally, I'd like to thank all the busy parents who graciously gave their time to be interviewed.

Introduction

Today's busy parents have to be organized or perish under the mounting piles of sweat socks that make it out of the clothes dryer but never into the dresser drawers, the school permission slips that always seem to disappear, or the morning chaos when everyone is frantically looking for "something" while trying to head out the door. Yet who has time to read lengthy how-to books on combating the pack-rat syndrome or America's bout of "affluenza"? Other time management and organizing books offer some comfort but often in the way of convoluted solutions to basic problems. "Create a cleaning roster" sounds like a great idea, but it's not practical for active parents. We need quick, effective solutions to manage our hectic lives so that we actually have time to hang out on the front porch reading with our children or build that fort together.

The Organized Parent: 365 Simple Solutions to Managing Your Home, Your Time, and Your Family's Life shows you how to stop feeling guilty about all that needs to be done by taking control of your day-to-day environment so you can actually have time to share in your kids' lives.

Are People Born Organized?

Although I'm much busier now than I was B.K. (before kids), I'm more organized and more productive than I've ever been in my life. I have a house that needs constant attention (we've been renovating it on and off for more than two years), a husband, three boys (six-year-old twins and a three-and-a-half-year-old whiner), and two careers (freelance writer and part-time ESL—English as a second language—teacher), yet I still make time every day to take an hour-long nap.

I laugh when I think back to my carefree twenties (everyone does) when I was just starting out as a struggling freelance writer, bartending at night to earn money. I had an enormous amount of time during the day, but instead of pounding away at my typewriter, I was consumed with writer's angst, moping and lamenting, "Oh, *why* can't I be a writer?" Consequently, I took months to write a 1,000-word article (these days it takes me a week). Now, as a woman rapidly ascending into her forties, I've finally learned how to prioritize tasks, simplify my life, and let go of useless clutter. (Well, not all the clutter—the garage is a constant battle, but we're working on it.) But it's taken me awhile to get there—I'm always reevaluating my methods, asking others how they do things, or thinking of new ways on my own to accomplish a goal or organize a shelf more efficiently. It's been a gradual process but an important one to my family and me.

All this brings me to an important question that my closest friend, the inspiration for this book and to whom it's dedicated, Gina Ferrara Bates, proposed to me. Are people born organized or is it something that is learned? Interesting question. I opted for the latter explanation, claiming that we take our cues from our parents as young children and then observe and often adopt the ways of our friends and roommates, our environment, and, ultimately, our mates.

Surely a person can learn to be organized—the military teaches it all the time. (I remember a guy from college who kept a fastidious kitchen, mopping the floor every evening after dinner. He blamed his time in the Marine Corps for his somewhat unorthodox behavior.) And what about kindergarteners? Have you ever walked into their classroom at the end of the day? They're not sitting on the floor watching TV and eating popcorn while their teacher puts toys and books away. On the contrary, these little kids are busy returning puzzles and art equipment to their proper homes. It's expected of them and they happily comply. (It's only when they get home that a parent takes over—doing everything for them, expecting little compliance in return.)

Yet for many parents, no matter how much they crave order in their lives, it eludes them. My friend Gina is a perfect case in point. She claims that she'll never be organized because it's just not in her nature. She struggles on a daily basis to get everything done, from doing the laundry to paying the bills. But to me, a best friend who has known her since the third grade (and roomed with her for more than six years when we were single), she is organized and gets an enormous amount done each day, especially considering the agenda she keeps. The reason she feels disorganized and overwhelmed, in my opinion, is that she constantly overschedules herself and her family (a common phenomenon in the twenty-first century).

Gina is (and always has been) a joiner, a can-do woman. Last told, she's active in more than three organizations, including La Leche League (which meets once a month) and KIVA (a dance group that practices twice a week in preparation for a yearly show). She also volunteers at her daughters' (she has two) school once a week, is active in her church, and dutifully takes care of an elderly neighbor by driving her to her weekly hair appointment and taking her trash to the dump every Monday morning. Oh, and did I mention that Gina works thirty hours a week as a dance movement therapist (and has a part-time job as a dance instructor in exchange for dancing lessons for her daughters)? And although there is certainly a prime spot in heaven for this mother, it's no wonder she's overwhelmed. Just writing this makes me tired.

How to Use This Book

You're a parent who needs a bit of direction. Your home is out of control or maybe just a bit misguided. You need sound advice on how to get on the right track. That linen closet is begging for attention, and you don't even want to think about the basement. And you want to get something done right now, but you don't know where to start. Fine. Let's go.

The Organized Parent contains nineteen management sections arranged alphabetically so that when a specific problem strikes, you can quickly find a solution. (Need more cabinet space in the kitchen? Turn to the "Kitchen" chapter for help. Want some advice on reorganizing your child's closet? Turn to "Children's Bedrooms." See how easy that is?)

Most chapters begin with **Key Organizing Tips**, general ideas to think about *before* tackling a major organizing problem (for instance, "Never leave a room empty-handed" is a tip for "Housecleaning"). Next, I offer specific solutions to each chapter's many topics. And because one resolution doesn't fit every family or every situation, they're varied and plentiful and broken up into two categories: a **Quick Fix**—something that you can accomplish right now with a minimum amount of effort or money or both but offers an immediate sense of gratification (such as putting your child's puzzles in resealable plastic bags—one puzzle per bag); or a **Major Tune-Up**—an idea that takes a bit more time or a bit more cash or both but has a long-range payoff (like finding additional space for your child's growing Harry Potter book collection by breaking through the existing drywall and recessing a tall, narrow bookshelf between the wall studs).

This double format—**Quick Fix** and **Major Tune-Up**—allows you the freedom to make changes either gradually or radically, depending on your time or current family situation. Although you'd love to redo your entire linen closet, the prospect of emptying its contents at this point in time may be too onerous, yet weeding out a few old, torn towels seems doable. You'll work on evaluating your sheets next week. And who knows? Maybe next month you'll be ready for that major tune-up.

Look for **Style Tips** throughout the book, too, when searching for functional yet tasteful design ideas, because even busy parents deserve to live in a home with a little panache and elegance. If your kitchen is low on drawer space, for instance, try moving the eating and cooking utensils to the countertops by placing them in old crockery, decorative baskets, or even painted terra-cotta flowerpots—anything striking that works with the theme of your kitchen.

Next, **Time-Savers** offer you a chance to cut down on the amount of steps it normally takes to complete a task. When it comes to changing the sheets on your bed, for instance, why not wash and dry the sheets that are already on the bed and then remake it? No folding laundry or having to put the clean set away in the linen closet. The same trick also works well with bathroom towels. (Don't worry about wearing out your linens too quickly—you'd be surprised at how long good-quality sheets and towels last.)

Real parents get a say throughout the book, too, by sharing their tales of woe or organizational enlightenment. For example, a working mother from Connecticut gave two thumbs-up for menu planning, a true time-saver. "Meals are always a challenge because we're vegetarians," she explains. "Most families can throw a piece of meat on the grill, fix a salad, and they're done. Our choices are more limited. By sitting down with the kids and planning two weeks' worth of meals, I can shop more efficiently, and when I come home at night, I don't stare at the stove and wonder what to fix."

The Beginning of an Organized Life

You're revved up and ready to go. Great. But before you break open your closets and dresser drawers, take some time to consider your family's lifestyle and schedule and how they impact all your lives. Become an efficiency expert by following yourself—figuratively, of course—for a few days, noting trouble spots in your daily routine (maybe dinnertime is stressful—you never know what to fix or your pantry isn't set up in the most efficient manner) on a pad of paper. When you have a clearer impression of where your day-to-day system breaks down, you'll have an easier time making positive changes.

Learning to Say No

To me, one of the most important steps to having a more organized life is learning to say no. Although it's important and valuable to participate in your child's school or volunteer at your church, you need to limit yourself and your family's time.

Prioritize everything, from social engagements to civic obligations. You may say to your young children, for instance, that they're only allowed to attend five birthday parties per year (or three, or one). Conversely, when their birthdays roll around, limit the number of guests they can invite. Soccer practice, tennis lessons, dance class, Little League—the list of after-school activities is endless. And if you have a household of kids, you often feel more like a taxi driver than a parent. Once again, sit with the kids and together set a limit. Say, for instance, that at the beginning of each school year, each child can pick one or two activities. Most likely, your kids will thank you. The pressure is off. They're now free to hang out in a tree in the backyard and contemplate life or play softball in the street with the other neighborhood kids.

Setting limits doesn't mean you need to sequester yourself inside your home. On the contrary—saying no opens up your life to a whole new world of possibilities. You now have free time to do exactly what you want to do—go to the beach together or hang out in front of the fireplace and play a board game.

It's Simple to Simplify

OK, so *simplifying* is the buzzword of the decade, but with reason. It's the antidote for Americans suffering from "affluenza," the need to consume mass quantities of stuff. Cell phones, satellite dishes, computers, a wardrobe of designer clothes and shoes for every mood, magazine subscriptions to periodicals that are rarely read, state-of-the-art toys with an insatiable appetite for AA batteries—the list goes on. And everything is getting bigger, too, from cars to houses. But is all this stuff helping you lead a better life or contributing to your sense of disorganization, preventing you from truly having fun?

Cutting back doesn't mean cutting out. It just means less chaos. Less clutter. Less to organize. Less to think about. As you read through the chapters of this book, scrutinize your life and decide on ways in which to eliminate useless diversions and worthless stuff that rob you and your family of your time, your space, and your hard-earned money.

Becoming Clutter Conscious

There's a lot of guilt associated with the accumulation of clutter. It's the number-one reason so many of us hang on to it for so long (not to mention a big obstacle in achieving an organized life). When purging our garages, kitchens, and dens of useless gizmos and gadgets, we face our mistakes head-on, like the exercise bike that we bought but never used. We feel shame when we think about littering our landfills if we do relent and throw stuff in the trash. We realize the waste of the doubling and even tripling of items that we purchased thinking we need them when one does just fine. All these emotions and thoughts are there when we begin to sort through the clutter, so it's often less painful to ignore it and pretend that it's simply not there.

But, hey, getting rid of useless possessions is invigorating. It's freeing. It's downright euphoric. It's finally removing the albatross that has hung on your back for so long. But go slowly. And to help ease the pain and guilt, donate the stuff. You may not need a dozen folding chairs, but the church up the street probably would welcome them. Or hold a garage sale and save the income for a family vacation. Give your old baby furniture to a friend who needs exactly what you have. Try to recycle, too. I always save Styrofoam peanuts that accompany mail-order packages out of environmental guilt, but after I save a bag or two, I head to my local pack-and-ship store, where they gladly take them off my hands.

And, ultimately, it is OK to toss some things. Learn your lesson. Become clutter conscious and try not to repeat the same mistakes.

Adopt the Keys

Organizing your life is an ongoing process that requires periodic checkups as your life and family change and evolve. Not only does it require physical changes to how you sort and store your belongings, but you'll need to adopt a few attitude changes as well. By internalizing these universal rules, you'll find making the transformation to organized family is not nearly as hard as you thought.

■ **One Day at a Time** Don't expect your family's habits and attitudes to change in a day, and certainly don't tackle organizing your entire house all at once, say, during a rainy weekend. That's just courting disaster. Instead, make a list of your goals and work by room or area. Implement new household rules one at a time (for instance, backpacks belong on hooks in the bedroom, not on the living room couch), too, and ask family members if it's helping or hindering family life.

■ **Everything Should Have a Home** One of the reasons you live with clutter is that it doesn't have a home—a permanent spot which you and other family members can return it to once you're done using it. This is where abundant storage solutions come into play. Pick and choose containers carefully, the right one for each job. If you can't find a home for one particular item, it probably means you don't really use it or need it. Donate it, give it away to a friend, or toss it.

■ **Think Small** Forget those cavernous toy chests or twenty-gallon containers with lids. When things are organized in small, palatable spaces, it is much easier to find what you're looking for and easier to put it back in its proper spot.

■ **The Rule of Use** Store it where you use it. Sounds pretty obvious, right? It saves time and frustration, yet you'd be amazed at how often people store their toilet paper in the hall closet instead of inside the bathroom vanity.

■ **Develop a Clear System** What exactly is a "system" anyway? (You'd better ask now; I use this word a lot throughout the book!) A system is a way of dividing a large group of things into a number of smaller, more manageable collections, and then storing each separate group in such a way that it's accessible and easy to keep track of.

Look seriously at each drawer, shelf, and cabinet throughout your home, and ask yourself, "What would make this function better?" Perhaps the answer will be labeled boxes with lids, a series of small wicker baskets, more shelves, or even simply moving one group of items closer to the spot where you use them most. Realize, though, that the first system you choose may not solve your problem. Don't be afraid to try again. Once you develop user-friendly systems in every room, it will be easier to keep clutter under control.

■ **Stop Buying** Beg, borrow, or rent rather than buy. Go camping once a year? Then why do you have a pop-up trailer parked in your driveway? Renting is always cheaper than buying something that you use only occasionally. The bonus? Less to store and maintain. Let someone else do that.

■ **Don't Expect Perfection** I may be organized, but let's get one thing straight, I'm not compulsive and by no means could you classify me as a neat freak. Far from it. On more than one occasion, you'll find clothes hanging from my exercise bike, I sometimes forget I have laundry in the washing machine only to find it five days later reeking of mildew, and the only real time I thoroughly clean my house is when company is on the way. What's my point? I'm human and so are you.

You Can Do It

Becoming organized involves breaking old habits and developing new ones. Take your time. Think it through. Decide where you want to go by analyzing your life and your family's habits. Peek in closets, drawers, and cupboards. Make a plan of action by prioritizing a list of ways to improve your current systems. Then attack.

You can do it.

Appointments

Whether you use little slips of paper taped to the bathroom mirror to remind you of an upcoming engagement or employ the old tried-and-true method of tying a string around your finger, juggling appointments is more than just knowing when your son has a dentist appointment or when you have to go out of town for an important business meeting. Busy families need to coordinate so much more—like getting the car into the mechanic every 3,000 miles for an oil change or cleaning the air filter in the furnace twice a year. It's a tricky business keeping it all straight, but if one person assumes the role of family secretary (Mom or Dad is the perfect candidate for the job) and uses simple organizational skills such as prioritizing (you've got to get those car brakes checked this week), proper scheduling (it would be hard to have your daughter at her swim meet *and* in for her yearly physical at the same time), and goal planning, the household will run smoothly, like a well-managed corporation. Hey, you may even show a profit. Well, at least it will seem that way when everyone shows up at the dinner table at the same time.

Keeping Track of Daily Appointments

The first order of business is getting into the habit of writing everything down! (And I don't mean by writing appointments on Post-It notes either.)

Every household needs one central family calendar. It's the simplest way of keeping track of family members' appointments and after-school events, social engagements, birthdays and anniversaries, even payday. Some families use a daily activity chart in addition to a calendar, but the cross-referencing from activity chart to calendar every day may prove to be too much writing for most of us. (See Figure 1.)

	Mom	Dad	Michael	Joseph
Work		8–4 P.M.		
Classroom Helper	8–11 A.M.			
Tennis	3–4 P.M.		3–4 P.M.	
Soccer		6–8 P.M.		6–8 P.M.

FIGURE 1. Daily activity chart

Assessing Your Needs

First, you have to decide how big of a calendar you'll need. For a large, busy brood, try a seventeen-by-twenty-two-inch desk pad calendar (available at all office supply stores). Tear off sheets monthly and hang them prominently in the kitchen for all to see—the best spot is near the telephone so you can quickly jot down an engagement or appointment—or keep it all together so that it's easier to plan several months in advance and hang it from a hook on the back door, or use it as a blotter on the kitchen desk. If this size seems a bit too big, you might find that a small desk calendar works just as well and is a bit more discreet.

You should use your calendar consistently to record all your appointments, but also think of it as a way to communicate with other family members—write down any unusual scheduling changes that will affect the family, such as a parent working late Tuesday night.

 STYLE TIP—To create a family message center, cover a square piece of corkboard with fabric (fold it over the sides and staple it to the back), and then crisscross strips of one-inch colored ribbon checkerboard style and staple them to the back as well. Tack the ribbon down in the front with sewing pins or buttons. Slip invitations, dry-cleaning claim tags, and so on behind the ribbon. (See Figure 2.)

Color Coding

To further help you understand your daily commitments at a glance, give each category a separate color—write birthdays and anniversaries in red, doctor and dental appointments in green, school activities in purple, social engagements in blue, business obligations in orange, and so on. If you're consistent in your color coding, you'll be able to tell if the month is too weighted toward one area of your life without actually reading it all.

Some families take a different approach to the color-coding system. Instead of assigning colors to different types of engagements, they assign each family member a different color—one daughter is pink, a son purple, and so on. That works, too, because everyone can see how busy or free he or she is just by looking for blocks of color.

FIGURE 2. Fabric corkboard

⏰ **TIME-SAVER**—At the beginning of each year, flip through your old calendar and transfer birthdays, anniversaries, and other important occasions into your new calendar. And don't forget to include weekly obligations, too, such as an evening class at the YMCA or the local community college.

Creating To-Do Lists

Do you routinely rely on your memory rather than refer to a map to get back to a place you've been but once? You slowly drive down the road, carefully scanning the roadside in search of familiar landmarks. Do you turn right here or is it the next street? You insist to your kids in the backseat that you have it all under control, but you can't shake a feeling of confusion and anxiety as you strain to remember which way to go. By sheer luck, you find the place (or maybe you relent and turn into a gas station to ask for directions or consult your map, hiding in the bottom of your glove compartment). Ah, ha! There it is! You knew it all along. You're triumphant! Until next time, that is.

That uneasy feeling you have as you blindly make your way down the street is similar to relying on your memory to tell you what needs to be done each day. All your energy is centered on remembering, for instance, that you need to pick up your son at four rather than five o'clock or that you have to call to make a dinner reservation at a new hot spot for next week rather than fully concentrating on your job, your family, or your own personal goals. Realistically, most of your errands will eventually get done, but at what cost? (You'll have to wait another month to get into that restaurant, or your son will be left waiting at school for an hour, wondering where you are.)

When you write a to-do list, whether it's daily, weekly, or even monthly, you don't waste energy trying to remember what needs to be completed. It's always right there in front of you to consult throughout the day. Making a list allows you to plan and prioritize your day, deciding what can wait or what must be done immediately. Besides, it's emotionally rewarding as you successfully check off each completed task.

Although writing a daily to-do list is helpful, it does have a disadvantage—some things inevitably don't get done and you end up transferring the same things over again to the next day's list. It's discouraging when the same chore keeps popping up day after day because it feels as though nothing is actually getting done. It's one of the reasons people eventually give up making lists. To combat the problem, however, try writing out more than one list. Create a *daily* or *weekly list* for chores, errands, and phone calls that must get done by the end of the day or week, such as filling out your daughter's summer camp application (it's due in two days!), but use a second *master list* for tasks that can be accomplished whenever you're in the neighborhood or you just find yourself with a little more time (picking up vacation photos from the lab is currently one example from my *master list*). You may even want to start a third to-do list, this one for *future projects* (such as finally putting all the family photos in albums or painting the bathroom). By creating separate lists, the pressure is taken off to complete everything in one day, yet all errands and projects have been notated so they won't be forgotten.

KEY ORGANIZING TIPS

■ **Keep It Simple** You may be tempted to write a copious to-do list. After all, a busy family is an important family, right? Wrong. If you give yourself too many chores to complete, errands to run, phone calls to make, and projects to do at home or work, you're putting too much pressure on yourself, and that's counterproductive. Instead, limit yourself to one or two phone calls a day (the bank and the plumber, for instance). Group your errands in one morning or afternoon after work, and schedule them for the end of the week. Pick one personal project at a time. List all other tasks on your master to-do list, and work off that if you have the time or inclination.

■ **Daily Update** Not only is simplicity important, but daily upkeep is paramount. Take a few minutes each morning before the family gets up or each evening before you go to bed at night and jot down what needs to be done for the upcoming day. Check the family calendar for appointments and social obligations; think ahead to future projects that maybe you could get a jump-start on tomorrow.

■ **If You Think It, You Should Write It** Keep your list with you always—carry it in your purse, your backpack, your briefcase, whatever your satchel of choice may be—and jot down ideas as they occur to you. When you're home, keep it by your family calendar or telephone. If you hold off writing your ideas down, undoubtedly you'll forget about them in a matter of minutes, and then the ideas are lost forever.

■ **Prioritize** Can someone else take the dog to the vet? (Say, your teenager on his way to football practice.) Learn the arts of delegation and deletion. The point of making lists is not to accomplish so much that you feel overwhelmed at the end of the day, but simply to get it all under control. Sometimes deleting and delegating make more sense than doing it all yourself.

■ **One Task at a Time** Don't measure your success by how much you scratch off your list. Some days you may have to abandon it altogether in favor of some other pressing matter. It's called life. But if you set your priorities each day, you'll be amazed at how much more you'll accomplish overall.

QUICK FIX

Making a daily to-do list sounds simple enough, but you'd be amazed at the number of different scenarios there are—scratch pad to leather-bound book. Take a look at the ideas listed, find one that feels comfortable, and give it a try. (On all these quick-fix tips, it's a good idea to include a small twelve-month calendar.)

■ **Just a Notebook, Please** The easiest way of getting into the list-making habit is to simply use a small, spiral-bound notebook (a five-by-seven-inch one works well). Choose one with subject dividers so that you can separate your *daily list* from your *master list*. At the top of your daily list, write out the date or the week and just list your tasks; then scratch them off as you complete each one. At the end of the day or week, tear the sheet off and start with a fresh one.

■ **Computerize Your Style** If you have access to a computer and want to customize your to-do list, more power to you. This idea works well when you want your to-do list sheet to have several categories on it, such as appointments, people to call, errands to run, and what to buy and what to cook for dinner. Design a master sheet, print up several each month, and place them in a three-ring notebook.

■ **Hit the Internet** Many organizing Internet sites have to-do lists that you can print for free. OrganizedHome.Com, for instance, has several styles from which to choose, including daily or weekly to-do lists and weekly or monthly menu planners. Print as many as you need and place them in a three-ring notebook.

The Word on Pocket Organizers

No doubt about it—technology has infiltrated all our lives and is changing them profoundly on a daily basis. Recently, you may have noticed more and more folks tapping away on strange little hand-held technotoys. They're called personal digital assistants (PDAs), and they're the new rage in computerized organization. If you've been curious if one of these fashionable little gadgets can help you get your chaotic life under control, read on.

What Is It? PDAs (a wealthy relative to the standard electronic organizer, whose main function is to track appointments and phone numbers) go by a variety of names (HandSpring, PalmPilot, and Pocket PC), but there are dozens of others out there ranging in price from $150 to more than $600! About the size and weight of a deck of cards, PDAs use a stylus with an on-screen keyboard and come with handwriting-recognition software so you can jot down notes directly onto the screen.

What Do They Do? Think of them as a replacement to the handwritten to-do list (although sophisticated models mimic a mini laptop computer) with files for addresses and phone numbers, calendars and to-do lists, a memo pad (this is where the handwriting-recognition software comes into play), calculators with currency converters, alarm clocks, and appointment reminders; more expensive models have nearly forty add-on features, from wireless remotes (to send and receive E-mail or surf the Web) and digital cameras to cell phones! The best feature of all, however, is a PDA's versatility. Simply plug your PDA into its port, and you can upload or download files directly from your PC or Mac. The downside is the small size and low-definition screen on some models, making it difficult to read in low-lit areas. (Newer models are offering high-resolution color monitors—for a price.)

Should You Buy One? It all depends on your lifestyle and your love (or distaste) for electronic gadgets. If you're a busy, professional parent with notes stuck everywhere from your refrigerator door to the inside of your day planner, you might consider one. If your life doesn't have that many different components to it, stick with an old-fashioned pen and pad.

MAJOR TUNE-UP

For years, whenever I'd see a well-written passage in a magazine article or book, I'd jot it down in my "good stuff" notebook that I kept in my office and periodically referred to for inspiration. I carried another pretty little notebook in my purse to mark down products and fixtures that I'd see on my travels and thought would look nice in my house. Moreover, I had another notebook for business mileage that I kept in my car.

All these diaries were very useful to me, but because they were spread out all over my house, I became complacent about using them. When I'd see them on occasion, I'd think, "Oh, yeah. I should jot down X, Y, or Z," but more often than not, I'd forget. Although they each served an important purpose, my system of organizing the information in separate locations was too convoluted, and consequently I gave the practice up. That is, until I decided to pool all my journals together to create one central repository called my *personal notebook*.

Before heading to my local office supply store to peruse the many different styles of day-timers, day runners, and other scheduling products out there, I sat down to decide exactly what I wanted my personal notebook to look like and the functions I wanted it to serve. In the end I bought several different items and added and subtracted from one notebook until I created the perfect personalized journal. (For instance, I added a calculator, lots of extra paper for note taking and list making, and subject dividers, but I omitted the phone directory and week-at-a-glance calendar.) You're free to customize your own notebook in any way you deem appropriate for your lifestyle. Here are a few suggestions.

■ **Calendar** Lots of variety here from day-, week-, or month-at-a-glance to a simple year-at-a-glance (my personal choice because I work off of a family calendar at home). Choose the model that best fits your needs. Remember, bigger isn't always better!

■ **Address Book** You may have a family phone book at home or emergency numbers keyed into your cell phone for when you're on the road, so an address book may be a bit redundant. If not, it's definitely an important feature to add to your personal notebook.

■ **To-Do Lists** Divide this section up into as many subcategories as you need: one for *daily tasks* (if you choose a day- or week-at-a-glance calendar, it's easiest to write your list directly on your calendar); a *master list* for errands and such that can be accomplished at your leisure; one for brainstorming *future projects* (such as redesigning garage space); and so forth.

■ **Business** Do you travel a lot for business? In this section record all mileage related to work and any other business expenses such as parking and meals (don't forget to get receipts, though).

■ **Family Members** Keep a personal page on each family member. Here you can write down current clothing and shoe sizes just in case you happen upon "a sale of a lifetime." Make notations about future gift giving, too.

■ **To Try** Have you ever been in the video store trying to remember the name of the movie your best friend saw a few months back and swears you'd love? If you'd just flip to your "To Try" section and hit the movies/videos subcategory, you'd remember. Go all out on this section and include items such as books, restaurants, wines, or anything else that you find appealing or important.

■ **House and Home** Include furnishing ideas or fabric swatches; the names of recommended craftspeople, plumbers, and electricians; include some graph paper in case you ever feel inspired to redesign your front garden while waiting for your dental appointment; or the name of flowers and shrubs to plant or tomato varieties to try.

■ **Groceries** Round up your grocery list on shopping day and place it in your notebook so it will never be left at home. You can also prepare your weekly or monthly menu planner here, too.

■ **Personal Journal** This, too, can run the gamut from humorous diary on life as a parent or inspired haikus to diet notes or a list of personal goals (hey, start that novel this fall).

Keeping Track of Household Details: Organizing a Household Log

There are so many details to running a household and organizing a family that it's impossible to keep track of it all in your head, no matter how organized you are. Your personal notebook will help enormously, but it would be difficult to have every aspect of household life listed there. For instance,

Setting and Achieving Goals

Writing everything down is an exhilarating experience—really. When a pressing idea or nagging thought has been solidified through writing, your mind is then free to concentrate on other matters. The same note-taking principle helps when setting and achieving goals—personal or professional. First, dream it (a two-week family vacation to England's Lake District next July sounds fabulous), plan your course of action by giving each step a deadline (choose the itinerary, send away for hotel information, set a vacation budget, and save the funds—see "Finances" for a few tips—make the necessary reservations, etc.), and then keep track of your progress on a regular basis. When you approach a goal systematically—no matter how lofty an idea—the results will rarely disappoint. Here are the six steps to success. Give them a try!

1. **Brainstorm** Let your mind explore the possibilities in life, and use your personal notebook to jot down your ideas. They can be for pleasure, such as learning to play the piano, or they can be grounded in your well-being, such as losing weight. Whatever ideas are running around in your head, make a note of them. It's fun. It's fulfilling. It's life affirming. And who knows? You may just achieve them.

2. **Categorize** Undoubtedly, you'll end up with dozens of goals (hey, you're a dreamer like me), so it may help during your brainstorming session to divide them into various categories, such as personal growth, family and friends, professional, financial, and house and home.

3. **Prioritize** Obviously, there's not enough time or energy to complete every goal you affirm. Prioritize your ideas by deciding which are more important or have more weight than the others (number them if you like), and then choose which one you'll begin working on today. (Save the others for later down the road.)

4. **Break It Down** It's not enough to just dream; you must now break your ideas down into smaller segments

and develop a strategy for achieving them. As you think through what it will take to reach your goal, write each step down. (What resources will you need to help you, both personally and financially? What specific tasks will you need to do?) Choose a target date for completion of your goal, and work backward, giving each step of your plan a separate deadline.

5. **Keep Tabs** Keep track of your progress in your personal notebook either weekly or monthly depending upon your goal. As you reach each individual objective, check it off of your plan. You're one step closer to achieving your dream.

6. **Reward Yourself** Perhaps the goal itself is the ultimate reward, but you can enhance the enjoyment of your persistence and success in some way. If your goal was to finally landscape your backyard, for instance, why not throw a big neighborhood bash in honor of all your hard work? Did you complete that French-language course you've always wanted to take? Why not enjoy a romantic dinner at the hottest little bistro in town? After all, you deserve it.

do you check your battery-operated smoke alarms and fire extinguishers on a regular basis? You should. When was the last time you checked? And how about when your baby-sitter comes over on Saturday night? Do you end up writing down your cell-phone number every time she comes, just in case? You shouldn't have to.

Details. Details. How do you keep them all straight? It's not as hard as you think.

Just as you created a personal notebook for all your daily tasks, thoughts, and ideas, keeping all household particulars in one spot saves time and energy. Start with a three-ring notebook and plenty of colorful subject dividers to help categorize every aspect of running your household, from an automotive maintenance schedule to a baby-sitter's information sheet. Head to your local office supply store to pick up a pack of paper with vertical columns to help you create a variety of logs, or use your computer (software such as Microsoft Works has a vast selection of household templates from which to choose). Take a moment to study your daily life and jot down some ideas. Here are a few to get you started.

■ **Automobile and Boat Maintenance** Begin by listing the basics, such as vehicle identification and registration numbers, as well as license numbers. Keep tabs on oil changes, tune-ups, and any other major repair work done. Note the names and numbers of your favorite mechanics.

■ **Caregiver Information Sheet** For the baby-sitter, list the essentials, such as all local emergency numbers; your address, phone number, and simple directions to your house; pediatrician's and poison-control center's phone numbers; family cell phone and pager numbers; and your next-door neighbor's and closest friend's or relative's name and number. Or, if you have a day nurse caring for an elderly relative, include the above plus diet and medication schedule.

■ **School Related** Here you can keep your children's daily class and after-school sports schedules, a list of names and numbers of school board members and office personnel, and don't forget a car-pool roster.

■ **House and Garden** Start with a house maintenance schedule where you can keep track of monthly chores, such as checking the batteries in your smoke detector, and seasonal tasks, such as clearing dead brush near your house in early summer (important here in Southern California) and checking the furnace and replacing the air filter every fall. Use this section for your garden almanac, too, where you can check off monthly chores, such as raking and composting leaves in the fall or sharpening gardening tools in the winter.

■ **Household Records** Keep a home inventory list for insurance purposes (read more about property inventory taking in the "Moving" chapter of this book) or a financial log where you can record credit card numbers and contacts, investment information, and insurance policies.

■ **Medical** Create a family medical history including vaccination information for every member of your household; keep tabs on your pet's visits to the vet, too.

■ **Emergency** If you live in a fire- or flood-prone area, list the location of valuables you'd grab in a moment's notice—Grandma's silver, your wedding album, and so forth. Write down practice instructions for fire, tornado, or earthquake evacuations, and keep track of yearly family drills.

What Great Timing!

No more Post-It notes for you! A family calendar, to-do lists, and household log—it may take a while to get into the writing habit, but once you commit, life does become easier because you'll no longer need to concentrate all your energy on remembering what has to be done every day. It's all written down right before you.

Bathrooms

In 1955, when my house was built, bathrooms didn't take top billing with many architects. Our main bathroom is a perfect case in point. Crammed into less than twenty-five square feet of space (I swear), it reminds me of an airplane lavatory. The shower stall is built into the wall and has no ventilation at the ceiling, so battling mildew is a constant challenge. Worse yet, there's only one small cabinet under the sink. Naturally, this room is on my hit list for a major renovation, but in the meantime, I'll continue to experiment with ways to carve out more space and make what room we have work more efficiently.

Many families share my complaint. The bathroom always seems too small considering the amount of traffic it sees daily. Moreover, it's a breeding ground for clutter. Who hasn't taken home those cute hotel samples of shampoo and lotion or been tempted to buy a new cosmetic just because they were giving away a free tote bag filled with little extras? But where do they end up? Stashed and forgotten with the dozens of others collected over the years under the sink or in a big basket hidden in the bathroom closet. The only way to bring organization back to the bath is to face each and every little bottle, tube, and barrette one at a time and make a decision—it's either you or them.

Where Do I Begin?

Find a quiet afternoon and arm yourself with lots of trash bags and a few small boxes for this job; then begin sorting through the mountains of cosmetics, half-empty bottles of mouthwash, old toothbrushes, and hair accessories hiding in the recesses of your cabinets. Not much to donate here; it'll mostly be a keep or scrap proposition. Divide what you do keep during this purging process into small boxes—one for cosmetics, one for hair-care products, and so forth. This way, it will be easier to decide what goes where when it's time to return everything to a new home.

KEY ORGANIZING TIPS

- **Check the Date** Confirm the expiration date on all medications and cosmetics, and toss the ones that are past their effectiveness.
- **Double Indemnity** Inevitably you're going to find doubles, even triples, of many products (we seem to breed toothpaste tubes in our house). As wasteful as it may seem, toss the extras, or at least group them together and work on finishing them off one by one. If you find two identical products, such as rubbing alcohol, with the *same* expiration date, it's OK to combine them and discard the empty bottle. (It's not advisable to blend two over-the-counter medications.) You can mix different shampoos together or even two separate conditioners, provided you're not finicky about the brand that goes on your hair. To avoid future doubling, get all family members to use the *same* brand of shampoo, conditioner, toothpaste, and so forth, so that you'll have only one bottle instead of five.

⏰ **TIME-SAVER**—If you don't have the heart to toss that extra roll of dental floss or half-used bottle of contact solution, store the item in a cosmetic bag and keep it in your suitcase so your toiletries are set to go when you're ready to head out of town in a moment's notice.

- **Medicine Man** Although most people keep their prescription medication in the bathroom cabinet, they usually take their pills in the kitchen during breakfast or dinner. Not only is placement in the bathroom inconvenient, but also humidity can destroy the drug's healing properties. Move all medication out of the bathroom and to another location—current prescriptions should go where you normally take them (bedroom or kitchen); products such as cough syrups and headache remedies can find a new home in the linen or hall closet. But wherever you choose to put them, make sure it's a dark, cool, dry spot out of the reach of young hands.

■ **Round 'Em Up** Self-adhesive bandages in one drawer, antibacterial ointment in another, and adhesive tape and a roll of gauze under the sink. You're ready for any minor emergency all right, but would you know where to find anything? During the eradication and sorting phase, round up all first-aid supplies and place them in a shoebox or even a large cosmetic bag (I'm sure you'll find an extra). Label the front—maybe with a big red cross—so you won't be tempted to toss it in the future, and store it in a practical place such as in a kitchen cabinet or with the rest of your medication on a hall closet shelf.

■ **Front and Center** Keep products and tools that you use daily in the most accessible spots, such as a top drawer or a shelf placed at eye level. Separate the remaining products into various categories—keep all hair accessories together in a small basket, for instance, or use drawer dividers to keep cosmetics tidy.

■ **Too Big** Don't house bulk items such as the one-gallon bottle of liquid soap in prime bathroom real estate; instead, transfer some to smaller dispensers and move the remainder to a secondary location, like the pantry.

*I*n my linen closet, I installed pull-out baskets on the shelves, the kind that slide out on tracks. Things are so much easier to see. Nothing hides in those deep, dark corners.

Clutter Control

Once you've gotten rid of the toiletry riffraff, divide the remaining survivors into several categories—hair-care products and accessories (clips, combs, and brushes), skin care and cosmetics (include shaving products), dental products (including toothbrushes), and, finally, grooming tools (nail clippers, scissors, and mirrors)—then assign an individual drawer, basket, box, or closet shelf for each.

QUICK FIX

It's not enough to weed out the old and unused posessions; now you've got to get back in there and put what you have left back in an orderly fashion.

The better your organization system, the easier it'll be to keep it all tidy every day.

■ **Top-Drawer Management** Use plastic drawer dividers for separating cosmetics (all makeup brushes in one compartment, lipsticks in another), grooming tools, dental products, and hair accessories.

■ **Bottle Battle** Forget lining up bottles of shampoo, conditioner, and body wash along the tub, and instead invest in a hotel-style shower dispenser that attaches directly to the wall. (Frontgate catalog, www.Front gate.com, has two stainless steel models.) Fill the dispenser once a week, and tuck those bottles back under the sink or in the linen closet.

■ **What's the Hook?** Utilize the backs of doors and walls next to the sink to install hooks for hanging bathrobes, wet towels, blow dryers, and curling irons.

■ **It's the Little Things** Give even the littlest toiletries an attractive home. Use decorative jars to store cotton balls or cotton swabs. Find a good-looking toothbrush holder so they needn't be tossed in a drawer or left on the counter after use. Use a liquid soap dispenser instead of bar soap to keep messes to a minimum.

■ **Toy Trouble** Collect all bath toys at the end of each soak, store in a mesh bag, and hang to dry from the bathtub faucet.

T om, Ken, and I had to share one bathroom. Instead of filling it with bath towels, I put hooks in their bedrooms specifically to hang their own personal towels. They'd carry their towels with them into the bathroom and then back to their rooms to dry on their hooks.

Finding More Space

It's a toss-up which bathroom dilemma is worse, finding more space or fighting mildew. Because I've covered the latter in the "Housecleaning" chapter, I'll examine the former here. Tossing out old or extra cosmetics and toiletries is a big help, but so is moving some items out of the bathroom altogether, such as medication and perhaps bed linen, and finding a new home for them. Most important, though, is to organize toiletries and accessories into zones.

Design Tips for Renovating the Bathroom

When the National Association of Home Builders surveyed 2,000 homeowners, guess what room topped their remodeling wish list (following the kitchen)? The bathroom, of course. These days, homeowners want their baths to be sanctuaries of style rather than just a place to hang a toothbrush. If you're thinking of a bath remodel, consider these tips first.

Beg and Borrow Before you think of adding an expensive addition, think first if you can make do with the space that already exists. Is there a closet or unused niche from the room next door that could be adjoined to your current bath? Knocking down a wall is a fairly simple procedure and could add much-needed space in your new design.

Extra, Extra Everybody wants them, but rarely do they use them. I'm talking about expensive extras like an in-tub whirlpool, European-style bidet, and even minibars. Before you pay thousands for these high-cost luxuries, ask yourself a question: are you including them in the design because they look good or will you actually use them?

On the other hand, many extras are worth their weight in gold. How about a fold-down ironing board attached to the bathroom closet door for a quick press before dressing for work? Or what about moving the closet into the bath so that if your spouse is sleeping, you can shower and dress without waking her? Although two sinks in the kitchen is rarely a good idea, a double sink in the bathroom is a must for cutting down on morning and evening traffic congestion.

It's a Separate Issue If space allows, having a separate room for the commode gives one person privacy while the other is free to get ready for work or bed.

Details, Details Swing radius is important. Always consider how your shower door will open. Will it knock into another fixture, such as the sink? Place the sinks—the most used fixture in the bath—out of the line of traffic. Allow for plenty of elbowroom on each side. And don't forget to install an exhaust fan to help remove excess moisture.

QUICK FIX

Even after a major reorganization of the bathroom, you'll sometimes come up short in the space department. Things like towels, toilet tissue, and toothpaste simply don't belong anywhere else, and you've got to fit them somewhere. Buying a bath caddy to keep shampoo and conditioner off the shower floor is one option, but there are plenty more. Follow these quick-fix ideas to find a solution that's right for you.

■ **The Land Down Under** You may have a pipe taking up most of the room under the sink, but you can easily fit plastic bins with pull-out drawers on either side of it (just measure carefully before you go out and buy them). Use the bins to store extra rolls of toilet tissue and other bathroom supplies. Or, investigate adding some kind of shelving unit under the sink; you can attach it to the cabinet door. Or buy two narrow systems with pull-out wire baskets to fit on either side of the pipe.

■ **Basket Bonanza** Place a few wicker baskets around the bathroom—put one near the toilet and fill it with toilet tissue or use a tall basket near the tub and fill it with tightly rolled towels. You can even use one for magazines. Or try hanging bike baskets (flat on one side, round on the other) to the wall. Don't just throw items inside, though; whatever you put on view should be neat and attractive.

■ **Hang It Up** Install plenty of towel bars to easily hang and air dry the family towels. If you're tight on wall space, think vertical by mounting one above the other every two-and-a-half feet. Assign Mom and Dad the upper bars, the lower ones to the youngest members of the family. For a contemporary look, try installing a floor-to-ceiling towel ladder (make it out of redwood—an excellent moisture-resistant hardwood). Or do away with bars and go for hooks—it makes a great design feature and uses up less room.

■ **It's a Shoe-In** Hang a plastic shoe bag on the inside of the bathroom closet door and store bottles of shampoo and conditioner in each compartment. You can even assign each family member a row of his or her own for personal use.

■ **Behind Door Number Two** Install additional shelves in your medicine cabinet. Most hardware stores can custom cut glass shelves.

■ **Corner Corral** Take advantage of unused corners with glass shelving built to fit this triangular shape.

⏰ **Time-Saver**—Keep a small bucket or plastic caddy with a handle filled with cleaning supplies in each bathroom. This way, when the mood hits—say, as you're waiting for the shower to warm up—you can grab a sponge and cleanser and scrub the sink or toilet.

MAJOR TUNE-UP

With a little more time, money, and imagination, you can easily create more space—short of knocking down the walls, of course.

■ **The Big Cover Up** What happens if you have a pedestal sink in your bathroom? Can you still use the space underneath for storage? Absolutely. If you're handy with a sewing machine, create a sink skirt. Attach the curtain to the sink with Velcro tape or glue small hooks to the underbelly of the sink and add grommets to the top hem (both ways make it easy to remove and wash the curtain).

I never had all my cleaning supplies in each bathroom; hence, they never got clean! I've wised up. It's so easy to keep the bathroom sparkling now that everything is right there.

■ **Bathroom Furniture** Even if you only have a twelve-inch section of wall in your bathroom, you can still place a piece of furniture such as a tall tower with shelves or baskets to fit the space both in size and in style. Or how about the unused area around the toilet? There are plenty of over-the-tank shelving units made specifically to fit this unused space (or simply build a set of shelves directly over the toilet). Check out Pottery Barn, holdeverything, Crate & Barrel, or even Lillian Vernon catalogs. Or stroll the aisles of Target, Costco, or IKEA to weigh your options.

■ **Walled Off** Adding a false wall with small nooks and shelves next to the toilet not only provides more privacy, but an abundance of storage opportunities, too.

■ **Above and Beyond** When thinking of more ways to use space, look up. Try installing a shelf directly above the window or just a foot below the ceiling over the bathroom door or even around the entire room, and store extra towels there. Or add decorative baskets to hide other bathroom basics, such as toilet tissue.

🕯 **STYLE TIP**—If you haven't the room or the money to add a master bathroom, consider adding a pedestal sink complete with mirror and shelf—boardinghouse style—in the master bedroom itself. It will help cut down on the morning and evening bathroom snarl. Use a decorative screen or dramatic curtain to conceal it from the rest of the room.

We have topical baskets in our bathroom closet—one for makeup, another for travel-sized items, one for feminine products, and even a samples basket. In the bathroom, all those items are way too small to sit on the shelf because they tend to topple when they stand alone.

Daily Dealings

Once you've made a plan and reassigned all your bathroom essentials to their new and proper homes, how do you keep the bathroom neat on a daily basis? You may be with the program tidying up each morning (after all, you're the one who did all the work), but what about the other messy members of your family? How do you get them to cooperate?

Start by giving a tour of the new system showing everyone where each item belongs. You can even add labels to each shelf, drawer, or basket to ensure that all products return to their new homes. Next, set a few simple ground rules.

Add a clothes hamper (even a laundry bag hanging on the back of the door will do) to round up spent towels and dirty clothes.

Color code toothbrushes and towels for each family member—white for Mom, blue for Dad, green for Junior, and so on. It keeps confusion to a minimum and you can keep tabs on who's the messy culprit.

Make quarterly inspections of bathroom shelves, drawers, and cabinets, and toss out expired or seldom-used items.

Insist that family members return all items to their new homes after use. Even small counters seem larger when clutter free.

Dan, Francesca, and I each have our own plastic baskets with handles that we keep in the bathroom closet. So, in the morning, say, Dan pulls his out and it has all his shaving stuff and comb—anything that's specific to him and not a shared item like shampoo. When he's done, he puts it back. It cuts down on clutter in the bathroom.

She's Been in There for an Hour!

Even if you weren't blessed with an abundance of bathroom square footage, you can still create a space worth lingering in. Once you've cleared things out and reorganized, go ahead and add a bit of style with new rugs and trash can, ceramic soap and tissue dispenser, a fresh coat of paint, some new towels, and maybe even a new mirror and lighting fixture. For just a few hundred dollars, you can improve the overall look and feel.

Everyone deserves a nice bathroom, and your family may even have more incentive to keep it organized if it looks good.

Children's Bedrooms

For the moment, our three sons are sharing a bedroom. (My husband and I need a bedroom for an in-home office.) The boys don't seem to mind though; in fact, they actually like sharing a room—for now. By the time privacy becomes an important issue, we hope we will have built an addition onto our home enabling one child to move to his own room.

Although I'm sure in twenty years my guys will look back at these times wistfully, remembering all the nights they giggled while hiding under the bedcovers, protected by the glow of their toy camp lights, or the great fun they had propelling Super Balls from the ceiling fan, I, on the other hand, will remember the daily challenge it was keeping the room neat and organized.

Organizing the Space

Before tackling any major room reorganization, especially a child's bedroom, you'll need to make a plan. Unlike Mom or Dad, who have several different rooms in which to conduct business and store their belongings, children sleep, play, and study in one room. Therefore, organizing their space can be a real challenge. But if you take a moment to consider your child's current needs and developmental stage before diving in, the task will be much easier. For instance, is your five-year-old getting more independent, able to dress himself? Then you might want to think of ways to make his clothes more manageable by lowering the rod in his closet to encourage him to choose his own outfits and dress himself each day. And what about his present interests? Is he an aspiring painter? Perhaps creating an art center complete with easel near a window with lots of natural light should be included in the plan.

Think of what you'd like from the reorganization as well. You may want to persuade him to play more in his room rather than pulling every toy out into the middle of the living room floor. In that case, try designing a play area within his room—a large colorful rug surrounded by a bookcase for his favorite stories and shelves filled with some of his toys. Maybe add an activity desk with built-in cubbies for all his art supplies.

STYLE TIP—Picture this: a stainless steel shelving unit running the length of your teenager's bedroom wall. (Many stores, including IKEA, Target, Costco, and Sam's Club, offer an inexpensive model.) Add a wood top to one shelf for a writing/desk area (clear the shelves underneath so he'll have legroom); add lots of square baskets and boxes on the remaining shelves to organize teen tools—games, sporting equipment, and memorabilia. The best part is, when he moves out, it dismantles easily and can go with him to his next home.

Yet what works for you and your child this year may not work for the both of you come next fall. Children aren't stagnant; they're constantly developing, and what might be a great arrangement one year will not hold up the next. Therefore, periodically reevaluate his needs (and yours) and make changes accordingly.

Choosing Furnishings

In choosing furniture for a child's room, think about the present as well as the future. An elaborate canopy bed may be stunning for your five-year-old daughter, but what happens when she gets older and thinks it's too frilly? Will you have to buy a new bed set? Juvenile furniture, regardless of how adorable, is rarely a good investment—kids grow out of it physically as well as emotionally very quickly. Instead, choose a design that will survive through many childhood stages. Remember too, that you may need to add additional pieces to the set as the years pass—a computer desk, for instance. A funky contemporary design may look good now, but how about finding a desk to match it in five years? It may not be easy. Stick to classic styles that can be mixed and matched with many other manufacturers' designs. The key to symmetry in a child's bedroom (and even yours, for that matter) is to keep it simple—a spot to sleep, a place to study, something for clothes, and an area for play and projects.

STYLE TIP—Instead of buying a changing table for your new baby, consider using a dresser instead. Remove the top drawer and add padding inside to make a removable changing station for the top. The empty space where the drawer once was makes a handy spot to store diapering necessities. When your little one grows out of diapers, replace the drawer and use it for its original intention—storing clothes.

In Francesca's bedroom we took one whole wall and built a ceiling-to-floor unit with an armoire for her clothes, drawers underneath, open book shelves, and cabinets with doors. Because of it we were able to get rid of a standing bookshelf, a dresser, and some hanging shelves. The room now is twice as big; it's saved an enormous amount of space because the unit only comes out about sixteen inches. Then, under her window, we built a window seat that lifts up for even more storage. There's no wasted space.

TIME-SAVER—Simplify your child's bedding by omitting the top sheet. This way she can make her own bed by simply pulling up the bedcover. Don't worry that the quilt will get dirty quicker without the sheet—just buy an inexpensive, machine-washable duvet.

Share, Share, That's Fair

Growing up, did you have to share a bedroom with a sibling? If you were like most kids, you probably did. I have a girlfriend who has nine siblings and shared a room with her four sisters! (The room contained two sets of bunk beds, plus a single bed.) My brother-in-law had to bunk in with a sister and a brother (his grandfather built a room divider so each sex could have a bit of privacy). Although young children find comfort in sleeping in the same room with a brother or sister, older siblings will eventually start the I-want-my-own-room whine, probably by the time they reach junior high. But what if there's not a room to spare?

QUICK FIX

Although sharing a room is a great lesson for the future—children learn to cooperate, compromise, and settle disagreements on their own—everyone needs a little retreat she can call her own. So, how can you organize the space so that each has a bit of legroom and privacy?

■ **Divide and Conquer** There are lots of creative ways to divide a room, allowing each child to have a completely separate space. Shop around for bamboo or wood screens and place between the beds. Use furniture as a natural divider—two tall bureaus back to back give each child a little niche. Or look for a tall bookcase with open shelving. (To prevent it from toppling over, be sure to anchor the side of the bookcase in the wall studs.) Go the sixties route, and hang a row of beads or suspend a rod from the ceiling and hang a curtain. If you're handy, you can inexpensively build a miniwall between the beds rising up three-quarters of the way to the ceiling. (The kids can use the top as a decorative shelf for plants or books.) Or think corporate and investigate in cubicle-style walls available at most office furniture stores (they come in a huge variety of colors).

■ **Don't Cross This Line** Giving each child a bit of privacy can be as simple as taking a side of the room. Cluster each person's bed and desk together and put the shared dresser in neutral territory.

■ **Think Small** Space-saving furniture leaves enough latitude to divide the room equitably. A tall chest of drawers takes up less space than a long dresser (place a full-length mirror on the back of a closet door), freeing up valuable wall space. Instead of two nightstands, try beds with headboards, or attach a small, single shelf into the wall studs directly next to each person's bed. (This idea is great for kids with bunk beds, allowing the top bunker to have a place for his nighttime essentials.)

■ **Color Code** If the roommates are young, consider color coding shelves, dresser drawers, or even closet doors—one color for each child's possessions. Ownership gives the illusion of privacy.

■ **Gender Gap** Help a teenager obligated to share a room with a younger sibling gain a bit of privacy by providing her with extra drawer space and shelves in your master bathroom.

I n our little Cape Cod–style house, Katherine and Olivia share a nine-by-nine-foot room. They share a dresser—two drawers each. The closet is wide but narrow, with only one bar across, so I placed a hanger with a bow on it in the center, marking the halfway point for each girl. The closet isn't big enough to house all their shoes. Because Katie is little, she puts her shoes in an old dresser drawer and slides it under her bed. Unfortunately, Olivia has three times as many pairs—she's one of those Imelda Marcos girls—so she puts hers in a shoe shelf in the closet. All toys are downstairs in the playroom; only stuffed animals are in the bedroom—they line the windows.

🗄 **STYLE TIP**—Got a teen in the house? Forgo the conventional bed in favor of a sofa bed or futon and frame. During the day, it's an informal den with plenty of room for friends to hang out but at night with just a bit of elbow grease, a cozy lair for one.

MAJOR TUNE-UP

Sometimes it's simply not possible to divide the room in two (perhaps there's only one window and one child would get "shoved in the dark," or the furniture arrangement makes it difficult for the other child to get out the door). Whatever the problem is, there may be a way around it.

■ **Larger Living** If possible, try to move the roommates to a larger room or, at the very least, a room more conducive to dividing. In our house, my boys are in the original master bedroom while my husband and I occupy a smaller room on the other side of the house. Their room is large enough to accommodate three beds, and the attached bath is a plus—no wet children running down the hall after bath time. (We don't mind sleeping in an eleven-by-eleven-foot room for now, but I am looking forward to one day having a new master retreat.)

■ **Invent a Room** Look for substitutes other than bedrooms. How about converting the attic or part of the garage? I know a woman who turned a small, out-of-the-way family room into an additional bedroom by adding folding doors to each entranceway. Another family transformed a rarely used formal dining room into a bedroom. With a little imagination, anything is possible.

Organizing Books and Toys

Did you ever see a child near a toy chest? He dumps the entire contents on the floor, chooses one toy, and walks away. In addition to the mess he leaves behind, the toys often get crushed and destroyed under the weight of so many others, or pieces to puzzles and games mysteriously disappear. Toys take on little importance or meaning when they're heaped together in one tangled pile. When thinking about organizing the millions (or so it seems) of toys in your child's room, forget cavernous toy chests.

Organizing toys into smaller categories, on the other hand, spotlights the toys' uniqueness, teaches children to respect their belongings, and helps them to learn how to classify and separate. Use plastic storage bins with lids in a variety of sizes to sort everything—one for Hot Wheels, another for dress-up costume jewelry, and so on—choosing the right size for the right toy. It's much easier for children to find the exact toy they're looking for without making a huge mess, and cleanup's a snap because they can sort the toys into the correct boxes and effortlessly stack them back up. No problem; no mess. You can even add color pictures on the outside of each box for a visual cue.

*I*n our house, we have toys areas in the bedroom, dining room, and living room because I don't think that children understand that they need to go to a bedroom closet to get a toy and then bring it out to the play area. To keep all the toys visually organized, we have colored mats on the floor in the corners of each of the rooms. If a toy is thrown back on the mat, it's in a visually contained space.

Style Tip—When decorating a child's room, don't forget a bit of whimsy. For instance, paint a tree in the corner, branches spilling out onto the adjacent walls. Where the leaves meet up with the branches, add a hook for stuffed animals or whatever else needs a home.

Storage

Before you head out to the store to start your collection of plastic boxes, baskets, and trays, figure out what you need first. Take an inventory of your child's toy collection and other memorabilia and decide on the number and size of containers rather than just guessing. The system won't work if you have a large wooden block collection, for instance, smashed inside a container that's barely big enough.

QUICK FIX

The world of containers has exploded in recent years as everyone gets on the organizational bandwagon. Just peruse the aisles of Target for a sampling of organizing products, or visit containerstore.com on the Web (they have a few great stores throughout the U.S.—check the website to see if one is near you). Start writing out your list now, but first check out these quick-fix ideas below.

■ **Sleeping with Dust Bunnies** Store large, garment-sized plastic containers under the bed for out-of-season clothing or large toys. Old dresser drawers make great under-bed storage bins, too. Just splash on a new coat of paint, some hardware, and four corner casters to help them roll in and out of their hiding place easily.

■ **Baskets Galore** Use laundry or wicker baskets to house oddly shaped train sets or car tracks.

■ **Cigar Box or Cookie Tins** Great for storing marbles, jewelry, dominoes.

■ **It's a Shoe In** A clear plastic shoe bag hung over the back of the bedroom door or over the back of a bed is great for storing little gems like jewelry and hair accessories or even a fashion doll collection; or hang it next to the baby changing station and park cotton swabs, nail clippers, and other baby paraphernalia.

■ **Milk It** Colorful plastic milk crates are inexpensive and stackable! Great for garaging trucks and other large, oddly shaped toys.

■ **Hanging Out** Hang a small hammock from the bedposts for stuffed animals.

■ **It's in the Bag** Store puzzles in resealable plastic bags—one puzzle per bag.

■ **Savvy Shelves** Use wire, wicker, and plastic baskets to subdivide a bookshelf more efficiently—one basket for CDs, another for comic books, and so on.

W hen I bought my son a bunk bed, I also purchased two large match- ing drawers set on rollers that fit snugly under the bottom bunk. The drawers are huge, running the length and width of the bunk. We can store all sorts of games and sporting equipment in each one.

MAJOR TUNE-UP

Look beyond the basics and get out your tool kit and paint palettes. Stor- age solutions abound if you're a willing wanna-be carpenter.

■ **Wallflower** If you can swing a hammer, you can create a bit more storage between the wall studs by breaking through the existing drywall and recessing a tall, narrow set of shelves (it should be about sixteen inches wide, the typical width between studs). Choose a spot near a desk to house schoolbooks or right above a changing table to keep baby supplies close at hand.

■ **Lucky Lockers** Transform a set of battered gym lockers that you can find at a yard sale or salvage yard with a coat of enamel paint, add track shelving inside, and you're in business. After the kids have outgrown them, move them to the basement to store pantry items or the garage to help orga- nize gardening supplies.

■ **A Lofty Idea** Build a high-in-the-sky sleeping loft. The comfort- able upper berth offers a bird's-eye view with plenty of space below to fit a desk or play area.

A Word on Books

Thin paperback children's books have always presented a storage problem. Because they have no spine, in the average bookshelf, it's nearly impossi- ble for a child to find the title she's searching for without pulling every other book out, too. What's the solution? Actually, there are two. The first idea came from my local library: purchase several small, rectangular plas- tic baskets (the kind that beauticians use to store their hair clips and rollers) and store books with titles facing forward. When a child wants to find a book, she can simply flip through the titles in the basket.

*O*rganizing library books has always been a problem in our house. I don't like them lying on the floor, yet if the kids put them in the bookcase then we forget about them when it's time to return them to the library. So, the kids made a special home just for these books by decorating a cardboard box with the top cut off and a "library book" sign pasted on the front. When they want a library book, they take one out of the box. When they're finished reading it, they know right where to put it. No more overdue books.

The second idea requires a little creative work, but your child will be a happy assistant. Collect several large cereal boxes and cut along the diagonal, eliminating one corner to create a magazine-type file box. Cover with decorative wrapping paper. They're great for storing books in a series. File all Arthur books in one, Clifford in another, Berenstain Bears in a third, and so on. For an added visual cue, color copy a front cover, and tape the picture onto the appropriate box.

*O*livia and Katherine found an old bookshelf at a tag sale. When we got it home, they painted it. It's now up in their room, and we moved all special books there, the ones they want to hold on to—hardcover, first editions, Harry Potter series, books that have been signed by the authors. For all other books, each girl has her own wicker basket by her bed.

Time to Weed

Most children would keep everything that they've ever come into contact with (if their parents would let them), from their first Happy Meals toy to a rock that they found in the park that they swear is a real dinosaur fossil. Even if it's broken or not played with any longer, a child will hold tight to his possessions. Yet the average child's bedroom couldn't possibly hold eighteen years of stuff—something's got to give. Several times a year—maybe right after her birthday or Christmas—go through your child's toys and books and decide which items can be thrown away, passed down to a smaller child, or given to a local charity.

Toss ripped or torn books (paperbacks can be put in the recycling bin); throw out old puzzles with more than a few pieces missing or trucks with missing wheels; retire dolls with missing limbs and ceramic tea sets chipped beyond recognition. And of course, toys that are just "too babyish" should be boxed up and given away.

QUICK FIX

If all this purging is just too painful for your child, think of a compromise. Realize that it may seem like junk to you, but it's pure treasure to your child. Some parents choose to weed toys when their young children aren't around (because most kids never notice when an out-of-favor toy disappears anyway) and stow a box or two in the attic or basement for a few months before tossing to make certain they haven't misinterpreted their children's ambivalence. Or, if you'd like, try one of these quick-fix ideas.

- **Into the Closet** Put hard-to-let-go toys in a box and place it in the closet for a few weeks. Chances are this transition will provide enough time for her to let go.

- **Memory in a Box** It may be a Barbie without a head, but it was her first, and that alone makes it very special. Give this twelve-inch American icon a place of honor in a memory box and store it in the closet. Every year visit the memory box and see which toys your daughter will agree can move out and into the trash.

- **Only One per Week** If there is a pile of stuff that's just begging to be tossed but your child flat-out refuses, try eliminating just one toy of her choosing per week.

Organizing Clothes

Fortunately, most young kids don't need a lot of clothes to make them happy—a bunch of T-shirts, jeans, and shorts, maybe the occasional clip-on tie or black patent leather shoes for that special party. If you have young kids, treasure it now, I'm told, because all bets are off as teens reach high school, and the fashion police roam the halls more often than a bewildered freshman on her first day of class.

QUICK FIX

There are plenty of solutions when it comes to organizing a closet or even a dresser bureau for that matter, but what about the everyday stuff such as pajamas and sweatshirts? How do you get them off the floor or off the corner chair for good?

- **What's the Hook?** Choose a wall (preferably close to the closet) or a portion of a wall and mount hooks at your child's eye level. You can

Helping Kids Help Themselves

It's not enough to have a newly designed, well-functioning room if you're the one who runs in daily to tidy it—the kids need to learn to do it themselves. But how do you get your child to want to clean her room? Try these steps below.

Plan Together When you ask your child for her input on how to redesign her room, she now has a stake in its outcome and is more likely to take an interest in keeping it clean.

Everything Must Have a Consistent Home She can't put her toys away if no home has been assigned. Everything needs a place, whether a plastic container, basket, box, or shelf.

Keep the System Simple and Centralized Legos in a box under the bed and wooden blocks in a basket on the top closet shelf may seem like a logical sorting system to you, but to your child it's just confusing and hard to remember. Create zones when designing the space (for instance, keep all building-type toys in different boxes but on the same shelf) and keep all similar items together.

Consider Ergonomics If her bed is pushed up against the wall, she won't be able to make it easily; if all her clothes are housed in the top dresser drawers, she won't be able to reach them. If her room functions well, however, she'll function well within it.

Develop Daily Routines Children function best when following a consistent routine. Develop a morning strategy, such as making beds and hanging pajamas following breakfast, as well as an evening routine, such as picking up toys off the living room floor right before dinner.

Motivate Consistently congratulate them on a job well done. Compliment them on how nice their rooms look or what a fine job they did on making their beds (but avoid the urge to straighten the bedspreads right in front of them).

Offer Rewards; Implement Consequences A well-chosen reward works miracles—a half-hour video, ice cream after dinner, or an extra bedtime story. By the same token, taking away privileges has equal impact. Set the timer—if the room isn't tidy within the allotted time, come up with an appropriate consequence, such as taking away the toys in question for the day.

keep it simple with just a few or make a decorating statement with a variety of sizes, shapes, and colors. Use one for his pajamas, one for his backpack, another for his various assortment of sweat jackets, an additional one for his baseball cap collection, and so on.

■ **Hat-Rack Jack** Not just for the corner by the front door, a hat rack can be a great place for your child to hang it all up. Many companies, including Pottery Barn Kids (potterybarnkids.com), make miniature models just perfect for your three-foot clotheshorse.

■ **Go Vertical** The word is out—vertical space is in. Hang a colorful gym rope from the ceiling (hey, it's a kid's room; she'll love it) and attach a hat or scarf collection with large clips.

■ **Peg-Board** Mount a Peg-Board on the wall, once again at eye level, and add an assortment of hooks. The best part is your child can change the design of the hooks as new stuff enters her life.

Into the Closet

What's in your child's closet? Toys given a "time-out" but left on the top shelf and forgotten? A couple of pairs of jeans that cousin Max handed down to your son but are still a bit too big? Chances are there are probably other clothes in there that he hasn't worn or fit into for a year now. Cleaning out a child's closet is a big project, and therefore most of us avoid it until we can't stand it another moment (or until we just can't get the door to close any longer). Redesigning the space will help your child function better in his environment, and it'll cut down on the daily "clean-your-room" bickering, too.

Reorganizing a closet is a several-step and, unfortunately, time-consuming project. Choose an afternoon or Saturday morning when both you and your child can go through its contents together. It'll help though, if you begin with some big boxes—one for toys in need of a home, another for charitable donations or hand-me-downs, a third for clothes that will go back in the closet—and some bags for the stuff ready for the trash.

🕰 **TIME-SAVER**—As you sort through and discard outgrown clothing, make a note of what each child needs for the upcoming season in your personal notebook. (See "Appointments" for more details.)

*B*ecause we get a lot of hand-me-downs and I shop the end-of-the-season
sales where I buy something for Nathaniel that will fit him next year, I
have lots of boxes with lids that are marked not with the size of the clothes,
but with the season and the year in which I should open them. So, right now
I'm opening the fall 2002 box, and I'm finding all the hand-me-downs and
the clothes that I bought ahead of time.

QUICK FIX

Once you've separated the junk from the treasure, take a few moments to
evaluate what's left and what you'll need to organize it all. But before you
go out and drop some serious cash on some new closet gadgets, consider
these quick-fix ideas. (And remember to measure twice! Mistakes are
costly.)

   ■ **Hot Rod** All you may really need to do is add an additional rod to
open up a bit more space. The simplest way to do this is to raise the original rod six to eight inches and suspend a second rod, half the size, on one
side of the closet with lightweight chains. Use this new two-tiered space
for short clothing such as shirts and skirts; use the second, taller portion
for longer garments such as dresses and pants. (See Figure 3.)

FIGURE 3. Second closet rod

■ **Shelf It** The upper shelf in a closet is definitely no-man's land. Hardly a kid under the age of ten could possibly reach its contents. But if you're not ready to do a total closet teardown, use this space wisely by storing special toys that require adult supervision, such as a prized doll collection, or warehouse out-of-season clothing or hand-me-down clothes ready to hit the closet in the next year.

■ **Color-Coded Closet** It's a great idea to organize clothes by type—all pants together, shirts together, skirts together—but it's not as easy for a child to remember to do it. To help, color code the rod. Paint a portion red, and hang pants in that section, blue for shirts, yellow for skirts, and so on. (Hang a coordinating color chart on the closet wall with cut-out pictures to help her remember.)

■ **Hey Baby!** Organize baby clothes more efficiently by hanging a tag listing the garment's size (six months, nine months, twelve months, etc.) and arranging sizes from smallest to largest.

■ **Back to Basics** Get rid of wire hangers that destroy and stretch clothing, and get child-sized sturdy plastic ones instead. Purchase several inexpensive shower curtain hooks, suspend them from the rod, and use them to hold umbrellas, belts, or ties. Keep two laundry baskets on the floor—one for dirty clothes, the other for empty hangers (teach your children to put the hanger in the basket as soon as they pull a garment from the closet). Consider installing a battery-operated light inside so your child can actually see what's what.

Wе have T-shirts hanging on a low bar in the closet and other clothes in open baskets rather than drawers. Nathaniel's five; he's not going to remember that his underwear is in his dresser drawer, but he can see them easily in the baskets.

 STYLE TIP—If closet space is minimal in your child's room, consider a freestanding armoire. Variety abounds when it comes to this beautiful European accessory, but most contain a small rod perfect for hanging young children's clothing as well as several drawers and shelves perfect for storing toys. Use the doors to mount additional hooks and don't forget to bolt the armoire to the wall to prevent it from tipping over.

MAJOR TUNE-UP

A major closet renovation takes time and money, but the investment will ultimately pay off every time your child helps himself to a shirt or actually puts his own shoes away. When good systems are set in place, it's much easier for children to keep clothes tidy.

■ **Prepackaged Paradise** Head to a home center and browse the collection of prepackaged closet kits, most designed to fit a typical five- to eight-foot-wide closet. You can customize the space to meet any child's need. There are many add-on components, such as shelves and bins, but be careful; many are not interchangeable with other manufacturers'. A few points to consider: ventilated wire shelving is less expensive and easier for the do-it-yourselfer to install than its laminated wood counterpart. Also, wire shelving and rods are adjustable, a big selling point for a child's closet—you can easily change the configuration as your child's needs change. Look for *continuous sliding rods* that allow you to move your clothes across the bar uninterrupted. To optimize space, buy two hanging rods and use the upper rod for an older sibling's clothing and the lower rod for the younger's—if the two share a room—or use the upper rod for out-of-season or special-occasion clothes for a child lucky enough to have his own room.

■ **Forget the Rod** If you want to encourage your young child to dress himself each morning, consider tossing out the clothes rod altogether and replacing the old system with shelves and pull-out wire baskets, further eliminating the need for a dresser.

■ **The Door to Enlightenment** To expand the space even further, consider enlarging the closet opening by replacing the old door with sliding doors, allowing easier access to clothes and toys. Or eliminate the door altogether for a true alfresco look!

■ **Trouble with Teens** Fifteen and female usually means lots of clothes and never enough space. Build her a walk-in closet by adding a floating wall about five feet from her existing closet; add a storage system to corral her clothes collection and accessories. (See Figure 4.)

QUICK FIX

The bedroom dresser can be a crafty apparatus—clothes go in but few come out. Things don't have to get out of hand, just follow a few guidelines.

FIGURE 4. Walk-in closet

■ **Purge Protector** Once a week as you put clean laundry away, take a minute to tidy up—pull out clothes that no longer fit your child and put in a box earmarked for charity or keep an ongoing hand-me-down collection.

■ **Within Arm's Reach** Put clothes within reach of small children by placing them in lower drawers (you can keep memorabilia and out-of-season and special-occasion clothing in top drawers). If two children are sharing a room, put the younger child's clothes in the bottom drawers, where he can easily get them.

■ **It's Your Turn** Clothes on the bottom of the dresser drawer rarely get worn. To make sure this doesn't happen, put freshly laundered clothes on the bottom of dresser drawers, moving the less-worn clothes to the top.

It's Child's Play

Although you'd love to see your child's room neat and tidy every day, realize that she is just that—a child—and it's her job to make a mess. Some organizational experts suggest limiting the number of toys you allow your child to pull from the shelves at a time to help control the clutter, but it's a child's job to explore and discover, and, unfortunately, that often means making a mess. Instead, try to look the other way—within reason—until dinnertime, and then have her put away her toys (and if she's young, give her a hand).

Closets

Linen, Entry Hall, and Utility

It used to be that a closet contained a rod and a shelf and that was it. Unfortunately, in its simplicity it also unwittingly became a tangled jungle for just about everything that didn't have a permanent home. These days, closets have taken on a more sophisticated personality. If you still don't believe me, just flip through the pages of a holdeverything catalog, where you'll find dozens of gorgeous products—maple shelves, baskets, and shoe cubbies—designed to sort and display your wardrobe, outer gear, accessories, and linens in style. If your budget suggests that you look elsewhere for inspiration, don't worry; you can still have a well-functioning closet without spending thousands of dollars on costly gear. (For information on organizing bedroom closets, however, see the "Children's Bedrooms" or "Master Bedroom" chapters.)

Where Do I Begin?

You'll get an enormous sense of satisfaction organizing your closets, much more so than any other household restructuring because the result is so positive, obvious, and immediate. Each closet will, however, take an afternoon of your time to complete. You'll first need to empty its entire contents; sort or discard every item; clean the inside with a broom and dust rag; set your new system in place with either shelves, hooks, or drawers; and then put everything back. With this in mind, it's best to work on one closet at a time rather than doing an all-out assault on your entire home. But even if that proves to be too much for you, try organizing *one shelf* at a time.

KEY ORGANIZING TIPS

■ **A Well-Made Plan** Before you tackle any closet reorganization, think about the function of each. For instance, is your front hall closet used primarily for guest coats or is it a launching pad to get out the door each morning and filled with coats, umbrellas, backpacks, and briefcases for you and your family? Deciding on each closet's role will help you determine which items belong and which should be moved to another location.

■ **The Golden Rule** When reorganizing your closets, keep one rule in mind—visibility. Every item needs to be seen so that you can quickly retrieve it. No more hiding stuff in the back of your closets; bring everything out in the open. You can do this by investing in pull-out baskets, wire shelving systems, and stackable plastic bins.

■ **Give a Tour of Your New System to All Family Members** There's nothing more frustrating than having spent all afternoon reorganizing a closet only to have your new system undermined with one wrong move by your significant other or kids. Give every family member a tutorial of what you've tried to accomplish. Ask for suggestions on how to improve the system.

■ **Tools of the Trade** Add a few extras, such as installing a battery-operated light to each closet or a step stool or retrieving pole with hook and pincers (available in houseware stores such as Linens-N-Things or Bed, Bath and Beyond) to help reach high shelves.

Linen Closets

In researching this section, I decided to organize my own linen closet. What I found surprised even me—a collection of thin, worn towels and sheets in the most hideous colors from my husband's bachelor days and old wool blankets pocked with holes. None of these items was worthy of donating to a local charity, but even I didn't have the heart to throw them in the trash. Out to the garage they went to begin a new life as workshop rags, drop cloths, and furniture covers—respectively.

While thumbing through your own linen shelves, do the same. If you haven't used something in more than a year, consider donating it to a local shelter. But if your bedding is beyond recognition, either toss it or reinvent it. (Keep them for camping trips, picnics, or to cover up out-of-season clothing to keep the dust off.)

⏰ **Time-Saver**—When changing the sheets, why not wash and dry the sheets that are already on your bed and then remake it? No folding laundry or remembering to put the clean set away (the same trick works well with bathroom towels, too). Don't worry about wearing out your linens too quickly—you'd be surprised at how long good-quality sheets and towels last.

QUICK FIX

We'd all like a bigger linen closet, but the fact remains that most of us are stuck with what we've got—one little stall with a half-dozen shelves. Fear not, there is a way to bring method to the linen madness.

■ **Ask for Accessibility** When reorganizing shelf space, keep most-used items such as towels and sheets at eye level where they are easiest to see, and move those rarely used blankets and heirloom tablecloths to lower or higher shelves.

■ **The Category Is . . .** Categorize every item so that it has a permanent home, not merely where it will fit on any given day. Place all sheets on one shelf, towels on another, and table linens on a third. You can break it down even further by separating everyday table linen from special-occasion linen or divide up bedding for each bedroom. If you store spare toiletries in your linen closet, they should be properly categorized, too. You can keep them corralled by sorting them into small plastic baskets. Or better yet, install pull-out wire baskets so you can see the contents in the back of the closet more readily.

■ **Together Forever** Store your matching sheets and pillowcases together—fitted sheet, flat sheet, and pillowcase—for easy retrieval. You can make assembling a set effortless by housing both sheets inside the pillowcase!

■ **Best Face Forward** Stack linens fold side out. It's easier to grab the number you need. (You never know what you'll get when the edges are facing out.)

■ **Under Covers** If you're short on closet space, try storing a set of clean linen under each bedroom mattress. This system makes changing the bed a snap because everything is right at hand the moment you need it.

STYLE TIP—If you're tight on space, you can create an open-air linen closet right above your washer and dryer by installing a series of decorative shelves for housing your towels and bedding. Or search tag sales and flea markets for vintage kitchen cupboards that will give your impromptu closet a country feel and keep dust off your linen at the same time.

■ **A Set of Your Own** If your kids have different linens than you (they've got the colorful cowboy; you've got the 200-thread cotton), store them in the room where they're used—either in a bottom drawer or on a shelf in the closet.

■ **Get a Move On** Move table linens out of the closet and into the kitchen (provided you have a spare drawer) to store them closer to where you use them. Or keep them in your dining room buffet. To prevent wrinkles, try placing sheets of thin cardboard between each set.

■ **Keep It Simple** Never stack your linens too high (install more shelves if you can), so they won't come tumbling down every time you take something out. Keep only two to three sets of sheets per bed or sets of towels per person (donate the rest). As they come out of the laundry, place the fresh linen on the bottom of the pile so all sets rotate over time.

A family of four needs a certain number of towels, and that's what we have. We don't have room for excess. When guests come, it's a little tight, but we make do. Every bed has two sets of sheets, and that's it. I would only have one if my kids would promise not to vomit in the middle of the night ever again!

■ **Sweet Smells** Line your closet with cedar planks (available at kitchen and bath stores) to help prevent moth damage, or scatter small sachets of dried flowers to keep everything smelling fresh.

*W*ith six kids, my mom was always washing and changing towels, so she *color coded. Each kid had two towels in his or her own color. You couldn't put your towels in the hamper until you were sure the other of that color was waiting on the shelf.*

MAJOR TUNE-UP

If you're ready to graduate to a major linen tune-up, pay close attention to these tips. With just a bit more effort, you can create a space even Martha Stewart would envy.

- **Label Lover** Label each shelf by content—bath towels, hand towels, washcloths, sheets, pillowcases, extra blankets, and so forth—so that it will be easier to put linen back in its proper place.
- **Hang Ten** To keep tablecloths wrinkle free, try installing a low-hanging rod in your closet or a towel rack on the back of the door, pad it (try rubber tubing), and then lay the cloths over it. Or hang each one from a good-quality hanger (place a tag around the neck to identify it—"Linen Christmas cloth for two-leaf table").
- **There Is a Season** Rotate your sheets by season—every spring, put your cozy flannels on the top shelf and pull down the flowery cotton prints to eye level. In the fall, reverse the process.
- **Room to Grow** If you have an older home with a small, unoccupied bedroom, consider transforming it into a walk-in linen closet to increase your storage space.

The Entry Hall Closet

In our first home, a 1906 Craftsman bungalow, we didn't have a hall closet (we didn't have a linen closet either, for that matter). So, when we moved into our current home, I was ecstatic to have an entry hall closet to call my own. Never mind that it's a mere four feet wide; it's a closet next to the front door and that's enough for me!

You'd be amazed at what I can fit in that small space—a vacuum cleaner; seasonal coats, jackets, and a various array of hats, scarves, and mittens; slippers and shoes (we don't wear shoes in the house); holiday and gift-wrapping supplies; and a cooler. How do I do it? Luckily, the previous owners had the foresight to add shelves just above the rod running the length of the closet, perfect for storing that bulky cooler and other seldom-used items, such as winter accessories. Next is a hanging shoe cubby for our everyday footwear. Every spring I move winter coats and rain gear (I put them in my office closet) and reverse the process every fall, keeping the number of hanging clothes to a minimum. Small, stacking drawers house slippers, and a wrapping accessory bag keeps my holiday bows and paper in check.

I get a lot of bang for my buck out of that tiny closet. Everything has a proper home. Everything is neat. But most important, I can find what I want when I want it.

QUICK FIX

Designate this space primarily as a get-out-the-door pit stop and arm it with work and school essentials.

- **Hook Heaven** Keep the hallway or entranceway floor clear of back-packs, diaper bags, purses, and briefcases by installing a hook for every family member on the back of the closet door—lower hooks for young family members, higher hooks for Mom's and Dad's paraphernalia.
- **Yeah, I Got That** Keep a laminated list of daytime essentials—house keys, cell phone, homework, backpack, bag lunch, and so on—taped to the inside of the closet as a last-minute reminder, so nothing is ever left behind. (Add colored picture cutouts as visual cues for the soon-to-read younger set.)
- **Hang It Here** If you're really tight on space and love to entertain, consider buying a folding garment rack. Set it up in a small niche or empty bedroom before guests arrive (store it in the garage, basement, or attic when not in use). No more stuffing company's coats into a tight closet or piling them high on your bed.
- **No Closet? No Problem!** Create the illusion of a front hall closet by adding a corner coat rack and hall bench with built-in cubbies to stow sports gear and shoes. Or install a peg rail along the wall.

The Utility Closet

My current home doesn't have a utility closet. (What? No basement, no attic, and now no utility closet? How does this woman do it?) Using a few inexpensive wire shelves and hooks, however, I have successfully found a home for every mop, tool, and cleaning product in my back porch area just steps from my kitchen. At the moment, the space is also my pantry and laundry room, but everything coexists happily.

QUICK FIX

Every utility closet should contain cleaning and maintenance supplies—that's a given. But how do you efficiently organize it all? Read on for a few quick fixes.

Make Way for a Mudroom

Every family, large or small, could benefit from a mudroom, a cozy corner of the house where family members prepare or unload for the day. The perfect mudroom contains a bench for putting on or taking off shoes with a rug to soak up moisture, a place for shoe storage (it could be as simple as a rack under the bench or a basket for muddy boots), and a place to hang coats, hats, and mittens. You should locate your mudroom nearest the door most used—in the garage next to the entrance to the house, by the back door next to the carport, or in the front vestibule next to the entry hall closet.

But what if you simply don't have the room? Just think small. How about creating a mudroom niche complete with a small triangular bench built into the corner (maybe with a flip-top to store hat and mittens inside), hooks running parallel along the wall for hanging up coats and hats, a basket for mittens, or maybe even a small bookcase for personal belongings such as backpacks and work folders? (See Figure 5.)

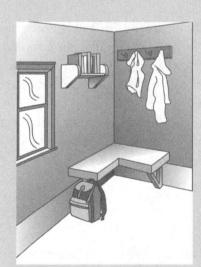

FIGURE 5. Mudroom corner

■ **Off the Floor** If you don't have a closet or cabinet to hide your mops and brooms, instead of sliding them next to your washer and dryer, install a mop holder on the wall and get them off the floor. Mount wire baskets around your laundry room to store cleaning supplies.

■ **Pare Down** To keep things looking neat, pare down cleaning products and tools that you haven't used in a year.

■ **It's in the Bag** Organize the sea of paper grocery bags by clamping them to a skirt hanger and hanging it from a hook. Put plastic bags in a dispenser, and pull one out as needed from the bottom. I found Hold-a-Bag at the Container Store (containerstore.com); it takes up little space and works flawlessly.

■ **Shower Power** Use a shower caddy or small plastic basket with handle to stow cleaning essentials. It's ready to grab and easy to carry around from room to room. Store from a hook on the back of the door or a wall.

■ **Basic Necessities** Use your utility closet to store all those odd items that never seem to have a home but are needed every now and then—flashlights and batteries, a toolbox with basic home-repair tools, and so forth. Hang extension cords from hooks (one for indoor use, the other for outdoor). Install a small sixteen-drawer hardware organizer on the back of the door or on an adjacent wall to store pushpins, small hooks, small nails, screws, and felt furniture pads.

MAJOR TUNE-UP

What if you're like me and you don't have a utility closet? If you have some space in your laundry room or back porch area or even a small alcove in your kitchen, you can create one. Here are a few ideas to get those construction juices flowing.

■ **Niche Kitsch** See a small recess between two cabinets in your kitchen that would be a perfect hiding place for your mop? Install a set of folding doors at the opening (head to a home center to find a pair that will match your kitchen's décor), or hang a rod with opaque curtains and then add rows of shelving and hooks on the inside walls.

■ **The Investment of a Lifetime** If you have space in your laundry room, consider installing prefab closet-size cabinets to keep your cleaning supplies organized and out of sight. Nearly every home center carries inexpensive store-brand cabinets that would be perfect for the job (Mills Pride at Home Depot would work nicely).

Close the Closet Door!

A hundred years ago, most middle-class homes didn't have many closets. And they certainly didn't have the walk-in wonders we see in all the model homes today! The reason? They didn't have much stuff to store.

Today, things are different. Sorting and purging will help get things back to a manageable size, and the abundance and variety of hooks, wire shelving, and baskets will keep the remaining essentials accessible and neat.

Daily Routines

The Morning Dash and Nighttime Wind Down

I n the Tinglof household, life is busy. Sure I'm organized, but some days it's almost chaotic. Although I stay home with my children, cutting down on some of the madness, I have three boys within two and a half years of each other (their ages range from three and a half to six at the time of this writing). That young, male energy constantly racing at top speed through my house alone often sends me in a tailspin. Obviously, we've developed a rhythm to our lives that works for us. It helps enormously, for instance, to have certain set routines.

Every member of the household has a morning and evening responsibility. In the morning, for instance, my husband is in charge of making breakfast for all while I see to it that the boys are dressed and ready for school. (Their duties include making their beds, hanging up their pajamas, and getting their backpacks.) In the evening, I handle dinner prep and homework; Kevin oversees showers and story time.

Like having a predictable schedule, prioritizing my days is a must, too. I take a moment each morning to think about how I want to organize my time—what problem, errand, or phone call needs to be addressed first. What project needs attention? Next, I envision how I want the rest of the day to play out, all other tasks falling into line, and then I tell my kids what's going to happen.

How to Minimize the Madness

What about you? Consider your scheduling problems. Maybe it's a little too stressful first thing in the morning when everyone is trying to get out the door at the same time. Or, perhaps evening is your trouble spot. The kids routinely have a meltdown just when it's time to settle down for bed. Take a moment and think about your family's life and pinpoint the time when problems emerge.

Come up with an amenable daily routine. Decide who will wake the kids, who will start breakfast, who will get the kids dressed and ready for school, and so forth. Conversely, work out an evening schedule, too. Who will make dinner? Will the kids eat first or will you eat as a family? Decide on a bedtime for all children and determine what chores and activities need to be completed before bedtime. If you want the kids to clean up toys, take a bath, and then read a family story—and all that takes an hour and their bedtime is eight o'clock—start directing them at seven.

The Morning Dash

If it seems like no matter how early you get up you just can't get everyone out the door on time, you're not alone. It's a top complaint of busy families everywhere. Instead of getting up earlier, however, take fifteen minutes before you go to bed every evening and prepare for the next morning. After the eleven o'clock news, for instance, I make the rounds, setting up the coffeemaker, organizing the kitchen, and laying out the kids' school clothes. Believe it or not, just these few things help streamline our morning.

Many tasks can be accomplished the night before—short of sleeping in your clothes—to make the morning dash less hectic. Try thinking ahead to the next day: is your son going on a field trip? Make sure his permission slip is signed. Is Thursday "Share Day" at your daughter's preschool? Help her pick out her treasure before her bedtime story rather than one minute before the car pool arrives the next morning. Assign everyone a chore or two each evening. Have someone set the breakfast table or have your children lay out their clothes for the next day (a huge time-saver for parents with fashion-conscious kids). Use timers wherever you can—to start the morning coffee or turn on your electric rollers.

If your family needs some serious morning reconstruction, however, it's best to start implementing changes slowly. Test-drive one or two ideas first (it will still make an enormous impact) instead of making sweeping amendments. By getting everyone slowly used to a new way of operating, they'll barely notice that they're doing something different. If you see time-management improvements, add a few more ideas.

QUICK FIX

Making small, effective changes is painless, yet the results are often astounding.

- **Sunday, Fun Day** Set aside fifteen to twenty minutes each Sunday evening to prep for the week ahead. Call a short family meeting, if you'd like, to discuss the upcoming schedule for the week—field trips, baseball practice, birthday parties. Next, assign everyone a task to get the Monday morning ball rolling (doing a load of laundry, checking homework, replenishing backpacks with gym uniforms, and so on). Make prep time the same each Sunday so it becomes part of your regular routine, and add a little fun by turning up some dance music.

- **Feed Me** Not only can you make your children's lunches the night before and leave them by the front door so they won't be forgotten, but you can pack their lunch bags every Sunday evening for the whole week—juice box, snack, and napkin, minus the perishables—and store them in the pantry.

- **Clotheshorse** Laying out school and work clothes the night before is an excellent way to reduce morning stress, but this idea, too, can be taken one step further by choosing outfits for the whole week. Choose a small hall closet and allocate each person his or her own shelf just for this purpose. Or purchase a six-pocket hanging closet organizer for your child—the sixth compartment is for shoes—and place a week's worth of folded clothes inside. Target sells one; One Step Ahead (onestepahead.com) offers a slightly larger version with additional side pockets.

MAJOR TUNE-UP

If you feel the need to succeed and are ready for a serious morning makeover, try these ideas. The tips are helpful as long as you don't mind moving some furniture!

Morning Pitfalls (and How to Avoid Them)

No one seems to have enough time in the morning, especially families with children. Yet if you take a close, critical look at how you handle the morning, you might be surprised to find that you and your family are slaves to a few of the following pitfalls.

Too Much TV Ever find yourself standing in front of the morning talk shows spellbound by a fascinating piece on the potato crop in Idaho? When you finally focus on the time, you realize that you're now twenty minutes behind schedule. You're not alone. Turn that thing off! If you simply must stay connected, try turning on the radio instead. NPR's *Morning Edition* runs news and features and cuts away for local traffic and weather reports—all without commercials. (Log on to npr.org/members for an NPR station in your area.)

You Snooze, You Lose Forget the snooze alarm and move the clock far enough away to make you get out of bed to turn it off. Once you're up, it's just a bit harder to justify crawling back into bed.

Cook to Order Instead of fixing pancakes and waffles, a delicious but time-consuming breakfast, make Monday through Friday "no cook" mornings. Instead, offer the family a selection of cold cereals, yogurt shakes, bagels, fresh fruit, and juice.

Shower Power If your household is constantly fighting for shower time in the morning, assign each person a designated time slot. Or, better yet, have younger children bathe at night (you, too, if you don't mind).

■ **Round 'Em Up!** Can't find your briefcase or car keys in the morning? Son's library books under his bed for six weeks collecting library fines? Well, here's your solution—you need one central spot where everyone can load and unload for the day. Call it a launching pad, the family garage, the corral—whatever you want—and try to make it near the exit that's used most frequently, not in the way of foot traffic, and large enough to accommodate your family's stuff. (A small alteration to the mudroom will bring it up to speed.) Use a bookcase tucked in a closet or a hall console near the front door: set backpacks and briefcases on the shelves; add color-coded bins inside drawers for wallets, sunglasses, and lunch money. Place a decorative bowl on top for car keys, incoming receipts, or letters that need to be mailed. Or hang several in-boxes on the wall. (holdeverything and Pottery Barn each make a smart-looking set.) Add hooks for backpacks and purses. Set some limits, though—you don't want it to look like a locker room. Tell the family that the corral is only a temporary holding spot for belongings.

■ **Command Central** Your corral takes care of the big stuff that your family hauls every day; now you need a spot for all the paper that they drag home, too. You know, a place to round up permission slips, school flyers, work-related memos, and so forth. If you already have a desk in your kitchen, it's just a matter of finding a filing system that works best. Create an in-box—anything from a basket to a dish—and instruct family members to use it for items needing immediate attention. Each evening, take a moment to go through and address each item. Sign that permission slip and tuck it in Junior's color-coded bin or assigned shelf. If you don't have a desk in your kitchen, however, you can still easily create a post. Place an in-box in the corner of your kitchen counter or on your dresser in your bedroom. It will take a few weeks before your entire family is on board with the system; just keep reminding them on a daily basis where to deposit their paperwork until it sinks in.

I have my keys on a mountaineering clip that's attached to the strap of my pocketbook. That way they're never at the bottom of my pocketbook. I feel that's safer for getting in and out of cars when you're parked in strange places. I never have to put Mia down to find my keys, either—I just reach back and get them. And when I come inside, I don't have to remember where I put them.

The Evening Wind Down

Evenings are rough for families. By six o'clock in most two-career households, both Mom and Dad are exhausted from the day, yet the kids are anxious to talk and share their experiences and at the same time wonder how long until dinner is ready. When one parent stays at home, dinner may be simmering on the stove, but the full-time caretaker is usually burnt out on crayons and juice boxes and anxiously looks forward to the other spouse to return home and offer some relief. Let's face it—the evening is a high-stress time of day when energy is low, bellies are empty, and everyone needs something!

Yet with a bit of foresight, the evening can actually be a loving time when families regroup and share their day.

When I was a child, I'd spend a lot of afternoons at my girlfriend Andrea's house. As I would leave around six, just as the dad was coming home from work, both the mother and father would sit together in the living room chatting, sipping cocktails. The lights would be dim, classical music would be softly playing, and you could smell that dinner was nearly ready. After I left, my girlfriend and her sister would stay in their rooms and do their homework, giving their parents time to catch up on the day. Promptly at seven, they all sat down to dinner together. To me, that scene seemed so peaceful and perfect.

KEY ORGANIZING TIPS

■ **Transition to the Evening** If you haven't seen your kids all day you'll need to find a way to transition from your daytime routine to your evening regimen. If you work outside the home, once you step through the door try to devote a half hour to catching up on the day with your kids. Don't answer the door or telephone. Keep the television off. Have everyone head to the kitchen for some communal meal prep and conversation.

■ **Keep to a Dinner Schedule** If you have dinner one night at five and the next night hold off dinner until 6:30 P.M., most kids won't respond well. It throws their little clocks off. Whatever time you choose to eat, keep it consistent.

■ **Assign Bedtimes** Give each child a set bedtime taking into account his or her age and sleep requirements; then stick to it each night.

■ **Develop Loving Evening Routines** Once the sun starts to set, turn your attention to the final wind down. Decide what needs to be done—dinner prep and household cleanup, homework, suppertime, showers, stories or songs together, bedtime—and assign each segment a time slot. Then count backward from bedtime to come up with a start time. For instance, if bedtime is 8:30 P.M. for all children and it takes two and a half hours to run your routine, then all children must be in the house at six ready to help.

■ **Give the Ten-Minute Warning** Most children, especially pre-schoolers, don't have a concept of time. It's very upsetting to them to suddenly be told to clean up their toys and get ready for dinner without warning. To avoid a tantrum or two, always shout out, "Ten minutes until cleanup!" Or "Ten minutes until dinner!"

■ **Limit After-School Activities** We all want our children to blossom and succeed in all that they do, and we want them to try new things, but when you have three kids running from activity to activity every day after school, it can create scheduling turmoil. Limit the number of sports or clubs that each child participates in.

■ **Keep It Peaceful** Although it may be tempting to head out to the driveway after dinner for a little one-on-one family basketball, exercising actually energizes rather than calms down most kids. Keep after-dinner events low key and tranquil such as reading, talking together, or watching a well-chosen video.

I *always made sure that the diaper bag was actually packed the night before. Obviously, I couldn't include snacks, but I had an extra outfit, extra diapers, baby wipes, little toys, and so forth. This way it wasn't a scramble in the morning when I wanted to get out the door.*

QUICK FIX

Now that you have the ground rules down, how about a few simple tips to cut down on the time spent cooking, cleaning, and shuffling the children off to bed?

■ **Menu Manager** Establish a set weekday menu—Monday pasta, Tuesday casserole, Wednesday Chinese takeout, and so forth—it keeps the dinnertime guessing to a minimum. (For more tips on streamlining dinner and other cooking quick fixes, turn to the "Mealtime" chapter.)

■ **Move the Machine** Screening phone calls is a must during dinner, but what good is trying to monitor your calls when your answering machine is all the way in your bedroom? Permanently move it to the kitchen, where you can easily hear who's calling while you're preparing dinner.

■ **Think Small** Little ones love to help in the kitchen. Designate a lower cabinet or drawer for dinnerware—plates, napkins, and cups, all within easy reach. Now your preschoolers can help set the table and you don't have to stop what you're doing to gather the supplies.

It's Just Routine

Life can be crazy. When kids enter into the mix, the days of lounging in bed on a Sunday afternoon are pretty much over. The good news is, however, that you can get control of the madness by establishing simple, everyday routines. Just a tweak here and a touch there to your family's day-to-day schedule, and presto, you'll be enjoying a bit of peace.

Even so, every family is different, and not all will be able to fit what they need to do each evening in a compact two-hour time slot. What happens if you work until eight o'clock? Do you hold dinner and eat as a family? What if your oldest son is a budding tennis star and can't get home from practice until seven o'clock each evening? What about doing his homework and his evening chores? All these are special considerations and need to be thought out carefully. But one thing is certain—consistency is the key to a peaceful evening. Decide as a family how you'll approach the end of the day together, and stick to it.

Finances

Some people hoard it; some people spend it even when they don't have it; others fear it. Then, of course, there are those who respect it. Whether you love money or hate it, you need it; and you have to find a healthy way to take care of it so that it will take care of you.

Money issues are deep rooted spanning back to our childhoods and most likely the result of how our parents viewed it. My mother, for example, the family business manager, was a frugal woman who carefully watched every penny go in and out of the house. First in line to sign up for an IRA when they became part of the financial landscape back in the seventies, she was a classic saver rather than an impulsive spender. My dad, on the other hand, was spontaneous to a fault. He once came home and announced that we were all taking a spring vacation to Spain. My mother flipped, but we went anyway. Another day he decided that we needed an addition to our house. Once again, my mother protested, but six months later we had a new family room.

I'm a blend of both these people. I'm a diligent saver, but I also have an impulsive side. (I once wanted to ship a $5,000 armoire that I saw in a Connecticut antique shop back to California, but when my husband threatened divorce, I backed off.)

My task here is simply to help you find ways to make your financial life easier and more secure both in the short term—bill paying and debt consolidation—and in the long term—retirement and college savings and estate planning—no matter what your personality is. As a financial planner once told me, money is a means to an end. There's nothing mysterious or mystical about it. What is baffling to most, however, is how to responsibly keep track of those precious bucks and make them work hard.

Setting Goals

About twice a year, I take a half hour or so and do a quick financial roundup and report my findings to my husband. Because I handle all the bill paying and hold the only checkbook, the poor guy has no idea where we're heading financially, much less if I've been funneling funds into a private Swiss bank account. This twice-yearly ritual is my way of keeping him informed, as well as having an open dialogue on our finances. I update him on our net worth (all assets—real estate, savings accounts, IRAs, insurance policies—minus all debt—mortgages, credit card bills, home equity loans) and recap what we owe and where. Next, we discuss whether we should make any investment changes. Finally, we reaffirm our short-term goals (like finally building our backyard deck) and long-term aspirations (early retirement sounds nice to us).

The conversation is pretty much the same each time, but restating our goals to one another is like renewing our wedding vows—it draws us closer as a couple knowing that we're on the same page. And apparently we're on the right track. According to financial experts, having an open dialogue about money and establishing fiscal benchmarks—deciding what you want to do and when—is paramount to a family's economic health. The reasoning is simple—when you set a serious goal you usually obtain it.

Put It in Writing

What do you dream of? Buying your first home? Taking a trip to Australia? Retiring in Tuscany? Sending the kids to an Ivy League school? Whatever your financial goals look like, it's important to declare them, own them. When you do, you'll be one step closer to attaining them.

Here's your assignment: during a quiet evening after the kids are in bed, both you and your spouse grab some paper and pens; then each of you must head to a quiet corner for a bit of goal searching. Don't hold back; anything goes. This first step is simply to proclaim your desires in writing (you'll compromise and hone your list later). The only rule is that you must divide your goals into three different categories: short-term goals (something you'd like, perhaps a car or a vacation, within the next twelve to eighteen months), midrange goals (something within two to five years, say, buying a new home), and long-term goals (building a substantial nest egg for retirement and the kids' college tuition).

When the two of you are done, head to the kitchen table for a look at each other's list. You might be surprised to learn that your significant other has secretly dreamed of something completely out of character, like trekking through Nepal. Maybe not this year, but who knows what will happen in ten years if you start saving those pennies now?

Prioritizing the Future

Once you've each taken a look at the other's list, start seeing what you both have in common, and work from there. Both want to buy a new car next year before the one you drive gives out? Great. Circle that one and move on.

Talk openly about your dreams, but be realistic and distinguish between the feasible and the fantasy. (I'd love to buy and restore a seventeenth-century villa near Rome, but that ain't gonna happen. Renting one for the summer, however, may be doable.) Try to keep each other focused on your future as a family, but compromise—you both deserve a bit of your dreams. Revisit your list twice a year to see if there are any changes—life has a funny way of surprising you with the unexpected (say, another baby or a big, fat inheritance). And remember, although it's important to save for retirement and the kids' college education, you're here now, and you may want to forgo the extra retirement savings for a few years in favor of saving for a new house in a good neighborhood with excellent schools or a safe car that can reliably get you to and from work.

Once you have your list of short-, mid-, and long-range goals decided upon, it's time to assign a dollar figure to each. Let's say you want to buy new bedroom furniture within the next eighteen months (a short-term goal). You've shopped around and found that you could buy a set for $3,500. Sounds like a lot, but if you sock away $185 a month in a money market fund that gives you 5 percent interest, you'll be reading the Sunday paper from your redecorated bedroom in about eighteen months.

When you break your goals down into smaller amounts, expensive dreams don't seem so hard to reach (that $185 a month for new furniture breaks down to a more palatable $46.25 a week). Knowing how much something costs and what it takes to get it helps to further focus your goals. Something that seemed important can suddenly wait once you see the price tag and figure out how long it will actually take to buy it.

Getting Out of Debt

When I was twenty-five, my girlfriend Gina and I went to Australia for a month. We had such a fantastic time in the Land Down Under that when we returned to the States, we tried to think of a way to go back for good. I was bitten with wanderlust, and there was no turning back. As I spent the next week deep in thought, reexamining my life and my goals (a concept very new to me), it quickly became painfully clear that I couldn't go back— I owed too much to my closetful of clothes. If I wanted to be free to pick up and travel at will (my job at that time allowed me to take as much time off as I wanted), I had to be financially free as well. My credit card debt was preventing me from doing the things that I truly wanted to do.

What an epiphany! That night, I cut up all my credit cards and promised to pay the balances off quickly. Within a year, I was debt free and on my way to Europe with saved, rather than borrowed, money.

Do you ever go to bed at night and lay awake thinking about the credit card bill due next week and how you are going to finance more than just the minimum payment? Does your rising debt make you uncomfortable? You're not alone. Americans have a love affair with consumerism, and it's eating us up. In fact, the Federal Reserve Board estimates that consumer debt in 1999 was a staggering $7 trillion, up from $3.55 trillion in 1990. That translates to approximately $9,000 per household. It's the number-one reason inhibiting financial success.

Take a look at your credit card statements, and add up just the interest charges from last year. Shocking, isn't it? Not all debt is bad, of course. In fact, some, like a home mortgage, is good. But when you keep refinancing to pull equity out of your home to pay off the rising credit card debt, that's a disaster just waiting to happen. Although that may allow you to deduct the loan interest from your taxes, if property values drop, you may end up owing more on your home than it's worth. It's important to understand the feelings behind your spending, but that's beyond the scope of this book; for a bit of soul searching, check out Suze Orman's *Nine Steps*

A Great Financial Tool

Wondering how I knew that if you invest $185 a month at 5 percent interest you can save $3,500 in just eighteen months? I'm no math whiz, but I do own a present-value calculator (financial calculator to some), a valuable tool that helps plan all sorts of saving scenarios. It looks just like a calculator that you buy at any electronics or office supply store (mine is Texas Instruments BA-35 solar), but it has six keys that your average calculator doesn't: *PV* (for present value), *FV* (for future value), *PMT* (for payment), *N* (for number of payments), *%I* (for interest), and *CPT* (for compute).

Say you have $12,000 saved for retirement, you contribute $300 a month to your company's 401(k) plan (which has been averaging 8 percent interest a year), and you want to know what you'll have when you retire in twenty-five years. No problem. By knowing four out of the five possible variables (CPT merely tells the calculator to do the math), you can quickly figure out your answer.

First, punch in 12,000, followed by PV (you presently have $12,000). Next, key in 300, then PMT (you save or make a payment of $300 each month). Now multiply twenty-five by twelve, followed by N (twenty-five years times twelve months a year; thus, 300 payments). Next, divide eight by twelve (.6666), and punch the %I key (8 percent compounded over twelve months). Finally, hit CPT, then FV (you're telling the calculator to compute the future value). Voilà! You'll have $197,225.

Want to know how much you need to save each month to get the $30,000 down payment for your first home in just two years (assuming you're investing in a conservative money market fund at 5 percent)?

PV: 0

FV: 30,000

N: 24

%I: 5 ÷ 12 = .4166

Answer? Hit CPT, then PMT, and you'll see that you'll need to sock away $1,191 every month before you can call the moving van (but don't forget that's only $298 a week).

to Financial Freedom (New York: Crown Publishing, 1997). In the mean-time, vow to get it together. You need to get rid of your debt before you can start saving for the future. Knowing that your debt is under control is more powerful and positive than having a garage full of stuff.

QUICK FIX

With patience, dedication, and willpower, you can be debt free. And although it certainly won't go away overnight, there are a few simple things that you can do today to take control and gain the confidence you need to fight for your financial freedom.

- **Think Before You Spend** Before you reach for your credit card, think, "Do I really need to buy this today?" (or write that phrase on a slip of paper and tape it to your credit card). Try to wait one week before you make any purchases of more than $50; wait one month for major purchases (you'll probably change your mind before the time is up).

- **Talk Openly with Your Spouse** Share your concerns about money and debt with your significant spender. It's impossible to do it alone; you need to work as a team by supporting each other. There is strength in numbers. Brainstorm together on ways to cut spending and pay off those cards.

- **Call Your Credit Card Companies** Most companies want to be competitive and will knock off a percentage point with little encouragement. Push a bit harder, and who knows?

- **Pay Off the Highest-Interest-Rate Card First** Concentrate on paying off the card with the highest interest rate first (paying just the minimum on all the others). When you've paid it off, cut it up, call the company, and cancel the account; then move on to your next plastic offender.

- **Cut Them Up** Choose one credit card to use in case of emergency (that doesn't mean a half-price shoe sale) and cut up the remaining. With temptation gone, it's easier to keep your spending under control. (If you aren't in deep debt, you may want to keep two cards, but we'll talk about that later.)

- **Consolidate** Look in the business section of your local paper, or check in financial magazines such as *Money*, for credit cards offering low rates. Then transfer all your high-interest credit card debt to just one low-rate card, but be sure that you continue to pay as much each month to the new card as you've been paying to all your other cards combined (you'll get out of debt months sooner). Be sure to read the fine print carefully, too.

Some companies' teaser rates (very low interest rates to entice you to sign on) don't last long, and many charge a higher rate for balance transfers.

C ash seems to hemorrhage from my wallet, so I try not to carry too much of it at any time. Instead I charge everything, even a $2 cup of coffee at Starbucks, to my American Express or Visa This way, at the end of the month when the bill comes in, I can keep careful track of all those little expenses. Besides, I want those two frequent flier miles!

MAJOR TUNE-UP

There are other, more drastic ways of cutting debt, but there's always a downside when you take a radical approach. Carefully analyze your situation before following any of the suggestions in this section. Realize that even if you do get out of debt, it's not a signal to repeat the behavior all over again. If it does happen twice, you may want to seek the help of a credit counselor or Debtors Anonymous (www.debtorsanonymous.org).

■ **Sell, Sell, Sell** Take a look around the house. Do you have an autograph, stamp, or coin collection that you don't care for any longer? Maybe it could bring in some extra cash. Take a look at your portfolio. Any stocks you've been thinking of selling? Savings bonds from your first Holy Communion? Consider family heirlooms carefully, though. You may regret selling them in a few years. (I once sold a gold coin that my grandmother had left me just to pay my college phone bill. It's more than twenty years later, and I still regret my actions.)

■ **Get a Job** It could be as simple as working in a department store on weekends or delivering newspapers from your car before you head to work in the morning. The extra money can quickly add up, and you won't be agonizing over whether to sell your great-grandmother's antique silver service.

■ **Use Your Savings** Got a few thousand hiding in a 3 percent savings account? Cash it out and pay off your debt. You'll be ahead of the game. (Keeping $2,000 in a 3 percent account gains approximately $60 in interest a year, yet a $2,000 balance on a 16 percent credit card account costs $344 a year in interest. If you pay off the debt, you'll actually *save* $284.)

■ **Borrow from a 401(k) or Life Insurance Policy** Both have major disadvantages. If you borrow from your 401(k) plan, for instance, you'll lose out on any gains that the stock market might make, thus possibly endangering your retirement. Also, if you lose your job, you may have to repay the loan within sixty days. Borrowing from a life insurance policy is a better option, but if you should die before you pay back the loan, your death benefit is reduced by the amount borrowed. Be sure to understand all the financial ramifications before cashing in.

■ **Take a Second on Your Home** A home equity loan sounds nicer than a second mortgage, but that's exactly what it is—*a second mortgage*. If you have equity built up in your home, a second might be a painless way to get out from under your debt. And although you may be able to deduct the interest from the loan from your taxes, closing costs can run in the thousands, pushing you further in the hole. Plus, you may be jeopardizing your most valuable asset—your home.

The Last Word on Credit Cards

Let's face it, plastic is convenient. And if you're careful about how you use it, it can be a valuable tool in building a solid credit history (important for major purchases like a new home). All you really need are two credit cards—a low-interest-rate card and a perk card—but consider these points before signing on the dotted line.

Low-Interest-Rate Card Think of this card as a white knight offering you peace of mind in an emergency (to purchase a last-minute airline ticket to attend a funeral cross-country, for instance) or a short-term line of credit (that dining room set that you've been planning to buy is on sale this week, but your bonus check to cover it won't come until next month). Do your research and find the lowest rate available (don't be duped by low teaser rates that end in a few months) and one with no annual fee.

Perk Card If you have the discipline to pay off your balance every month, then add a credit card that offers perks—everything from frequent flier miles to money to use toward the purchase of a car. If you charge just about everything on this card, from groceries to haircuts, the benefits add up quickly. But find a card with a perk that you'll actually use, and be sure to pay off your balance each month; otherwise, you'll be back in the black hole of consumer debt before you know it.

Making a Budget

With your debt under control, it's time to set up a budget. Say the *B* word and the average person rolls his eyes. With today's fast-paced family life, most parents say there's no time to sit down and crunch the numbers. Unfortunately, it's the only way to organize your finances and save for the things you truly value. Fear not—budgeting doesn't have to be distasteful; there are many quick tricks and software programs out there to help you. And once you get the framework in place, it's relatively painless to follow (provided you were realistic in your calculations).

Make a Note of It

Why do some people claim they can't afford to buy what they need? Simple. They haven't a clue where their money disappears to on a daily basis. To get a handle on the situation, you have to understand exactly what comes in each month (income) and what goes out (expenses). One reliable way to monitor your spending is with a pad and pencil. Carry it with you everywhere and track even the minor expenses, like the quarter you give your daughter for the gumball machine. Get into the habit of asking for receipts, too; it's much easier to follow what went where at the end of a long, busy day. Follow your income as well. In addition to your salaries, you may occasionally get some freelance income, interest income, or my personal favorite, the birthday or Christmas check.

Do this for a month or two (possibly three if your expenses vary greatly), and then sit down and list every expense you have, such as rent or mortgage, utility bills, groceries, preschool or private school tuition, clothing, medical expenses, home repair, magazines and newspapers, birthday presents, car washes, fast-food snacks, pedicures, video rentals, library book fines—you get the idea (but don't forget to record occasional expenses like car repair and vacations)—then divide your expenses into major categories.

Armed with this information, you can now make informed decisions on what to spend where (that is, make a budget). You might be surprised to find, for instance, that those seemingly innocent café au laits that you buy every morning for $2.25 before heading to work cost you $45 a month, or $540 a year. Or you may think that your $520 a month grocery bill can't be cut any further. So be it. On the other hand, maybe you could start fixing your laits at home and save that $45 a month for one of your short- or midterm goals. The decision is yours. But isn't it nice to have the choice? For once, you'll be directing your money rather than your money directing you. Spend and save the way you live—not the way you think you should or the way your neighbors do.

QUICK FIX

Once your budget is set up with a dollar figure assigned to each category, it's time for a test drive. Here are a few simple ways to keep tabs of your monthly finances. (Some families prefer to assign yearly figures for each category rather than monthly. When you work from an annual financial plan, it's easier to budget and keep track of occasional expenses such as car repair, property taxes, and vacation funds.)

■ **The Write Way** At the beginning of each month, set up two columns on a sheet of legal-sized paper or a notebook page—one for income, one for expenses. On the income side, list all the money coming in for the month. On the expense side, write down all your expense categories that you decided upon from the above exercise (skipping lines for daily and weekly entries between each category) and the target price for each (e.g., groceries, $520; gasoline, $160; gifts, $35; entertainment, $200; etc.). At the end of each day or week, total your expenses carefully, watching that you don't go over the target price (if you do, you may be able to "borrow" from another section; but remember, there is only so much money to go around, and it might be better to simply cut back or do without for this particular month). At the end of the month, add up both your income and your expense columns, and then subtract expenses from income. If you come up short, you'll need to make some adjustments. If you have a positive cash flow, however, congratulations! Take the surplus and put it toward one of your many wonderful goals.

■ **The Envelope, Please** Each time you deposit your paycheck, immediately write a check for each fixed expense (items that don't change from month to month such as mortgage or rent, utilities, medical premium, etc.). Then take what's remaining in cash and divide it into labeled envelopes—one for groceries, another for gas money, and so on. Use the money from each appropriate envelope as you need it. Try to collect receipts so that you can see at the end of the month how well you did.

When a specific envelope is empty, wait until next month to make the purchase from that category, or if you have to, "borrow" from another (be sure to keep a record so that you can make adjustments at the end of the month).

MAJOR TUNE-UP

There are dozens of computer software programs and financial Internet sites that can help you organize your finances and figure out a budget. If you're willing to put in the time to enter all your financial data, they can be very helpful in keeping a careful eye on your cash flow and even your whole investment portfolio.

Two of the most popular software programs, Quicken and Microsoft Money, are easy to learn and navigate. You simply set up expense categories (they have an extensive list, but you're free to create your own) and type in all your "payees," from the phone company to the mortgage broker. The program notifies you when a bill is coming due and charts monthly (pie, graph, or bar—it's your choice) where your money goes for such things as clothing, housing, entertainment, and so forth (a very helpful as well as eye-opening tool).

There are a few small inconveniences to these programs, though. First, it takes time to log in all your expenses (although you'll have to spend time notating them in a handwritten ledger, too), and if you let it lapse for a week or two, it's hard to catch up. Second, even though you log your bills in your checking account register, you need to also record them in the computer program—essentially doing the same task twice. Finally, it's difficult to balance the "cash" account. Even tiny, day-to-day expenses—a quarter for the meter—must be accounted for; otherwise, what you have in your pocket won't match what the program says (some days I'm off by $20).

Bill Paying

How do you pay your bills? Do you meticulously write checks the day they arrive in the mail? Or do you throw the pile into a basket and sift through them once a month? For most people, bill paying is a twice-monthly, time-consuming ritual that we'd all rather forget.

Budgeting Pitfalls

It's not easy for some families to stick to a budget. But it doesn't have to be painful. Here are a few common mistakes and how to avoid them.

Writing Up a Budget Without Knowing How You Spend Your Money Before you can think about drafting a budget, you need to see exactly where your money goes each month. The only way to do this is carefully documenting every nickel and dime for several months. Only then can you decide how much you should be spending (or cutting back) on each aspect of your life.

Feeling Powerless Your money does not control you (although it often feels that way). You control your money. It isn't hopeless no matter how often you've tried to budget.

Thinking on a Grand Scale No need to cut your grocery bill in half to make a budget work. Actually, it's constant, incidental spending that ruins most budgets. Instead of all the premium cable channels, try just basic cable. Four magazines arriving in the mail each month when you really only have time to read just one or two? Cancel them. Always opt for valet parking? Park down the street and walk instead. Each one may not seem like a lot of money, but add them all up and the amount can be considerable.

Not Allowing for Any Guilty Pleasures Budgeting means watching your money carefully, not depriving yourself of every pleasure in life. Love having a pedicure once a week? No need to cut it out completely; just try limiting it to once or twice a month.

Not Using Enough Categories to Track Spending If you find that your miscellaneous column is the biggest entry at the end of the month, then you haven't listed enough categories. You need to see exactly where your money goes each month, and you do that by breaking down your spending into very specific areas (we even have a category for film and photo processing to track my camera-buff husband's hobby).

Not Keeping a Running Tally You may have decided that you're only going to spend $50 a month on gifts, but you're always surprised when you run over. It's probably because you don't keep a running tally of your expenses. Write down the amount of every gift you purchase, so that when you reach $43 for the month, you'll only spend $7 for the first-grade teacher's gift instead of $15.

KEY ORGANIZING TIPS

- **Select Two Bill-Paying Days per Month** Depending on the days your bills are due, decide on two days each month—say the eleventh and the twenty-sixth—that you'll pay bills, and stick to the schedule. Having two consistent days will help avoid late fees and possibly a poor credit rating.

- **Review Bills the Day They Arrive** Don't let the mail sit on the kitchen table for a week—sift through it daily. Open bills immediately and check for accuracy. If there's a discrepancy, call customer service right away or place it in your "phone calls to be made" file and follow up as soon as possible.

- **Notate the Envelope** Once your bill has passed inspection, place it back in its original envelope (minus all the advertising supplements) and write in the lower right corner the date it's due and the amount owed. Then file it.

I'm the one who takes care of all the bill paying and investing in our family. Yet it occurred to me one day that if I should die suddenly, Brenda won't know what's what. So, I typed up a list spelling everything out for her and locked a copy of it in our safe-deposit box.

QUICK FIX

You may have been paying bills since you got your first job, but you still feel your system needs a bit of help. Not to worry—there are plenty of painless tips to make the process run a bit smoother.

- **Pull into the Bill-Paying Station** Set aside an area of your house—an office desk, a kitchen drawer, a nightstand cubby—and designate it as your permanent bill-paying residence. Keep a supply of pens, stamps, and a calculator nearby, and instruct all family members that borrowing is forbidden. It's helpful to have your station close to your household files (more on that in the "Paperwork" chapter) so that as you pay your bills, you can file the receipts in the appropriate folders.

■ **All Systems Go** There are many ways to organize your bills, but here are the three most popular systems. Just designate one weekday hour twice a month to take care of business.

1. **Labeled Folders** All you'll need are two folders—one labeled "bills due first through the fifteenth" and the second labeled "bills due the sixteenth through the thirty-first." Then sit down around the twenty-sixth to work on the former folder, around the eleventh for the latter.

2. **Vertical Wire Organizer** If you like to see your bills to get a visual idea of what's due next, invest in a vertical organizer (available at office supply stores) and file your bills—one wire slot for each bill—chronologically, making sure the due date written on the envelope is facing out.

3. **Baskets** Neat and pretty, a small basket on your bill-paying station is a perfect solution for those who want to keep things looking nice. Just remember to always stack chronologically, with bills due first on top; otherwise, you may miss paying a bill that gets buried under the pile.

■ **Once Is Enough** Rather than paying homeowner's/renter's/medical/car insurance bills monthly, pay your premiums annually (or at the very least, quarterly). No more monthly hassles of getting the payment in on time, and as an added bonus, you'll save money, too, because most charge a monthly service fee of $2 to $3 for the privilege of paying monthly.

■ **Same Day, Same Way** Phone bill due on the fifth? Cable bill due on the tenth? And gas bill due on the twentieth? Forget about it! Simplify the insanity by calling each company and asking if they will change the due dates—say, all on the fifteenth—so you can pay and mail them all at once.

■ **Stamp It** Invest in a personalized return-address stamp with built-in ink pad (available at stationery stores). It saves time and aggravation.

MAJOR TUNE-UP

Technology can be a wonderful thing, especially when it comes to bill paying. These days, it's easier than ever to manage nearly all of your finances online. Following any one of the suggestions below, or using a combination of several, will save you scads of time—a huge bonus for busy families.

■ **Pay Online** Nearly every company lets you pay your bill online. Look through the literature that comes in your monthly bill to see if this service is offered. You simply log on to the company's website and enter your account number and credit card or checking account number. That's it. The rest is done through cyberspace. Although it's fast and convenient, many companies still charge a service fee for the privilege—always check the fine print first.

■ **Debit Delight** Authorize your mortgage, utility, or insurance company to automatically debit their monthly premiums on the same day each month from your checking account. Although the ultimate time-saver, there is a downside. Automatic debit plans, unfortunately, work on a set schedule, not allowing you the monthly flexibility of deciding which day you want to send the funds. In addition, some companies still charge a fee (like my car insurer) for the service.

■ **Bills in Space** Rather than logging on to each individual company website to pay your bills or writing out dozens of checks each month, sign up for electronic bill paying through your bank or an independent company such as CheckFree.com. With just a few clicks, all your bills are paid. Convenience does have a price, though, around $5 to $15 per month, but if you write a lot of checks each month, it pretty much pays for itself because you won't have to buy stamps or extra checks.

■ **Cyber Invoicing** Some brokerage firms not only offer online bill paying, but electronic invoicing, too, where you'll receive your bills electronically. No more paper! The cost? Well, Fidelity Investments says "free" if you maintain a total minimum balance of $30,000 in all your Fidelity accounts (fidelity.com).

■ **Take Charge** If you're a responsible credit card consumer (you pay your entire balance every month), then consider using your "perk" card (see "The Last Word on Credit Cards," above) to pay for many of your monthly bills, such as your Internet provider, long-distance phone company, newspaper delivery—whomever will accept a credit card. Not only will you earn points or miles, but it's easy to keep track of expenses each month when you review your credit card statement. The best part is, you write only one check to cover it all.

Creating a Savings Plan

To reach your financial goals, you must make saving a habit. There are all kinds of ways to save money. Some obviously produce better results than others, but don't always turn to the one that gets you the biggest returns; the trick is finding a method that works best for you—a system that you can stick to month after month.

⏰ **TIME-SAVER**—Have your paychecks direct-deposited into your checking account (your pay is wired from your employer to your bank). No more waiting in line at the bank, and the funds will be available at predictable times each month, helping you plan for bill paying.

QUICK FIX

For some, putting money aside each paycheck is painful; for others, seeing the accounts grow and the interest compound is enough to make them giddy. If you find yourself in the former group, maybe one of these little mind games will help you amass some dough.

■ **Bill Yourself** Add a new monthly statement to your bill pile—one for your services as a hardworking parent. Write up an invoice (you can print several at once on your computer), and attach an envelope addressed to your bank with a deposit slip. If saving money is a new concept to you, try shooting for $25 a month and slowly increase the amount as you feel more confident.

■ **Automate** With as little as a phone call to your local bank or brokerage firm, you can have a set amount of money withdrawn from your checking account or paycheck each month and deposited directly into a money market or mutual fund of your choosing. When it's done automatically each month, it's by far the easiest, most pain-free way of saving some big bucks.

■ **Take Five** Never spend a five-dollar bill again. Every time you see Abe Lincoln in your wallet, pull him out and stash him in a coffee can. When the can is full, deposit the proceeds in the bank.

■ **Coin Saver** This is a great way for the whole family to get involved. Find a large glass jar and every evening have each member of the household deposit all his or her change inside. When the jar is full, have the kids roll the coins and take them to the bank. You won't fund their college education this way, but it's a great jumping-off point toward a family vacation.

*W*hen *I first worked as a waitress, right out of college, I used to come home with at least five dollars' worth of coins after every shift. I looked at this as gravy money that I threw in a piggy bank. About once a month, I'd roll the coins and deposit the proceeds in the bank. It was a painless way to save.*

■ **Group Dynamics** Find a group of willing (and trustworthy) savers and have each contribute a set amount of money—say $15 a week—to a communal kitty. At the end of the month, one person takes the pot and personally invests it for her own family. The following month, someone else gets the loot. And so on. If you have eight people in your saving gang, that's $480 every eight months. Or open a joint mutual fund with a friend and each contribute a set amount of money each month (you can have it automatically deducted from your checking accounts).

*A*nytime *we get "free money," say, like the Bush tax-cut check, it automatically goes into Francesca's college fund. We don't even think about it. Off it goes.*

MAJOR TUNE-UP

When it's time to get serious about saving, one of these methods is sure to deliver.

■ **Tax Saver** My brother-in-law swears by this method for saving money. He takes zero deductions from his paycheck, thereby ensuring a big, fat refund check from the IRS every year. Once in his hands, the check is socked away or used for long-awaited big expenses—vacations, furniture, home improvements. (Some financial experts argue that this isn't the best form of saving because Uncle Sam, not you, earns the interest on your money over the past year. They argue that you should adjust your withholding so you'll neither collect from the IRS nor owe. But if the tax-refund system works for you, ignore the naysayers and keep up the good work!)

■ **Freelance Funds** Thinking of doing a little freelancing on the side now that the kids are a bit older? Live on your salary just as you have been doing, but save the freelance money for short- and midrange goals.

I used to have two speech clients twice a week that I'd work with in my home office after school while Jenna and Cara played quietly upstairs. It wasn't a lot of money, maybe $100 or so a week, but when I got those checks, I put them directly into our travel account. When I had a few thousand, it was time to call the travel agent.

■ **Raise to New Heights** Whenever my husband gets a raise, we up his contributions both to his 401(k) plan as well as his automatic deduction to our short-term savings account. The secret to success here is to increase your deductions as soon as you hear the news about your raise, well before you get too used to the extra money in your paycheck.

Organizing for the Long Term

Goals established? *Check.* Debt under control? *Working on it.* Budget established? *Check.* Will set up? *What? There's more?* Yep.

It's time to start organizing for the latter half of your life. You know, those carefree, fun years that you haven't seen the likes of since you were four and could ride your bike in the driveway all day. You've got to plan for those, too, with wills and life insurance, in addition to properly investing your nest egg. Confused? Read on.

Do You Need Life Insurance?

Got kids? If you're reading this book, I'm assuming you do. Therefore, if you—the major or sole breadwinner of the family—want to financially protect your young brood in case you die prematurely, then you'll need life insurance. (The chances that you'll die young are slim to none, but if you do, the financial consequences could be devastating to your loved ones.)

There are all kinds of formulas to determine how much insurance you'll need. The old rule of thumb said two to three times your annual salary; these days agents say five to six times (sometimes ten). But the truth is highly more individual—it all depends on your current assets (and whether the surviving spouse will be willing to liquidate them), your liv-

Spring Cleaning: Organizing for Tax Time

There are two types of tax preparers—those who are chomping at the bit every January and race out of the starting block, calculator in hand, once their final W-2 arrives in the mail and those who vow to get started earlier this year but find themselves once again pulling an all-nighter come April 14. Sound familiar? Organizing and filing your taxes takes time, but there are a few tips to make the process go a bit smoother.

Make a Date Circle the first weekend in February on your kitchen calendar, highlight the date in your pocket organizer, or notate it in your computer's appointment search. Do whatever it takes to set this time aside for organizing your tax file. By then you should have all your necessary documents from employers and brokerage firms. If not, start making phone calls to check the status of the missing documents. Then . . .

Check It Twice Check your package from the IRS to make sure you have all the forms and schedules you'll need. If something is lacking, either call the IRS (800-829-3676) or download copies of what you need from their website (irs.gov). If you've used a software package like TurboTax or MacInTax before, go online to Intuit (intuit.com) and download your federal and state programs. It's faster than heading to the store to buy them, and there's no extra packaging to discard or file. Also compare your employer's W-2 with your last payroll stub of the year. If there's a discrepancy, ask your employer for a corrected W-2. Then . . .

Divide and Conquer Spread your tax file out before you and separate receipts and documents according to schedules. Paper clip each pile together with the appropriate schedule. Then . . .

Begin Early filers get their refunds faster than those who file late (this year, it took all of two weeks to get mine). Besides, when you have the luxury of time, you're less likely to make a costly mistake. Schedule three to four weekday evenings to fill out your forms. And finally . . .

Put on Your John Hancock Don't forget to sign your returns, make a copy for your files, and place it in the folder with receipts. Keep all prior tax returns indefinitely.

ing expenses and liabilities (your mortgage and child-care costs, for example), future expenditures (kids' college tuition), whether you want the family to simply live off the policy interest alone or have them tap into the principle, and, most important, your comfort level—how much your budget can actually afford. It's important to run the numbers every few years as your life changes (more kids, big inheritance, divorce).

What the heck is term insurance anyway? Simply put, term insurance allows you to buy a policy for a set period of time—ten, twenty, thirty years. When the term is up, you stop paying premiums. And because you buy it solely for the death benefit, you get nothing when the policy ends. It's the least-expensive form of insurance and the best for young families because you can determine how long you'll need the coverage. To guarantee that your premiums will not rise as you age, look for "level-premium term," where your monthly payments stay locked in for the duration of the term, but make sure it remains the same for the *entire* term, not just the first half. (Other types of insurance, such as whole life, act as investment vehicles that not only pay a death benefit, but are also invested in a cash account. Although you can borrow against them in case of an emergency, the premiums are more expensive and the invested account typically does not perform as well as stocks.)

QUICK FIX

Avoid the high-pressure sales pitch of insurance agents and use the Internet to your advantage. You can shop for quotes day or night and compare several companies all at once and even begin the application process right online.

■ **Quotesmith.com** View twenty life insurance companies in one click, plus their ratings (all companies are rated A++ to F based on their financial strength and operating performance).

■ **Insweb.com** Very easy to read and navigate. Allows you to compare several companies and their Standard & Poor's rating at a glance. Shows monthly rather than annual premiums (great for calculating your monthly budget).

■ **Quickquote.com** Compare quotes from several companies; then narrow it down for a more detailed side-by-side comparison.

Wills

I admit it. My husband and I have only recently written up our wills. Many reasons I'm sure the more than 70 percent of Americans who haven't written theirs will understand: it saddens me to think about the prospect of both my husband and I dying and leaving our children orphaned; we couldn't decide who to assign guardianship of our three boys; it seemed costly and confusing.

But if you have kids, you need a will. If you should die *intestate*, that is, without a will, the court will divide up your assets and your kids according to the laws of your state (and take a percentage of the estate in the process to offset the work that's involved). Think about that for a moment. The courts may decide that your sweet, loving sister isn't the best choice as guardian for your children but someone else in your family, for whom you may not have warm, tender feelings. In a will, however, you name an *executor*, a family member or trusted friend who ensures that your wishes are carried out.

QUICK FIX

Contrary to what many may believe, you don't need a lawyer to write a will. If you have a complicated estate (large assets, numerous beneficiaries—including stepchildren and charitable organizations) and long, involved wishes for dividing things up, hiring a lawyer is clearly in your best interest. The cost will range from a few hundred dollars to several thousand, depending on how organized you are in presenting the information to him or her. But for the rest of us, though, once we get over our uneasy feelings about drafting a will, it's really quite easy and inexpensive.

■ **Go Online** Several Internet companies (such as Legaldocs.com) offer wills online. Just answer a few questions regarding how you want your estate divided and whom you want to designate as guardian of your children. Click and presto, you have a will. Fees are usually cheaper than buying software (Legaldocs charges about $8.95 for a simple will, $27.95 for an estate plan).

■ **Buy Software** Just about every financial software publisher has an estate-planning program. Check out WillMaker 8.0 (Nolo Press) and Quicken WillWriter (The Learning Company). Although more expensive than doing it online, the software programs let you update your will as often as your mood strikes. (If you're part of a young family, chances are you'll write several wills in your lifetime as circumstances change, such as a new baby.)

Saving for the Long Term

I'm no financial expert, but statistics tell the story—when you're investing for the long haul (retirement and sending the kids to college), nothing beats investing in the stock market. In fact, stocks have outperformed all other investments—an average of 10.6 percent annually, and that takes into account the crashes of 1929 and 1987. When it comes to saving for your children's college education and your retirement, a variety of options are available.

Saving for Retirement

When faced with either saving for retirement or college, always maximize your retirement savings first. Why? Although there are many resources to help pay for college (e.g., student loans, grants, scholarships, tax credits, part-time jobs), there is no aid for retirement (with the exception of Social Security, of course). So, how much will you need to finance your retirement? There are countless formulas that finance books and websites offer you, far too complicated for me to get into in just a few paragraphs. Suffice it to say, save as much as you can and then save a little more. But which saving vehicle is best for you? Read the summaries below and then do your own homework.

QUICK FIX

There's only one quick fix, and it really is a painless way to save for retirement. It's your company-sponsored retirement savings plan, called a 401(k). You can invest up to 15 percent of your salary, up to $11,000 annually (this amount will slowly increase through 2006), in a tax-deferred account. (Most companies offer a variety of investment options, such as stock and bond mutual funds.) Your contributions are taken out from your paycheck *before taxes* (a huge savings because it actually lowers your adjusted gross income). In addition, most employers generously match your contributions anywhere from 25 to 100 percent (25 to 100 cents for every dollar you put in) up to the first 5 to 6 percent of your contribution. Another advantage: you can borrow the money (usually up to 50 percent) before you reach the age of fifty-nine and a half at a reasonable interest rate without penalty. If you change employers, simply roll your 401(k) over into a traditional or Roth IRA and begin a new 401(k) with your new employer. Contact your human resources or benefits department for more details.

MAJOR TUNE-UP

If you work for a company that doesn't offer a 401(k), you won't be left out in the cold when it comes time to retire. The choices out there are plentiful—just find the one that best matches your situation.

■ **Roth IRA** If your company doesn't have a 401(k) or you're contributing the maximum percentage that your company matches, turn next to a Roth IRA. Although you won't get a tax deduction for your contribution and there are income limitations (your adjusted gross income must be less than $95,000 for an individual, $150,000 for married couples filing jointly), your money grows tax-free—you won't pay a dime to the government when you pull it out during retirement.

■ **Traditional IRA** Make up to a $3,000 tax-deductible contribution each year (with increases due through 2008) and watch your money grow tax deferred until you begin withdrawing the funds at age fifty-nine and a half. Disadvantage: you're subject to income limitations—your adjusted gross income can't exceed $34,000 for an individual, $54,000 for married couples filing jointly.

⏱ **TIME-SAVER**—Track the progress of your financial portfolio quarterly, not weekly. You will save time and aggravation as well. You won't be tempted to sell stocks, bonds, or mutual funds when the market is down. Remember, those who trade the most usually lose the most. Do your homework, invest wisely, and sit back and relax.

Saving for College

The good news is that the percentage of high school students going on to college is growing each year. The bad news is that the cost of college room, board, and tuition is rising exponentially—far outpacing inflation. Most students, however, receive some kind of financial aid—nearly 70 percent—in the form of federal student loans and government grants. Plus, there are always scholarships. Do you have a budding Tiger Woods in your midst? Maybe he can get a free ride to a four-year university. Yet your child doesn't have to be a first-rate jock or whiz kid to get a scholarship. There are thousands out there just waiting for your child to cash in. For a good place to discover a few hidden gems, log on to scholarships.com or pick up a copy of *The Scholarship Advisor*, by Christopher Vuturo (New York: Princeton Review, 2001).

QUICK FIX

A quick fix for college saving is a bit of an oxymoron; it takes discipline and hard work whichever way you choose. Yet some ideas are easier than others.

■ **Equity Economics** If you own your own home, concentrate on paying off your mortgage as quickly as possible by adding additional money to the principal each month. (Use your financial calculator to figure out how much you'll need to add to reach a zero balance by the time Junior hits his senior year of high school.) When your child nears the end of twelfth grade, apply for a home equity line of credit, and write tuition checks against the equity in your home. (I'm assuming you have great credit and can qualify for the loan.) The benefits are twofold: first, you use only the amount of money you need when you need it. Second, the money from a home equity loan is usually tax deductible.

■ **Uncle Sam Wants to Help You** Did you know that there are two tax credits to help families with children in college? (A *tax credit* is deducted directly from the tax you owe, making it more valuable than a *tax deduction*, which merely reduces the portion of your income that's subject to tax.) The *Hope Credit* covers the first two years that your child is in college by allowing you to deduct 100 percent of the first $1,000 and 50 percent of the second $1,000 of college tuition and fees (not including room and board), for a total of a $1,500 credit per student per year. To qualify, your child must be at least a part-time student working toward a degree or certificate. *The Lifetime Learning Credit* covers the third year and beyond of college but is limited to 20 percent of the first $5,000 of tuition and fees, for a maximum of $1,000 (as of 2003, it is limited to 20 percent of the first $10,000, for a total of $2,000). Although there's no minimum course-load requirement, it is calculated on a per-family basis, not per student. Both of these credits are subject to income limitations: $40,000 adjusted gross income for individuals, $80,000 for married couples filing jointly. Also, you can't take either credit the same year that you withdraw money from an Education IRA (see below).

MAJOR TUNE-UP

Perhaps you rent your home or the equity won't be enough to cover all your children's educations. Not to worry—there are plenty of other saving options to investigate. All have their advantages and disadvantages, barely covered in this short amount of space, so research each one more carefully before proceeding.

■ **Custodial Accounts: UTMA/UGMA** Although *each* parent or grandparent can contribute up to $10,000 annually to these accounts (also known as Uniform Transfers to Minors Act and Uniform Gifts to Minors Act, respectively) without paying any gift tax, the first $750 in interest that these accounts generate is tax free, the next $750 is taxed at the child's rate (typically 15 percent), and the remainder is taxed at the parent's rate (you can cut the amount of taxable capital gains by investing the money in a low-turnover mutual fund such as an index fund or in low-dividend growth stocks). Other disadvantages: a custodian (typically a parent or guardian) controls the account until the minor (your child) reaches eighteen or twenty-one, depending on the laws of your state; then the child takes control over the account. Perhaps college is the last thing on your youngster's mind, but a new convertible is. Plus, having money in your kid's name reduces the amount of financial aid you'll be able to qualify for.

■ **Education IRAs** Although money deposited in these accounts for anyone under eighteen years old is nondeductible, the interest does grow tax free and can be withdrawn tax free, too, as long as the fund is used to pay for college. Advantage: if your child opts out of college, the money can be transferred to a sibling, tax free. Two disadvantages: first, the tax-free withdrawals are disqualified from the Hope and Lifetime tax credits if taken in the same year; second, the money must be used by the time your child reaches thirty years old. One last note—deposits are limited to $2,000 per year.

■ **Title 529/State-Sponsored Savings Plans** This program, named after the section of the tax code it covers, allows you to save money for college, tax deferred, through a state-sponsored agency. (All fifty states offer some kind of savings plan.) The money is invested more aggressively when your child is young and then more conservatively as he nears college. When the money is withdrawn, it's taxed at your child's lower tax rate (around 15 percent). Advantages: first, you can invest far more money than in an Education IRA. Second, it's considered an asset of the parents rather than the child (a plus when applying for a student loan). Disadvantages: you have no control of how the money is invested, usually far more conservatively than most parents would like to see. For more information, contact the *National Association of State Treasurers* at 877-277-6496, or log on to collegesavings.org.

We're in the Money

Although this chapter has outlined the basics for budgeting and saving, it is hardly enough explanation for families in serious need of restructuring their fiscal life. If you fall into that category, head to your local library and check out the dozens of books on the market (with more arriving every day) that explain each subject in depth. Whatever you do, do it today.

Garage, Attic, and Basement

Whative hen I was growing up back East, my family home had a finished basement where my mom set up a laundry area and secondary pantry space to keep those once-a-year cooking supplies and my dad had a workbench where he pretended to putter and fix small appliances with a collection of neatly organized tools. The rest of the room was devoted to the kids in the form of a spacious playroom complete with pretend classroom and dance floor. We also had a large attic that stored out-of-season clothes, luggage, and a few pieces of mismatched furniture. Finally, there was a two-car garage that actually had more than enough room to park both our cars.

Yet when I ventured out on my own after college, I was surprised that not every dwelling was so well endowed. My first apartment in Los Angeles, for instance, had a mere locked cubby perched over my covered parking spot. My first home (a 1906 Craftsman bungalow) wasn't much better. Still, it was a step up, although it didn't have a garage or basement, just a crawl space for an attic. To reach it, my husband, Kevin, and I had to balance a ladder over the washing machine, climb up, and carefully pull ourselves through a narrow opening in the ceiling. We did use the space for storage, however, but only after laying sheets of plywood across the rafters. My current home has just a two-car garage, but to us it seems like we hit the jackpot.

With this in mind, I realize that every home or apartment has different architectural attributes and flaws. While reading through this section, keep in mind that many of the ideas presented here for an attic, for instance, can be adapted to fit a basement or a garage. And if you're one of the lucky ones who have all three—please, remind me what that's like again!

Where Do I Begin?

The Big Three—garage, attic, and basement—are the weakest links in the organizing chain. Because we don't utilize them on a regular basis and they're used almost exclusively for storage, they can quickly become dumping grounds for all sorts of belongings. Therefore, organizing them is a huge undertaking and requires willpower when it comes to weeding and purging. Most of what you'll come across will be deadweight—unlabeled boxes. Yet before you dive in and start pulling out dusty boxes from your childhood, rusty garden tools that you swear you've never seen, and gaudy furniture that you couldn't possibly give away because you inherited it from your Great Aunt Mable in Tulsa, envision how you want these spaces to look and function.

KEY ORGANIZING TIPS

■ **The Role of a Lifetime** Think for a moment about the role that you want each room to assume and the types of tasks you hope to accomplish there. For instance, you may be an aspiring woodworker and want to set up a workbench in the garage. Or maybe you'd like to have a craft center in the basement to help organize all your sewing projects. Jot these ideas down and the equipment that should accompany them. Sketch up a floor plan showing where you'd like everything to go.

■ **In the Zone** Whether it's the garage, attic, or basement, each room often has many functions—workshop, laundry area, gardening shed, and let's not forget, storage room. Assign each category a separate area or zone—trash and recycling, tools, long- and short-term storage—and set up a separate system for each—shelving for a secondary pantry, labeled containers with lids for seasonal decorations, wall hooks for summer lawn furniture. (See Figure 6.)

Basement

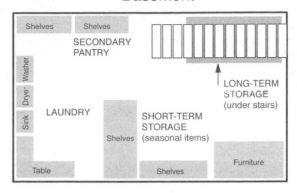

Attic

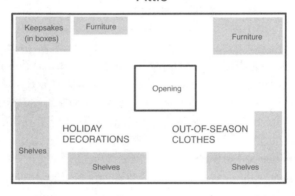

FIGURE 6. Organizing storage zones

■ **Rule of Use** The universal rule of use—keeping your tools, supplies, and equipment in the area closest to where you'll use them—applies to the basement, garage, and attic, too.

■ **A Clean Spot** Before you put things back in their new homes, clean the spaces with detergent and a bucket of water. Painting the walls (if you can) will cut down on the amount of dust and dirt (and even mildew, in the basement).

■ **For Love of the Label** Because it's probably been years since you've seen their contents, go through all of the boxes to see what they contain. Toss or donate ruthlessly, paring down your possessions as much as possible. Then sort the remaining belongings into new boxes (clear plastic bins with lids work best), making sure like items remain together. Finally, carefully label the boxes, listing their contents so you'll be able to find exactly what you're looking for in the future.

▪ **Hazy, Hot, and Humid** Make sure both the attic and basement are properly ventilated and insulated to prevent dramatic swings in temperature. In the basement, have some sort of dehumidifier and perhaps even a sump pump to remove excess groundwater. (By the way—the basement, attic, and garage are not the ideal places to store photographs, 16 mm home movies, or videos. Heat and humidity can destroy them in no time.)

Organizing the Garage

Our first home was a jewel in the rough. We bought it with the intention of restoring it to its turn-of-the-century glory. Consequently, over time we acquired a wealth of tools, both big and small. With no garage, however, storing them was a dilemma. The solution? First, for the smallest hardware—nails, screws, hooks, tacks, and so forth—we mounted a twenty-drawer organizer on the wall of our utility porch. Next, we headed to Sears, where we invested in a two-tiered, ten-drawer rolling tool bin that we fit sideways between the back wall of the utility porch and the refrigerator. Whenever we needed a tool, we carefully wheeled it out, took what we needed, and then rolled it back in place. For the largest equipment—saws, rakes, shovels, and such—Kevin built a shed at the side of the house. All in all, it was tight going, but we made do with what we had—everything had a place, and we always knew where to find what we were looking for.

QUICK FIX

Because the garage is rarely seen by others and isn't in line for any interior design awards, you can get away with using many recycled clunkers and kitchen castoffs. As long as it's functional, who cares what it looks like? So, before you throw anything away, ask yourself if you can use it in the garage for storing stuff.

▪ **Wallflower** Hang Peg-Boards on the walls and use S hooks to hang all sorts of small tools and gardening supplies.

▪ **Bikes and Trikes** Get those two-wheelers off the ground (and make some space in the process) by hanging them on the wall with bicycle hooks, or take the executive approach and paint specific parking spots with each rider's name directly on the concrete floor.

■ **Instant Shelves** No shelves in the garage? No problem. You can easily build a set in less than a few hours by stacking one-inch-thick plywood boards (have the lumber yard cut them twelve inches wide and no more than forty-eight inches long) on cinder blocks. For safety purposes, don't make the unit more than four feet high.

■ **Play Ball** Sporting equipment always winds up in the garage. House an assortment of balls in a clean plastic trash can. For baseball enthusiasts, mount a piece of triangular scrap wood in the corner and bore one-and-one-quarter-inch holes to keep the balls from rolling off and cut out bat slats with a coping saw. Add hooks nearby for cleats and mitts. (See Figure 7.)

■ **Save It for a Rainy Day** Mount rain gutters on garage walls to store long, lightweight objects such as extra wood molding or pipes.

■ **Roll the Tape** Electrical tape, masking tape, duct tape—how can you store them so they're handy? Slide them onto a paper towel roll and mount it to the wall near your tools. (This works well for string and twine, as well.)

■ **Nuts and Bolts** Store small items such as nails, nuts, bolts, screws, washers, and so on in clear baby-food or condiment jars. To see what's inside at a glance, mount a sample on the lid with glue.

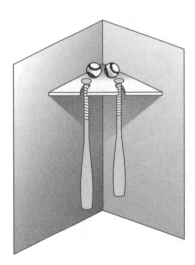

FIGURE 7. Organizing sports equipment

- **What's the Hook?** Install a series of rubber-coated ladder hooks up the wall studs every two to three feet. They're great for hanging extra chairs, insulated coolers, or other big items.
- **Nozzle Nightmare** Keep hose nozzles in one spot by drilling one-and-one-quarter-inch holes into a strip of two-by-four scrap lumber and then mounting the holder right near your hose.

📋 **STYLE TIP**—Never forget where all your hand tools belong by creating a silhouette tool board. First, wrap your tools in heavy plastic wrap; next, place them on the board (Peg-Board or plywood) using nails or hooks to mark their proper place. Spray the wrapped tools and board with a brightly colored paint. When it dries, unwrap the tools and hang them back again in their designated spots. Their shadows will remind you where each item belongs.

MAJOR TUNE-UP

Have a spring afternoon with nothing to do? Head to the garage for a major tune-up. Wear your grungiest clothes, though—you're going to get dirty.

- **Do It Yourself** Need a workbench but don't have the room? Try mounting a long sheet of one-inch plywood or particleboard to the wall by attaching large hinges to both the bottom of the bench and the wall studs. Flip the board up and rest it on flip-out blocks also mounted to the wall studs underneath the bench and, voilà, instant workbench. Flip it down and it rests flush to the wall when you're done.
- **One Man's Junk** Are you about to renovate your kitchen or do you know someone who is? Don't throw those old cabinets away, no matter how ugly. Hang them from ceiling to floor in a corner of the garage. Label the front of each cupboard with its contents. For instance, "garden fertilizer and herbicides," "carpentry hardware," or "barbecue supplies." (Don't forget to add padlocks to those cabinets that contain either dangerous chemicals or power tools.)
- **Look Up** Most garages have open ceilings with two-by-four rafters running the length of the room, perfect for storing stuff out of the way. Head to a home improvement store and purchase sheets of half-inch plywood. Balance each sheet across at least two rafters, distributing the weight of the board evenly. Use these handy pallets for once-a-year or dead-paper items—camping equipment, holiday decorations, or old tax documents. To

make it easier to find what you're looking for, confine like items together. You can even label the bottom of the pallet in big letters so when you look up, you'll know instantly what lies there.

■ **What a Stud** The space between the wall studs is a perfect out-of-the-way spot to hold gardening rakes and shovels. Nail strips of scrap wood horizontally across the outside of exposed studs one foot from the floor and then another set about three feet off the ground. Slide tools behind.

■ **A Cute Cubby** Using many small spaces to organize your paraphernalia is better than one massive spot where it's difficult to find anything. A set of cubbyholes—the kind that you see at preschools—is the perfect solution. Screw together one-by-twelve-inch pine boards for the top, bottom, sides, and shelves. Then rout narrow slots along the shelves at six-to twelve-inch intervals and slide in one-sixteenth-inch plywood dividers. (See Figure 8.)

■ **Shed Some Light** If you have space next to your garage, consider building a shed to store all your gardening tools and supplies. (If you live in a planned community, check with your homeowner's association for restrictions, if any.) Or go the prefab route—Rubbermaid makes durable outdoor storage units. With a minimal amount of assembling, you're in business (rubbermaid.com).

FIGURE 8. Set of cubbyholes

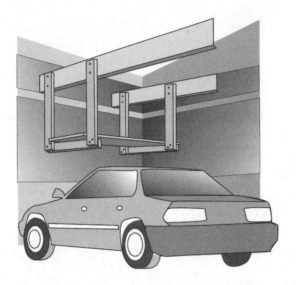

FIGURE 9. Garage storage loft

■ **Car Loft** Store your stuff up and over the front of the family car with a storage loft by attaching two-by-fours with lag screws from the garage rafters and then adding a one-inch sheet of plywood. (See Figure 9.)

Organizing the Attic

Attics have always had that haunted, get-out-now-while-you-still-can reputation. It's about time we've changed this room's image. An attic is a great asset to any home and can house a huge inventory of household stuff (or act as a spare room, for that matter). That is, if you dare venture inside its dark, dank interior.

QUICK FIX

Let's face it, the attic will never be the best-looking room in the house, but with a little elbow grease, it can be one of the most functional. The key here is to fit your storage to the unique shape of the space. Follow a few of these tips to get you started.

■ **Knock on Wood** Have a wealth of old furniture pieces sequestered in the attic? Put them to good use by making them storage units. Line the bottom of a dresser drawer with cedar planks for instance, and store out-of-season clothes inside (label the outside of the drawer for easy reference of its contents), or use a hutch to house boxes of old tax forms, the kids' school memorabilia, or holiday decorations.

■ **Doesn't Stack Up** Resist stacking boxes on top of one another, especially on furniture where too much weight will weaken their joints. In addition, stacked boxes provide the perfect breeding ground for rodents to nest. Instead, set up inexpensive shelving units and place the containers there. (Try the wood-and-cinder-block model in the "Quick Fix" for organizing the garage.)

■ **For Keep's Sake** The attic is a great spot for storing personal keepsakes such as prized school- and artwork, baby clothes, or even your old love letters. Assign every family member a clear plastic box with lid to keep his or her own personal belongings.

⏰ **TIME-SAVER**—Forget about the yearly ritual of untangling your holiday lights. Instead find a piece of eight-by-eleven-inch cardboard and cut two notches in the short ends so it resembles the letter H. Wind your lights around.

MAJOR TUNE-UP

If your attic is unfinished, you may want to consider insulating it to maintain a consistent temperature. Extreme swings in temperature—heat in the summer, bitter cold in the winter—make it a hostile environment for delicate items such as books, photographs, and heirloom linen. Add a three-fourths-inch plywood floor to make navigating the room much easier.

■ **All About Eave** Get the most use out of the undereave wall space by constructing a knee wall—a short interior wall built directly under the roof rafters—making sure it's at least four feet tall. By cutting off the angular grade of the room, you can now use the defined interior space for another purpose, such as shelving, while a small door can provide access to the space behind the knee wall, which can be used for storage. (See Figure 10.)

■ **Out-of-Season Clothing** Don't take up valuable floor space to hang out-of-season clothing. Instead, construct a makeshift closet by installing lengths of closet rod between attic rafters and hanging zippered linen garment bags there.

FIGURE 10. Attic knee wall

Organizing the Basement

The land down under could be as primitive as a root cellar or as elaborate as a bonus room complete with media center. Whatever yours looks like, to make it truly functional, you'll need to separate your basement storage into zones—laundry, food pantry, seasonal, and short- and long-term storage.

QUICK FIX

The number-one problem with most basements is flooding! Even if you have a sump pump to help with excess groundwater, be sure to store *everything* up off the floor. And if your budget allows, consider waterproofing it.

■ **Stair Master** The dead space underneath the basement steps is a great spot for long- or short-term storage, depending on how accessible the area is.

■ **Pantry Pride** If you want to locate your primary or secondary pantry space in the basement, set up shelving units near the steps for easy access and, if possible, on the cool north or east end of the house or away from heating and plumbing pipes.

■ **Fine Wine** The cool, dark basement environment is perfect for storing wine. If you've always dreamed of having a wine cellar, it's easy to set up. If you have a separate closet in the basement, line the floor with

Just in Case

If you live in an area that's prone to flooding, earthquakes, or tornadoes, it's a good idea to have emergency supplies on hand. Keep them in a backpack or duffel bag in a cool, dark place such as your basement so that if you need to evacuate quickly, you can just grab the satchel and go. First, you'll need a three-day supply of food and water. (Canned goods have a shelf life of approximately one year, so rotate them into your household pantry annually. Water will last six months.) You'll also need a few other supplies.

Cooking Tools A camp stove with full can of propane, paper plates and utensils, and a manual can opener.

Basic Tools A wrench is a must for turning off the gas or water line. Take a moment now to ensure you know where both shut-off valves are located.

Light and Communication A portable radio and a reliable flashlight, both with fresh batteries stored separately, candles and matches.

First-Aid Kit with Instructions

Clothing A change of clothes for each family member and walking shoes.

Blankets or Sleeping Bags

Basic Hygiene Items Toilet paper, soap, toothbrush, and toothpaste.

Emergency Phone Numbers Include the names and numbers of family members outside of your area.

terra-cotta tiles, install an overhead light, and choose among the dozens of wine racks now available from Sur La Table, Williams-Sonoma, and even Pottery Barn and Crate & Barrel.

The Perfect Playroom

Kids and their toys often spill out of their bedrooms and into every part of the house. And although you may not want to mandate a "no toys in the living room" policy, living among miniature cars, dolls, teacups, and Legos can be challenging. (Have you ever stepped on a square wooden block barefoot?)

Give kids the space they need to explore their world and, at the same time, a secondary location to stash their stuff by converting the attic or basement into a playroom. You don't need much room; actually a broad hallway or second-floor landing will do just fine.

Start by sprucing up the place by painting the ceiling to resemble a clear blue sky. Let the kids decorate the walls with colorful handprints. (Use semigloss rather than flat paint for easy cleanups.) Add some curtains and bright lighting.

Control the clutter with an old colorful trunk (you can find one at a tag sale or local antique shop) filled with dress-up essentials. Add some sturdy bookshelves built under the eaves (bolted to the wall studs for extra safety) to house toys and books and a craft table and supplies (use large, empty tin cans to house crayons, markers, and paintbrushes).

Create a bit of whimsy by painting a winding toy-car track directly on the floor. Add some game boards, too—hopscotch, checkers, tic-tac-toe. (No more board versions needed!) Just be sure to top them all off with a few coats of nonyellowing sealer to protect them from the hard knocks of childhood. Or how about fastening an old-fashioned tin-can telephone from one end of the room to the other?

Encourage your child's creative side by adding a raised platform—sort of a miniature stage—at one end of the room where she can act out her own plays. Add some authentic details such as track lighting, a large painted backdrop suspended along the back wall (try fabric paint on inexpensive white canvas), or a set of curtains hanging in the front.

Surprising Surplus Storage

Having a garage, attic, or basement to corral and store those once-a-year supplies and long-term keepsakes is a true blessing. Make the most of these spaces by organizing them in a way that fits your family's lifestyle. They may not be the most attractive rooms, but they certainly can be the most functional.

Home Office

It's a trend that started to take off in the nineties and has continued to grow. Is it the variety of risotto dishes appearing on restaurant menus? Not exactly. Rather, it's the number of Americans who work from home. Some say nearly twenty-five million people do at least part of their jobs from the comfort of their abodes (others put the estimate even higher), and the count continues to grow by nearly 5 to 10 percent each year.

You may love the idea of setting up a separate office space in your home or apartment, but you have no plans of churning out millions of dollars of revenue from your little efficient retreat; you just want a quiet spot to pay the bills, surf the Internet, or make written observations in your journal.

You're not alone. Most folks who have a home office use it just for those very same, important reasons.

Carving Out Space

The most difficult question to answer when setting up an office is, "Where shall we put it?" Some folks may find that an extra bedroom works perfectly for their needs. Even for families tight on space, finding a spot for an office is not as difficult as it appears. All it takes is a bit of brainstorming and, on occasion, some carpentry skills.

KEY ORGANIZING TIPS

■ **Serene Surroundings** When deciding where to set up shop, go with where you feel most comfortable rather than picking a spot just because the desk fits. There may be room in your finished basement, for instance, but if the dampness and lack of light leave you cold, you'll probably never use it. Instead, build an office in a part of the home where you feel you'll be most productive (you may have to move furniture or kids to another location).

■ **Separation Anxiety** When you have a home office, the boundaries between work and family life often become blurred, and the self-employed often feel as though they have no free time. It's therefore important to find some way to separate the two either with a door, curtain, screen—whatever—so that you can mentally walk away at the end of the day.

■ **The Story on Storage** While designing your space, make sure you plan for adequate storage for reference books, household as well as business files, and all the other accoutrements that go with working from home (don't forget to allow for growth). But before you go out and purchase those cute little wicker baskets that fit so neatly in your bookshelf, decide exactly what your needs are and find the right tool for the job. Don't buy something simply because you like the way it looks; make sure it will serve a particular function in your new office such as an in-box for organizing bills or a hanging file to keep current customers' reports close at hand.

Sharing the Space

How many different roles will your home office take on? If you're like most people with a part-time office tucked in a spare bedroom, you'll not only do some work there but you'll also use the room to store out-of-season clothing, your sewing machine, or holiday wrapping paper. Many home offices double as a guest room—corporate craziness by day, private guest suite by night.

If you, too, need to use the room for many different activities, break up the space accordingly into zones. Use furniture as a makeshift wall. Situate an open bookcase to divide your work space from your hobby center, for instance. Designate specific shelves, bins, or even an entire closet for work-related items where they will be off-limits to the younger family members. It's important to keep your workplace a separate entity from the rest of the room to stop the temptation of using your desk as a dumping ground for all sorts of misplaced household objects.

QUICK FIX

If you plan to work full-time in your home office, architects recommend at least 100 square feet of space (a standard ten-by-ten-foot bedroom). If you'll have clients visiting, add a couch or table and chairs. A separate outside entrance to the room is ideal, as is access to a powder room. Yet if you're looking to set up a part-time office—one where you'll do a bit of paperwork, pay a few bills, and house your computer—there are lots of overlooked places in your home that can easily fit a workstation.

■ **Daring to Share** Do you have two young, same-sex children, both occupying their own rooms? Perhaps combining them into one large bedroom will open up space for you. (Read over the "Share, Share, That's Fair" segment of the "Children's Bedrooms" chapter for some timely advice.)

■ **Double-Duty Room** There are lots of tricks to make a guest room–home office function: try using a daybed with a trundle or sofa bed instead of a full-sized bed, which takes up an enormous amount of floor space (or get a Murphy bed, which disappears into the wall completely). Disguise a two-drawer filing cabinet by placing a round section of particleboard on top, covering it with a table skirt, adding a lamp, and voilà, instant side table. Store files and other office equipment in a closed cabinet or closet rather than on shelves to keep the room's appearance neat.

■ **Screen Saver** If you have a spare corner in either your living room, family room, or even the master bedroom, try using a screen, open bookcase, curtain, or even miniblinds attached to the ceiling studs to separate the office area from living space. Just be sure to keep the office furniture in the style of the rest of the room.

■ **Closet Cubby** Have a spare closet? Transform it into a mini-office by removing the clothes rod and adding shelving and a computer workbench (call an electrician to add outlets for lighting, computer, and printer, plus a phone line). Choose a chair that will fit under the desk and out of the way when not in use. The best part is, at the end of the day you can close the door, concealing all office clutter.

■ **A Nice Niche** That small, dead-end niche at the end of the hallway would make a great office outpost. Build a narrow desktop so it won't

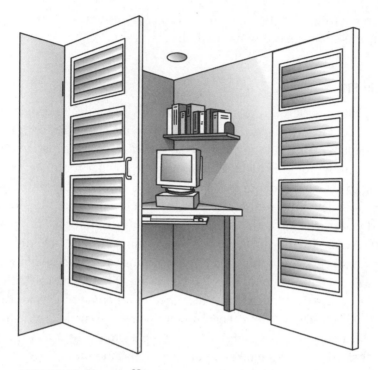

FIGURE 11. Home office in a corner

interfere with foot traffic and add shelves above to store supplies. Or, how about the landing at the top of the stairs? Surely you could tuck a computer desk under the window.

MAJOR TUNE-UP

If time and money are on your side, you can create a beautiful part-time office by following one of these tips. Although you won't need an architect, you'll probably have to call in the electrician to wire your space, and if you're not handy with a hammer, get the name of a trusted carpenter.

■ **The Corner Office** Not a bedroom or extra closet to spare? How about a corner then? Make an inviting office alcove by building a false wall with full-length folding shutters (available at most home stores) three feet out from an unused corner. Set up a triangular workstation and shelves inside. Paint the new doors the same color as the room so it will blend right in with the rest of the room. (See Figure 11.)

FIGURE 12. Home office under the stairs

■ **Dare to Stair** If you live in a two-story home, often the space under the main staircase goes unused. Try designing an office underneath the highest section—you'll need about a five-foot-wide segment. It will require you to break through the existing drywall enclosing the side of the stairs and finish the now-open niche to look like the rest of the hallway. (See Figure 12.)

■ **Don't Construct, Conceal** If changing your existing floor plan isn't turning you on, there is another option—buy a large armoire specifically meant for office use. Dozen of furniture manufacturers make hutches designed to fit your computer and files. Open it up and you have room to spread your work out and organize your files; close it and the cabinet blends in with your home's décor. Place it wherever you have the room—master bedroom, family room, or even the living room. Check out IKEA and Target for models under $1,000, but if style is more important than the price tag, head to Pottery Barn, Crate & Barrel, or even Ethan Allen.

Choosing the Right Furnishings

You've picked the perfect spot to establish your home office and now it's time to think about furnishing it. Before you hit the furniture or office supply store, take a moment to assess your needs.

KEY ORGANIZING TIPS

- **It's Definitely the Décor** Choose furnishings that match your home's décor if your office will occupy a corner of an established room. If your office is in a separate room, on the other hand, feel free to express yourself in any style you choose.
- **Buy Once; Measure Twice** Always take careful measurements of the area to be sure the new furniture will fit properly.
- **Proper Flow** Make sure you have proper clearance for a filing cabinet, about thirty-nine inches. Ditto for the space behind your chair. Allow thirty-five inches in front of shelves.

Desk or Workstation

When it comes to choosing an office desk, size does matter. You'll need space to not only fit your computer, but also to spread out paperwork on either side of you (look for a minimum of sixty inches long by thirty inches deep). Not only is the size of your office desk important, but the shape plays a vital role, too. If you'll be working from home full-time, an L-shaped desk offers the best layout because you'll be able to reach your phone, fax, files, and computer without leaving your chair. Look for a desk with a pull-out keyboard tray (or add one yourself) to make typing more comfortable. And before you write the check, take it for a test drive—sit down and see if you're comfortable (no knees knocking the legs) and feel at ease.

The Chair

Make no mistake, good office chairs cost a bundle. For maximum comfort, look for an adjustable chair, maybe one with a variable lumbar support feature. Find a model with good padding (for obvious reasons) and wheels, for mobility.

Storage

Because the selection is so vast when it comes to storage, you need to evaluate your needs carefully. Do you have lots of paperwork? Then you'll need a network of filing cabinets. But before buying one, establish the size of your files. Some cabinets accommodate letter-sized paper only; others can hold legal sized. If you need to house a multitude of reference books, look for bookcases that will fit in the closet or on an adjacent wall or install bookshelves above your desk. Use desk trays to organize supplies like pens, paper clips, and stationery. Consider using the space above your desk to install space-saving vertical trays and stock them with frequently used paper supplies.

The most important element to remember when purchasing storage units—buy 50 percent more than you need now to allow for future growth.

Lighting

Good-quality lighting prevents eyestrain. To avoid light glare on your screen, move your computer away from the window (or add sheer curtains to the windows to cut down on the brightness). Combine ambient lighting with task lighting. Position task lighting near your computer so you can adjust the beam on your current project. Keep it below eye level (so you can't see the bulb).

Wiring

You can never have too many outlets in your office. Your equipment alone takes up a bundle—computer, fax, printer, and desk lamp, just to name a few. To guard against electrical spikes, invest in a good-quality surge protector. Replace it every few years because it ultimately loses its effectiveness. (If your house is older and your outlets are not grounded, a surge protector will not work—call an electrician.)

How about phone lines? If you're a full-time entrepreneur who conducts most of your business on the phone, consider installing several lines to separate your office and home needs. Obviously, if you'll be using the office part-time, you can get by with less. Although two will do the trick—one for home use, the other for business, Internet, and fax—you can make do with just one (just get voice mail, available in most areas, added to your phone features—it answers all incoming calls when the line is tied up so the caller will never get a busy signal).

Step into My Office

Working from home either full-time or part-time, for business or for pleasure, is rewarding, especially if you've created an inviting space that allows you to be productive and innovative. Use your imagination and professional skills to construct the home office of your dreams.

Housecleaning

I'm not a compulsive cleaner. In fact, if you'd interview the handful of roommates that I've had over the years, you'd hear just the opposite. You might learn, for instance, that when I was in college and living with three other women in an apartment, I rarely if ever cleaned the bathroom. This, I found out on the day of graduation, was a source of contention for one roommate in particular, who had made up a cleaning schedule. I never knew it existed until the day I was moving back home and found it taped to the inside of the bathroom closet. Next to the list of my chores were large red check marks. It seems that every time I skipped a household task (which I admit was often), she would march to the list and slap me with a red demerit.

Which brings me to my second point—I hate cleaning logs of any kind. If you're overwhelmed with what needs to be done on a daily basis, you're certainly not going to follow a rigid cleaning schedule where you'll dutifully clean the bathrooms every Monday and scrub the kitchen floor every Wednesday evening. Life will undoubtedly get in the way—the dog needs to go to the vet on Monday, there's a movie that you've been dying to see on cable Wednesday night, and before you know it, you've thrown that schedule in the trash. And if you do have the wherewithal to write a detailed cleaning schedule and you actually follow it, then you certainly don't need me to tell you how to organize your life. I think you've got it covered. But if you're looking for a simple way to organize your housework without it interfering too much with your busy lifestyle, then you've come to the right place.

KEY ORGANIZING TIPS

- **Asian Invasion** People in Asian cultures have always removed their shoes before entering a home for thousands of years. Every family should have such a practice! Not only does it cut down on the amount of dirt entering the house (which translates to less vacuuming and sweeping), it also helps to prolong the life of your carpets and rugs. (Health experts stress that it's healthier, too, because pesticides and other toxins lingering on the soles of your shoes aren't brought into the house.) Place a large shoe tree in the closet nearest to the door most used or place a basket under a bench in your mudroom so family members and guests can easily stow their shoes when they arrive. Offer a selection of slippers or thick socks as inside replacements.

- **In the Mood** Clean the moment the mood hits you. The idea is to take care of a problem the moment it enters your consciousness, which ensures it will get done.

- **My Hands Are Full** Never, never leave a room empty-handed. Get into the habit of always checking around to see if something needs to be placed back in its proper home before exiting.

- **Meals on Wheels** It's tempting to occasionally eat dinner in front of the television or let the children chow down on a bowl of Fruit Loops in the playroom, but roving diners mean crumbs and stains everywhere. Fight back by mandating that all family members eat meals or snacks only at the kitchen or dining room table.

- **Volunteers of America** Enlist the aid of family members. Small children love to help with everything from dusting to setting the dinner table. Start them early and offer lots of praise. Things won't sparkle at first, but with a bit of practice, they'll get the hang of it.

Getting the Kids Involved

It's hard keeping a house clean when you have so many dirty little hands eager to touch everything. Just moments after you wipe off the kitchen table, *poof!* It's covered again with milk spills. Yet when you turn those dirty little hands into helping hands, now that's progress. Not only is delegating household chores to your children a help to you, but it also teaches them time-management skills, cooperation, and teamwork, and praising them for a job well done promotes their feelings of self-esteem.

Chores for Three- to Four-Year-Olds

- Setting the table (if you provide the raw materials)
- Clearing the table (encourage them to use both hands)
- Picking up and putting away toys
- Gathering trash cans for emptying (an older family member takes them to the garbage)

Chores for Preschoolers (All of the Above, Plus)

- Making a bed (don't expect perfection)
- Simple food preparation such as stirring a pot (with adult supervision), washing vegetables, making a salad, or gathering condiments from the refrigerator for the table
- Dusting, wiping, sweeping
- Separating laundry into whites and darks
- Feeding the family pet
- Taking silverware from dishwasher (minus sharp knives) and sorting correctly in cutlery drawer

Chores for School-Age Children (All of the Above, Plus)

- Simple yard work—raking leaves, watering garden, shoveling snow
- Putting away groceries
- Taking out evening trash
- Cleaning their rooms
- Emptying dishwasher
- Folding clothes and matching socks
- Vacuuming
- Washing the car

Chores for Junior-High Children and Beyond
(All of the Above, Plus)

- Preparing a school lunch
- Helping with dinner (or starting it)
- Changing bedsheets and starting laundry
- Ironing clothes (with adult supervision)

Cara and Jenna have recently begun doing their own laundry. Once every five to six days, they come downstairs and dump their clothes in the machine. If something has a stain on it, I'll give them a hand. It's freed up my time tremendously.

QUICK FIX

Once the kids reach kindergarten or first grade, it's time to assign everyone a daily or weekly household task. (I know I said I hate schedules, but this is for *them*, not you!) They're old enough now where you can (and should) begin to count on them regularly to help out around the house, an important aspect of being a part of a family.

It's better to assign chores to people who don't mind completing them; they're more likely to get done. For other ideas, scan the list below.

■ **Wheel of Chores** Who says housework has to be drudgery? Turn it into a game with the *Wheel of Chores*! Begin by cutting a circle from a piece of poster board. Color in pie-shaped wedges—one for each chore, such as setting the dinner table—and attach an arrow with a paper fastener. Have each family member take a spin to see what fate lies ahead. (See Figure 13.)

■ **Pick a Card** Write out chores on small slips of paper—empty trash cans or feed the dog—and turn it into a game where everyone picks a slip from a large jar.

■ **Chore Chart** No negotiations here, just a permanent assignment for each family member (you can change duties every fall and spring if you have a bunch of disgruntled butlers on your hands). Make a grid using a sheet of eight-and-one-half-by-eleven-inch poster board. Set up seven rows across the top and write the days of the week. Down the left side list your chores. Fill in the spots with family members' names. To be fair, alternate unpopular jobs throughout the week.

FIGURE 13. Wheel of Chores

om was always neat, well groomed, everything in order, so I never had to teach him how to be organized. Ken, however, was a challenge. The rule was, just keep your door closed. As long as I didn't see it, it's OK. I never forced him to clean up his room. I simply gave up. But there was no food allowed. It was either going to be that he had a clean room and we never got along, or we got along and his room was going to look the way he wanted it to look. I'd rather get along with my son.

Doing Laundry

You can ignore a dirty kitchen floor for a good week or two, and cobwebs in the corner look pretty as they sway in the afternoon breeze, but, unfortunately, when you run out of underwear and socks, it's time to do a load of wash.

KEY ORGANIZING TIPS

■ **Use Visual Cues to Clean** As you put clean clothes away, take an extra few minutes to reorganize drawers and pull out outgrown or damaged clothing. By taking a moment each week for maintenance, the drawers will never need a complete hour-long redo.

■ **Laundry Central** Regardless of where your washer and dryer are located (basement, garage, closet, or laundry room), set up a spot where you can easily reach all your cleaning supplies, treat stains, fold towels, and sort clothes (the top of the washer and dryer will do—just have supplies within easy reach). If you have the room, invest in a three-bin laundry sorter. On wash days, have each family member deposit his or her dirty clothes in the appropriate bin by a certain time, say, by 8 A.M.

■ **Fill 'Er Up** Save time and energy by washing full loads only. Although you may miss your favorite sweater (because you probably won't have a full load of delicates each week), you'll soon discover other favorites hidden in the recesses of your closet as substitutes. (Remember, though—*full load* doesn't mean *overload*, which not only may destroy your machine, but also produces excess wrinkles in your clothes.)

■ **Treat Stains Immediately** The key to making the full-load-only rule work is proper stain triage—quickly assessing and treating the problem as soon as it happens. Some clothes may not get washed for two weeks, and a stain can do some serious damage if not taken care of right away.

■ **Ironclad Rule** No one likes to iron. It's time-consuming, boring, and sometimes dangerous! Luckily, these days many fabrics are virtually wrinkle free. Before buying any new article of clothing, carefully consider its wrinkle quotient by crumpling the fabric in your hand. If it bounces back into shape, you have a keeper. For clothes that are wrinkle prone, however, get to them before the heat of the dryer has a chance to set in creases by pulling them from the dryer while they're still damp, hanging them up, and letting them air dry the rest of the way.

🕮 **STYLE TIP**—Build or install several decorative shelves just above your washer and dryer and use them as an open-air linen closet. Sorting becomes a snap—sheets and towels go directly from the dryer to the ledge above instead of making the long trip to the hallway linen closet upstairs. (This system works well for families with limited closet space or for folks with a small, single-story home where the laundry room is closer to the bathroom than the linen closet.)

QUICK FIX

You can't make the wash and dry cycles go any faster or somehow stop your son from getting his knees covered in grass stains every day, but you can organize the sorting of your laundry both before it hits the washing machine and after it leaves the dryer. These quick-fix tips will help you clean up in no time.

■ **Two Is Better Than One** Instead of doing an all-out assault on laundry every Saturday, where piles of dirty clothes permeate every inch of the laundry room floor, try having two laundry days—one for darks and the other for whites and delicates. When you break the task up, it's not as overwhelming.

Every Friday morning, Cara and Jenna strip their beds and take their sheets to the laundry room. I throw them in the wash with my bed linens and then head upstairs to shower and get dressed for work. When I come down for breakfast, I put the linens in the dryer. Just before we all head out the door, everyone goes back upstairs with the freshly washed linens and remakes her bed. We run the same routine for towels on Mondays.

■ **Job Sharing** This trick works well for us—I put a load of wash in before I leave for my evening job. When my husband comes home, he puts the wet clothes in the dryer and sorts them when they come out. When I get home, at 9:30 P.M., I put the clean clothes away.

■ **Color Code** Assign each family member a small laundry basket (a separate color for each), and have everyone leave them in the laundry room on wash days (after they've sorted their dirty clothes). As the clothes come out of the dryer, sort each person's apparel and place it directly into his or her designated basket. Family members can pick up their own baskets at dinnertime (younger ones may need help getting theirs back to their rooms). During the rest of the week, have them use their baskets for their own dirty clothes.

■ **Color Code Two** Buy a different-color mesh lingerie bag for each family member (use the same colors as the laundry baskets). Instruct everyone to deposit his or her socks and underwear in the bags (hang the bags in each family member's closet, next to the laundry basket). On laundry day, toss the bags in the washing machine, and then the dryer, and finally back in their laundry baskets with the rest of their clean clothes. No sorting and no matching socks!

■ **Dot It** To help distinguish your kids' clothes (a big plus as they come out of the dryer), place a dot on the label of your oldest child's clothes, two dots on the second oldest's clothes, and so on. As clothes get passed down, just add a dot.

■ **Sock It to Me** Buy each child his or her own "style" of socks—one-stripe sweat socks for the oldest child, two stripes for the middle child, and so on. The same technique works well for underwear, too. Have each child pick one color or one cartoon character.

> With six children, my mom insisted on our pinning our socks. She simply wouldn't wash socks if they weren't pinned together, so we all learned to comply. With all those Catholic-school navy kneesocks, it was a lifesaver for her.

■ **Shelf It** Install a single long shelf above the washer and dryer and assign a spot for each family member (you can tape a name tag along the side). As clothes come out of the dryer, fold and place them in the rightful owner's spot. Have everyone pick up his or her clothes before dinner.

■ **Bag It** No room for a three-bin laundry sorter? No problem. Just hang three hooks on the wall near your washing machine, hang three laundry bags, and tie a ribbon on each one—a colored ribbon to indicate colored clothes; a white ribbon on the second for sheets, towels, sweat socks, and so on; and a lace ribbon on the third to specify delicates.

■ **Air Dry** Install a closet clothes rod between two laundry room cabinets, about eighteen inches in front of a sunny window (and about three feet from the ceiling). It makes a perfect spot to dry delicates.

■ **It's Off to the Laundromat We Go** Fill resealable plastic Baggies with a premeasured amount of detergent, and store your supply in the empty detergent box. On wash day, pull out the number of bags you'll need (no need to haul a heavy, cumbersome box inside the laundromat with you).

> I never let anything get to the point where it's overwhelming. Every morning when Dan and Francesca take the dog for a twenty-minute walk, I completely vacuum the house, mop the kitchen and bathroom floors, touch up the bathroom, and make the beds. We have a 100-pound black Lab—he sheds. Nothing ever gets to the point where I say, "Oh, no, it's Saturday. I have to clean the house." I clean as I go.

The Need for Speed—Housecleaning in Thirty Minutes or Less

It's not often that I torture myself with a deep clean, where I take up an entire morning or afternoon scrubbing the whole house. If I've been keeping up with all the tips that I've mentioned throughout this chapter, there really is little need for it except when company comes to spend the night. On occasion, however, I will speed clean, where I time myself and cut loose. It may not be perfect, but then again, neither am I.

Get Ready Put on a T-shirt and some sweatpants, gather your cleaning materials in one bucket (don't forget to include a clean paintbrush to dust off light fixtures and a toothbrush to clean grungy grout), and turn the music up loud. (Think of it as an aerobic workout.)

Ignore Interruptions Don't answer the phone (let the machine get it), and forget about the doorbell (it's probably a salesperson anyway).

Turn on the Timer Set it for thirty minutes and go (remember to pace yourself—don't spend too much time in any one spot).

Start in the Bathroom Suds up the bathroom and take off to clean the rest of the house while you give the chemicals a chance to perform their magic.

Work from Top to Bottom Start with sweeping the cobwebs from the ceiling; then brush the walls. Next, move onto dusting and cleaning all glass surfaces. Finally, end with a good vacuuming.

Use Two Hands Make the most of your body by spraying with one hand and wiping with the other.

Work in One Direction Don't retrace your footsteps. Start in one room and work in a clockwise direction.

End in the Bathroom Just in time to rinse before the timer goes off.

Cleaning the Bathroom

With four males in my house, the toilet is my least favorite apparatus to clean (if you, too, have lots of household testosterone, you know what I mean). Even harder to clean than the kitchen, the bathroom requires constant upkeep and care.

KEY ORGANIZING TIPS

■ **Use Visual Cues to Clean** Take a moment to scrub the tub before you settle in for a long, luxurious bath (the reward will be all that sweeter); scour the vanity sink or toilet as you wait for your little ones to finish up with their bath.

■ **Keep a Small Bucket Handy** Keep glass cleaner, scouring powder, sponge, and paper towels in a small bucket below the sink. This way when the mood hits you to swab the decks, you can act upon your impulse quickly.

■ **Mildew Madness** Once it sets its slimy paws on your bathroom tiles, mildew is nearly impossible to get off. Your best line of defense is *prevention*—get to it before it gets to you. Invest in a squeegee (Target sells one in a storage case with suction cups, to affix it to the wall of your shower). It takes only moments after a shower to quickly wipe off moisture from the walls and shower door, but the payback is significant. Not only does mildew not have a place to grow, but you won't have to deal with stubborn mineral deposits left by your hard water as well.

Next, if you don't have an exhaust fan in your bathroom, open the curtain or door immediately following your shower, allowing the steam to escape (if you have a curtain, however, be sure to close it before you leave the room so it too can dry out and mildew won't have a chance to form in the creases). If the weather permits, crack a window open to further dry out the room. Finally, once you exit the bathroom, leave the door open. The point here is to let moisture escape, airing out the room.

QUICK FIX

A swipe here while the shower heats up, or a swish there right before you exit the room, and your bathroom will rarely need a major cleanup.

- **More Mildew Madness** Soak new plastic and cloth shower curtains in salt water for a few minutes before hanging (it will help stop mildew
from forming).
- **Better Aim** Help the little men in your household develop better
aim by placing a waterproof decal in your toilet as a target.
- **Drop a Tablet** Use a chlorine bleach in-tank tablet to stretch the
days between cleaning. (Or, for an organic approach, pour a cup of white
vinegar in the bowl every few days and let it sit overnight before flushing.)
- **Sponge Savvy** Keep a small sponge in the tub and give a scrub
around the waterline before stepping out of the bath. It'll help prevent bathtub ring.
- **Forget the Bar** Stop using bar soap; it gets too messy when wet
and is very unpleasant to clean up. Instead use liquid soap and a dispenser.
- **Sponge or Bristle?** When it comes to really cleaning the toilet,
invest in a *sponge* rather than a bristle brush. It gets into those hard-to-
reach spots under the rim better than its rival.
- **Rub a Dub Dub** For a quick clean of the tub, add one-quarter cup
of dish detergent and fill with hot water. Let it sit for thirty minutes and
then drain. Wipe the sides clean.

Cleaning the Kitchen

The kitchen is where we all live: it's the room where guests congregate at
a party; it's where the kids hang out after school telling of their day while
eating cookies. These days, nearly every family is renovating the kitchen
to make it larger and more of a gathering spot for family and friends. The
kitchen has been brought out to the forefront of the home, a showcase room
no longer hidden in the back of the house. The heart of every home, the
kitchen is also a breeding ground for huge messes.

KEY ORGANIZING TIPS

- **Use Visual Cues to Clean** Take five minutes each week before
you put away your groceries to clean out the refrigerator: toss leftovers
more than three days old and randomly pull out two shelves to thoroughly
wash them (if you use the two-shelf system of cleaning every time you put

groceries away, within a few weeks you'll have a self-cleaning refrigerator). Or try wiping down the front of two cabinet doors each time you empty the dishwasher.

■ **Make the Most of Your Dishwasher** If you open your dishwasher and can't tell if your dishes are clean or dirty, you're doing it wrong! Most models have a quick rinse cycle using a mere two gallons of water (refer to your owner's manual). After breakfast or lunch, turn it on—it will rinse the dishes for you. Now stop rinsing!

■ **Grease Is the Word** It's everywhere—on your cooktop, on your ventilation hood, on the oven door. Outsmart grease by incorporating healthier cooking techniques—rather than frying or roasting food, try steaming or grilling outdoors.

■ **Clean as You Cook** Get into the habit of cleaning up as you pre-pare dinner. Rinse the cutting board and put it away while you wait for the vegetables to steam; stack the dishwasher while your sauce reduces, and so forth.

QUICK FIX

You'll still have to scour the sink nightly, and the stovetop will get spills and stains no matter what you do, but there are lots of quick-fix cleanup tricks in the kitchen.

■ **Step Up to the Plate** Never place packaged meat, fish, or poultry directly in the refrigerator without a plate underneath it. The plate will stop the item's juices from spreading throughout the shelves.

■ **Liner Notes** Use a fresh sheet of paper towel to line vegetable bins. Replace it when it gets dirty.

■ **Take Cover** Cover pots and pans as well as food heading to the microwave to prevent unnecessary splatters.

■ **It's a Wrap** Use a sheet of aluminum foil over the broiler pan for easy cleanup. Use a sheet at the bottom of the oven, too, to catch spills.

■ **Blend Right In** To quickly clean your blender or food processor, add a few drops of liquid detergent and water, cover, and pulse for thirty seconds. Rinse.

■ **Speed Clean** Remove dried-on food from the microwave easily by first taking a cup of water mixed with a tablespoon of baking soda and nuk-ing for two minutes; then wipe clean. Freshen up your garbage disposal by first running a tray of ice cubes through (the ice sharpens the blades and removes small bits of trapped food) and then following with chopped lemon peel (it will keep it smelling fresh). Keep tile countertops free from ugly mildew stains by saturating paper towels with bleach, leaving them on the counter for fifteen minutes, giving a light rubbing, and rinsing. Finally, run a cup of white vinegar through a dishwashing cycle to prevent mineral deposits.

M*y mom gave each of us kids a special mug to drink from for our non-mealtime drinks. If it was dirty and you wanted a drink, you had to wash your own mug and use that. It really cut down on glasses in the sink and all around the house.*

Everyday Chores

There's more to a clean house than the kitchen, bathroom, and laundry—albeit those are a tremendous trio. What about a few other tricks to keep things humming along? Here are a few to get you going.

Apply a thin coat of car wax to windowsills to prevent dirt, dust, and grime from sticking, making them much easier to clean. Try it on ceiling fan blades, too.

Try using the two-bucket system when washing a floor—one for cleaning solution, the other for rinsing.

Invest in *two* vacuum cleaners, one for each floor of the house. If a vacuum is easily accessible, you're more likely to use it.

Cover the kitty's favorite spot on the couch or your bed with a towel to prevent cat hair from sticking to the furniture. Toss the towel in the wash as needed.

Stop buying knickknacks for your home—it will cut down on the amount of dusting that you do. And forget about dusting each bric-a-brac. Instead, fill your sink (lined with a hand towel to prevent breakage) with sudsy water and soak ornaments for a few minutes; then wipe dry.

The Last Word on Clean

With so many different cleaning products out there, it's hard to know which ones do the trick. Most of us end up buying more than we need, and these cleaners end up gathering dust on our pantry shelves. But did you know that most professional cleaners rely on just a few products to do the job? Think about it—all you really need to clean your entire home is a multi-purpose cleaner (such as a glass cleaner) to handle chrome in the kitchen and bath, countertops and windowsills, windows and mirrors; a tile and grout cleaner for tough mildew stains in the kitchen and bath; an abrasive scouring powder for tubs and sinks; and finally, for today's contemporary kitchen, a stainless polish for tough food stains on cooktops. That's it.

In the weeks that follow, as you begin to organize your laundry room, pantry, or wherever else you keep your cleaning supplies, take a long hard look at them and decide when was the last time you used them. If the answer is more than six months ago, toss them and vow never to buy them again.

Keep cleaning simple.

Kitchen

How much time do you spend in your kitchen? If you're like most families, probably a lot. Not just for cooking, the kitchen has a multitude of other functions—it's where the kids end up munching on cookies after school and spinning tales about their day on the playground or doing homework while Mom or Dad whip up dinner; it's where family meetings are held, nightly meals unfold, or bills are paid; it's where everyone congregates during a cocktail party.

Although much of our day-to-day business centers in the kitchen, it never seems large enough. (If you want to see *small*, however, head to a New York City apartment where tenants must walk sideways in a space no wider than a hallway. When my aunt opened the oven in her Gramercy Park apartment, it hit the opposite wall!) Yet it's not the square footage that's the problem (at least for non–New Yorkers); it's the excess cookware, the throng of utensils, appliances both large and small, outdated condiments, spices, and canned goods from the Reagan administration that clog every available nook and cranny that make it nearly impossible to find anything or let cooking be pleasurable.

KEY ORGANIZING TIPS

■ **In the Zone** A simple reorganization of your kitchen should begin with designating zones or work centers based on what you use your kitchen for—meal prep, cooking and baking, cleanup—a separate area for each one. Keep specific tools and equipment in each zone for fast and easy use.

■ **In the Right Place** Place things where you use them rather than where they fit best—dishes near the dishwasher, pots and pans near the stove and cooktop, and so on. Keep everyday items like the coffeemaker and toaster no lower than knee level or less than a foot above your head. Put seldom-used items, like your slow cooker and electric mixer, out of the way, perhaps in the cabinet above the refrigerator. Store china or lightweight items such as crystal on high shelves, or if you only use them during the holidays, try storing them in a hutch in the dining room or a spare closet in another room. Store heavy items, such as a blender or food processor, on low shelves. (Try not to place them on top shelves, where they could accidentally fall on the person trying to get them down.)

■ **Use It or Lose It** When sorting through drawers and cabinets, think seriously about the tools you have and how often you actually use them. Give duplicate items or odd pieces of glassware and china away to charity. Donate old cookbooks or toss them in the recycling bin after cutting out a favorite recipe or two and storing them in a recipe file.

■ **Think Before You Buy** A major kitchen reorganization will entail buying some sort of shelving units and wire racks, but before you head to your local home store, take careful notes. Decide what is in need of organization (spices, pot lids, cookie sheets, etc.), and find the product to match it. Measure your drawers and cabinets carefully and accurately to ensure a proper fit. Don't be tempted to buy something simply because it's handy or cute without first thinking what you can use it for—that's just a waste of money and one more thing to clutter your home.

■ **Remember the Kids** Designate a lower drawer or cabinet for snacks, so the little ones can easily help themselves. If you have a craft-savvy youngster still at home, try allocating another drawer for crayons and construction paper. The mood to create often happens when you're busy at the stove fixing dinner, but now she can get the supplies herself.

All About Cabinets

When it comes to kitchen cabinets, unless you're planning a major (and guaranteed costly) renovation, what you see is what you get. But don't let that deter you from creating a family friendly, chef-inspired environment. Set an afternoon aside to pull the contents out of *every* cupboard to weed through the good, the bad, and the outdated, and then reassign what's left to a new home. (If working on the kitchen as a whole is too vast a project, try writing out an overall plan deciding what will go where and then working on one drawer or cabinet at a time over the course of several weeks.)

QUICK FIX

It's easy to organize and create more space in your cabinets without tearing them down and starting over. The solution can be as simple as adding hooks in the dead space underneath shelves to hang coffee cups and mugs.

■ **Great Gear** The simplest way to add additional space and an organized touch to your cabinets is to add coated wire racks in upper cupboards (plates stack on top, bowls slide underneath); and to keep bending and lifting to a minimum, add pull-out shelves in the lower cabinets (for pots, pans, and cleaning products). Or install wire baskets with top-mounted runners underneath shelves to take advantage of dead airspace. Circular caddies (lazy Susans) and step-up or tiered shelves are great for organizing condiments and canned goods. Door racks are perfect for corralling spices and plastic wraps. Use plastic drawer dividers to separate cooking utensils and silverware efficiently. These are all low-tech, low-cost ways to add more space.

■ **Cheat** If you have a lot of headroom between shelves, try moving the shelving closer together and adding additional shelves at the top.

■ **All in a Row** Organize your cookie sheets, cutting boards, and platters upright in cupboards so they'll take up less space by slipping them in metal folder racks (available at office supply stores).

■ **Hey, Bartender** Instead of arranging tall glasses behind short glasses, requiring you to reach behind when you need the former, arrange glassware the way bartenders do—in horizontal lines from shortest to tallest. This way, any glass of your choosing is right at your fingertips. (See Figure 14.)

■ **A Tisket, a Tasket** Use small plastic baskets in cupboards to file seasoning packets and salad dressing mixes or to gather up small, hard-to-find items such as vanilla extract and toothpick holders.

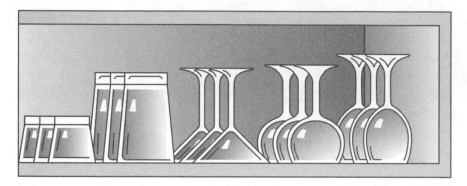

FIGURE 14. Arranging glasses

MAJOR TUNE-UP

Eager to do more? You can expand your space with a bit of imagination, a few tools, and a willing do-it-yourselfer.

■ **Peg-Board Perfect** Install a sheet of Peg-Board on the inside of a lower cabinet door, add hooks, and hang skillets and shallow pots.

■ **Tall and Lean** If you have a narrow kitchen that won't accommodate a standard twenty-four-inch base cabinet along a spare wall but you're in serious need of more lower cupboards, consider installing a twelve-inch-deep pantry cabinet instead.

■ **Up and Over** Although the average refrigerator stands twenty-four inches or more from the wall, the average cabinet placed over it only extends twelve inches. If you need more space, remove the old cabinet and add a new twenty-four-inch one.

■ **Island Fever** If you have a kitchen island that divides the kitchen area from the dining room, consider installing cupboards with glass doors, on the front and back, running parallel overhead. It's a perfect spot for storing china and glassware, and the glass doors allow for plenty of light.

Rethink Your Pots and Pans

Some professional kitchen organizers swear that the average cook can function nicely with merely three pots—an eight-quart stockpot, a two-quart saucepan, and a ten-inch sauté pan. Although your jaw may drop at such a bold, minimalist view on cooking, the message is clear—the average kitchen contains way too many pieces of cookware. (If you like the idea but couldn't possibly function with just three, try adding a twelve-inch fry pan—a sauté pan has straight, tall sides; a fry pan has lower, gently sloping sides—and an old-fashioned cast-iron skillet.)

Let's face it: cookware takes up a lot of space. It's heavy and cumbersome to store and retrieve, too. Rather than keeping every piece, hang on to the ones that you use on a daily basis (store these near your stove or oven) and a few you use during the holidays (these you can keep in a secondary location like the pantry, utility room, garage, or basement). Weed out the ones that you no longer use, have worn out, or contain broken handles and either toss them or give them away to a local charity.

For even more storage space, consider installing a pot rack either directly over your stove or cooktop or over a kitchen island. Pot racks come in all sizes, styles, and finishes and add an attractive statement to your kitchen. You can even make your own. Many years ago, after seeing the foreign film *Like Water for Chocolate*, I made a small replica of one I saw in that movie. I took a thick tree branch, drilled holes in the wood, and screwed in four C hooks; then I suspended it from the ceiling with cowboy-style rope. I got many compliments on the western design, and it only took an hour to make.

A few points to remember here: display only the items that you use most frequently, make sure they're in good shape to showcase, and keep the scale of your rack in proportion to the size of your kitchen. For safety, be sure to mount the hardware in ceiling studs to ensure the rack can bear the heavy weight.

Drawers

Some kitchens are very low on drawer space. If you find yourself in this category, there are a few tricks. Place plastic wraps and Baggies in a wire rack that mounts on a pantry door specially designed to fit those odd-shaped boxes. Pull the dish towels out and keep them in a basket above the refrigerator. Or put paper napkins in a caddy and keep them on the kitchen table where they're more likely to be used.

Cutlery

How many times a day are you or the kids in and out of this drawer and you still don't have a silverware tray? Go out and buy one today. And while you're at it, consider an organizer for your steak knives, too. Look for one with individual slots for each knife; it'll protect the blades and your little ones' fingers, plus it'll keep the drawer tidy. A magnetic strip mounted on the counter wall works well to keep carving and paring knives at the ready. And if you have young kids, move cutlery (minus the steak knives) to a lower drawer to help encourage them to set the evening dinner table.

⏰ **TIME-SAVER**—Sort your silverware as you place it in the dishwasher—all spoons in one bin, forks in another. It saves time when you empty the dishwasher every morning. Just make sure that your cutlery doesn't stick together in the dishwasher; otherwise, it won't get clean.

🗄 **STYLE TIP**—Not enough drawer space for cutlery and kitchen utensils? Make them part of the décor by arranging them in old crockery, decorative baskets, or even Mexican-style flowerpots and displaying them on your countertop or kitchen table.

Utensils

You'll be amazed at the difference a few plastic organizing boxes placed inside your utensil drawer will make. Simply dividing wooden spoons from stainless utensils makes an enormous difference.

For still more space, add a Peg-Board or wire rack with hooks over your stove, cooktop, or adjacent bare wall and hang your ladles, cheese graters, and wire whisks. And although the theme song so far has been weed and purge, it makes sense to keep an extra set of frequently used utensils such as measuring spoons and cups in more than one location, such as your food-prep area and your baking area.

Junk (aka All-Purpose) Drawer

Ah, the infamous junk drawers, where anything can hide (and often does). We all have them, and most of us would say we can't live without them, but that doesn't mean they have to be a disaster to open. Once again, plastic drawer dividers work well. If you can, have more than one, so you can categorize the contents. For instance, in our house, we have a three-drawer stack—top one for household goodies (screwdriver, tape measure, furniture leg pads), the center drawer for electrical paraphernalia (extension cords, lightbulbs, and such), and the bottom for batteries and flashlights.

Small-Appliance Jungle

No doubt about it, appliances have made our lives much easier. Yet, like cookware, warehousing appliances is a challenge. First, get them off your countertops and store them in cabinets. It looks neater and frees up prep space. Place everyday appliances, such as the toaster and coffeemaker, where you use them. This could be in a small cabinet near the kitchen table or a lower cabinet shelf near your food-prep area.

Next, move sometimes-used devices to a secondary location. I store my mammoth mixer at the bottom of a baker's rack in the back porch, just steps from the kitchen. Or, try creating an appliance center—a pantry shelf, corner cabinet, or even a box with a roll-up door—where all appliances stand together at the ready.

🖈 **Style Tip**—Cramped on dining space? Do hungry guests need to walk sideways to get to their chairs? Build a banquette (or booth) along the wall. Now you can move the table in tighter and do away with a few chairs, opening up more aisle space.

Creating More Space

Spent the afternoon purging and reorganizing but still in need of more space? There are a few tricks to help ease the crunch. Read on.

- **Add a bookcase along a spare wall or at the end of a counter.** Store cookbooks in the shelves. Display your best mixing bowls on top.
- **Mount a cutting board directly over the sink.** It frees up counter space and is convenient to the garbage disposal.
- **Invest in a rolling butcher's cart.** Use the top for extra counter space, and store the food processor and other tools in the cabinet

Renovating Your Kitchen

In the past two years, three of my neighbors have renovated their kitchens (and so have we). Hey, our houses were built in the fifties, and the dark cabinets and white linoleum flooring looked a bit dated. It was time. If you're in the mood to change the look of your kitchen, here are a few tips to help you find your way.

Choose Your Cabinets Wisely Prices vary widely, from top-of-the-line custom-made to moderately priced semicustom to the biggest-bang-for-your-buck—stock cabinets. Shop around; home centers are not always the cheapest source. Cabinets also come in all sizes, so carefully determine your needs by taking a survey of your cookware and appliances. For instance, if you have a plethora of small electronic gadgets, consider a lazy Susan in a corner cabinet; if you bake a lot, choose a cabinet with horizontal dividers for cookie sheets; if you have no other spot to store staples, pantry cabinets with pullout drawers and shelves will make your mouth water. And don't forget a cabinet with pullout recycling and trash bins.

Consider the Space We've heard it before—when designing a kitchen, connect your three work spaces (food prep, cooking, cleanup) through a triangle. Make each leg of the triangle no less than four feet but no larger than nine feet. Try to avoid traffic snarls by moving stations away from major thoroughfares. Don't block prime counter space by placing the dishwasher directly underneath the food prep area where the chef will collide with the person cleaning up.

Double or Nothing Although a double oven sounds like heaven to most aspiring chefs, it takes up an enormous amount of space and it's expensive (besides, that usually means the microwave will end up on the counter). Many families feel they'd benefit from having two sinks, too—one for food prep, the other for cleanup—but statistics show that most cooks work solo. And some large families are installing two dishwashers but then use the second only during the holidays. Before writing that very large check to cover the cost of appliances, remember that two is not always better than one.

It's All in the Details Two-sided sink or single basin? And what about the faucets? Levers allow you turn them on when your hands are dirty without touching the fixture, but some people like the look of cross handles better. What about a wine rack or bookcase for cookbooks? Don't forget to add plenty of drawers in the right locations, such as several near the oven or cooktop to store potholders, dish towels, and utensils. Make sure your refrigerator door swings open in the correct direction, too; otherwise, you'll need to buy an additional kit to adjust it. Check to see that you have enough electrical outlets, including one or two on a kitchen island. Then there's lighting. You'll need plenty of ambient light in the form of recessed lights to brighten up the room, but you'll also want task lighting over each workstation.

Step into My Office You only need a nook no larger than thirty inches wide to create a kitchen office, but the benefits will make it feel 100 times larger. Even if you have a home office, an additional work space in the kitchen will help you separate home business from corporate business. Use the space to organize and file recipes, cookbooks, and menu planners; to read and sign permission slips and report cards; and to write up the next day's to-do list, review your family calendar, and pay the family bills. Best of all, it's an extra desk, which comes in handy when two children sharing a bedroom are vying for privacy while studying. Simply set up one child in the kitchen, and each has his or her own personal space.

It's All for the Kids Kids love to be in the thick of things and that usually means underfoot in the kitchen. Make it a kid-friendly environment by choosing easy-to-care-for fabrics and flooring, rounded corners for tables and countertops, and even a minirefrigerator at their level for cold juice and healthy snacks (so they don't always need to open and close the family fridge).

Move Heaven and Earth Even if your budget is modest, you can still make construction modifications to increase the size and usability of your kitchen. For instance, we knocked down a breakfast bar that separated a narrow dining room from the kitchen. Making the dining room part of the kitchen gave the whole space a wonderful openness. With the extra room, we were also able to build a small island that we use for added counter space and as an informal buffet station.

below. When not in use, keep it in the utility closet or in the corner of the kitchen.

- **Look for a kitchen table with either a marble or stainless steel top.** Both surfaces are great for food prep, they clean up easily, and their contemporary designs look great in today's kitchen.
- **Install undercounter appliances.** They're smaller than their countertop rivals and are real space savers.
- **Use a baker's rack with a maple top for counter space.** Use the shelves above for pantry staples, the ones below for cookbooks and cookware.
- **Install a small shelf on the wall above the counter.** Display kitchen essentials such as olive oil, salt and pepper, and even frequently used spices.
- **Mount a flip-up leaf at the end of the counter.** Flip it up for additional work space; fold it down when you're done.
- **Hang stemware from an undercabinet rack.** Or hang coffee mugs from hooks.
- **Install a long wire shelf high up along an empty wall, in the empty space between cabinets or over the sink.** Store seldom-used items on top, and hang kitchen utensils from hooks underneath.
- **Add a bowl or plate rack on the wall.** Display your favorite pieces.
- **Place a pot stand in an unused kitchen corner.** The tall, narrow tower with built-in shelves is ideal for displaying large cookware.

A Proper Pantry

Wouldn't you love to have a walk-in, butler-style pantry where everything you need for cooking and entertaining is right at your fingertips? Large, flat drawers for properly storing tablecloths; clear glass cabinets for crystal; and rows of shelves for every staple you could think of?

Alas, most of us will never know the pleasure, but you can try to create something similar for canned goods and staples using the space you already have. A utility closet, for instance, makes a fabulous pantry (simplify cleaning supplies and move them elsewhere; hang the mop and broom from a wall hanger).

When I was growing up, for instance, my mom converted a linen closet right off the kitchen into a pantry. It had ample deep shelves to store canned goods, dry goods, and large bulky items, such as the ever-present gallon of olive oil (we're Italians!) and her old but outrageously large KitchenAid mixer. She moved her table linens to an antique chest in the living room; bed linens were stored in bathroom cabinets.

A pantry can come in all forms; it just needs to be accessible to the kitchen. In my home, for instance, there's little cupboard space to accommodate any kind of pantry (yes, even after the kitchen remodel), so I created a storeroom in my back porch area where my washer and dryer are. It's small, but very functional. First, I moved all cleaning supplies and mops off the floor and placed them in wire racks and hooks that I installed next to the washer and dryer. On the opposite wall is an eight-foot-tall stainless steel shelving unit that I bought at IKEA (Target and Costco have similar models). Although it came with four shelves, I bought an extra shelf and "cheated" some additional space. Tiered shelves keep all my staples accessible. I also added deep stainless steel baskets that hook to the sides where I keep potatoes, onions, and bags of chips. With just eighteen inches left before my back door, I found a three-tiered wire basket on wheels (at Crate & Barrel) that fits perfectly in which I store bottles of mineral water, juice, soda, and wine. And I have just enough room to squeeze my ironing board in before you hit the back wall. Everything I need—pantry staples, cleaning supplies, and laundry equipment—neatly arranged, easy to locate, all in less than thirty-five square feet of space.

🗄 **STYLE TIP**—Create a butler's pantry along a long hallway off the kitchen by installing narrow, six-inch-deep shelves from ceiling to floor. Keep the appearance orderly and interesting with old crockery and china, colorful folded table linens, staples displayed in clear glass containers, or jars of preserved food.

KEY ORGANIZING TIPS

■ **Follow the Group** Keep all like food items together—boxed pasta in one section, cereal boxes on one shelf, canned soup in another. And always keep them in the same spot: most-often-used items at eye level and least-used items, such as baking supplies, on lower shelves. Consider labeling shelves to help family members keep it orderly, too.

■ **Step to the Front of the Line** To see what items you have on hand at a glance, add a step-up or tiered shelf. As you unpack your groceries, place new items in the back, moving the older items up front where they'll be used next.

■ **Just a Slight Adjustment** Make the most use of your space by eliminating dead space—the area above your staples—by adjusting each shelf down a peg. You'll probably end up with extra space at the top of the cabinet to add an additional shelf or two.

■ **It's Very Clear** Transfer packages of dried beans, nuts, rice, and noodles to clear glass jars with lids. It reduces spills, looks neater, and is easier to see contents.

■ **Move It Out** Store overstocked staples (all those on-sale items you sometimes buy) in another, secondary pantry, such as in the utility room, garage, or basement.

■ **Don't Touch That** For items that you don't want family members to break into (like the roasted peppers or canned baked beans for Sunday's barbecue), come up with a no-touch symbol, such as a big, yellow star stuck to the lid.

Kiss the Cook

Your kitchen may be small, but with a bit of imagination you can give it a big heart. Just remember to reevaluate your lifestyle in relation to your kitchen and how you want it to reflect your family's interests.

Living Room and Family Room

Although my kids have a great big bedroom filled with a host of toys, every weekend morning they drag boxes of blocks, Legos, a train set, and whatever else strikes their fancy out onto the living room floor and begin their day of play. Within a half hour, the entire floor is covered with roadways, wooden buildings, and tiny, little cars. Truth be told, it drives me nuts! I spend the rest of the day stepping over them or, worse yet, on them. I hold my tongue until six o'clock, when I yell, "Time to clean up!" Only then does the toy city disappear back into boxes, and I can once again reclaim my living room.

Sound familiar? Kids want to be where the action is, and that means wherever Mom and Dad are. Parents of teenagers tell me to enjoy it now. Before I know it, they say, my boys will retreat to their rooms to play seemingly endless computer games, and I'll miss the days when they were constantly under my feet.

We'll see about that.

The living and family rooms have always been high-traffic areas, communal watering holes for family members and friends to gather and hang out together. Unfortunately, with so many different people coming and going, they're also spots where clutter builds easily. The kids come home from school and kick off their shoes and grab a bag of chips before they hop on the couch to watch a bit of TV; parents deposit parcels or briefcases as soon as they enter the door; newspapers scatter on Sunday morning; board games get left out overnight; and videos, CDs, and other electronic equipment are always in need of a home. It's enough to make any parent cry, "No more!"

Where Do I Begin?

Before jumping in with revamping your home's communal living space, take some time to consider your family's interests. Is watching TV top on their to-do list yet the set is hidden in the corner of the room where few can easily see it? Then perhaps you'll want to create a high-tech home theater with a big-screen TV taking center stage. Or maybe you're a family of readers with piles of books scattered throughout your living room with no permanent home. If so, perhaps a cozy library-style room is more your thing. Yet some families love to play games, whether its cards, board games, darts, or even pool. Whichever direction or personality your living or family rooms take on, keep them in line with your family's lifestyle.

Not only do you want to make them comfortable and functional for all those who live under your roof, but you'll also want to make them pleasing to look at, too, because these are often the first rooms guests see when they walk through the front door. Yet sometimes they look messy even after you've just spent an hour tidying them up. Why is that? Probably it's because the rooms have too many roles—playroom for the kids, media center for the family, and even a home office. When reorganizing, think of ways to visually separate each function, or transfer one or more activities to another spot in the house. Could you move the kids' toys out and perhaps set up a playroom somewhere else? (Turn to the end of the "Garage, Attic, and Basement" chapter for a few suggestions.) How about putting up some sort of dividing wall between your home office and the rest of the room? Next, try a no-fuss décor—a few well-chosen pieces of furniture cleverly arranged and even fewer accessories.

⏰ **TIME-SAVER**—An antique paperweight collection may hold sentimental value, but it takes up valuable space, often looks cluttered, and requires dusting week after week. Pare down knickknacks and objets d'art to a bare minimum.

Choosing and Arranging Furniture

To make your family or living room a true communal retreat, carefully look at your current furniture. Each piece should serve a specific function or purpose. Furniture with shelves, niches, cubbies, or drawers are all practical allies. But as you survey these rooms, you'll notice that some pieces are simply deadweight with no real purpose. They're just taking up valuable real estate and need to move on. If you can't part with the Chippendale chair, however, at least move it to a corner where it will take a place of artistic honor, out of the line of traffic.

W*hen you live in a small house, as Dan and I do, every inch of space counts. You just can't have a coffee table; you have to have one that lifts open so you can put stuff in it. You have to be very creative about the space.*

Pay attention to traffic patterns, too. Note how the living and family rooms are connected to the others in your home and how family members move in and out on a daily basis. Having the sofa directly in front of the TV may make for comfortable viewing, but if your kids need to navigate around it several times a day just to reach the kitchen, then perhaps you should move it. Experimenting with various furniture floor plans is fun. Once you've hit on the right arrangement, the payback is enormous yet the effort was minimal.

I*t seems like I'm always touching up the paint on the walls. Instead of hauling heavy paint cans from the garage inside to do the job, I've filled small, sponge-tip bottles with the matching paint. They look like shoe-polish bottles (I found them at a crafts store), and I keep them in my laundry-room closet. It makes touching up the walls easier.*

KEY ORGANIZING TIPS

■ **In the Zone** Allocate a specific area for activities that your family enjoys. Move the reading chair and light close to the bookcase, for instance. Arrange the sofa to visually separate the living space from a home office or a child's play area. If you have a table for meals, move it closest to the door leading to the kitchen for easy setup and cleanup.

🗜 **STYLE TIP**—Leather is a die-hard furniture fabric. It can take a lot of abuse and requires little or no maintenance (wear actually enhances its character). If you pick a classic style, it could very well last until the kids go off to college. Wrought-iron coffee and end tables are great for the same reason. And don't underestimate the durability of hardwood floors.

- **Stay in Focus** When arranging furniture, choose a focal point for the room—a dramatic fireplace, an interesting window arrangement, or even the TV—then work your seating around it in a way that will show it off favorably.
- **Take a Seat** When designing a living or family room, seating should be your number-one concern. Make sure you have enough room for the family to be together at the same time. Two smaller sofas (love seats) are easier to position than one large couch (most people prefer to sit on an end with an armrest rather than in the middle anyway).
- **Mix and Match** Use a variety of closed cabinets and open shelves to house electronic equipment and other household gear.
- **All Clear?** Pay attention to space between the furniture as well. Chairs and sofas need a minimum of one and one-half feet of clearance between them (more if they're positioned in the middle of the room).

🗜 **STYLE TIP**—Functional yet cozy, window seats are making a comeback. You can add one easily by installing two twenty-four-inch-wide kitchen base cabinets (twenty-four inches deep) side-by-side underneath your favorite window. (To create a true niche, however, also add floor-to-ceiling bookcases on each side.) Top with a one-inch-thick piece of plywood wrapped in fabric (staple in place underneath) and add a four-inch-thick matching fabric cushion. The cabinets allow for abundant storage, and the seat offers comfort and sunshine.

QUICK FIX

It could be a "girl thing," but I just adore furniture shopping and browsing through design magazines (my husband, like many males, would rather build the furniture in his workshop). Stores and magazines are great resources for gathering ideas for your own home. And there's often no need to spend a fortune to redesign the room—many simple solutions abound—

from rearranging the furniture and borrowing a few pieces from the attic or another room to adding a few baskets, boxes, or cabinets to contain the clutter and improve the overall appearance.

- **The Seating Solution** When seating the entire family is next to impossible, try adding large, plush floor pillows to the room. Not only do kids love lounging on the floor when watching TV, but also pillows stack up easily in the corner at the end of the evening and can be tossed in the wash when they get dirty.

- **Recess Is Best** Turn that unused niche under the window into an intimate seating area by moving a small couch underneath or building a window seat.

- **No More Traffic** Doors need a three-foot clearance in a room and are often the cause of many a traffic snarl. Consider removing them. Not only will it increase the flow in and out of the room, but also the space will feel more open.

- **Fabulous Fabric** If you're in the market for some new furniture, choose fabrics that hide stains, for example, dark colors, prints, and plaids. White and pale pastels are all begging for spots and the evidence of children. If your budget begs you to wait, consider slipcovers. These days, they come in a variety of colors and patterns and are more affordable than ever. In fact, pick up two sets and rotate them depending on the season or your mood.

- **Double-Duty Solutions** Make your furniture work overtime—choose coffee or end tables with drawers and shelves to house living room gear such as the TV remote, board games, knitting supplies, or the latest paperback. Be inventive. Use that old steamer trunk in the attic as a coffee table and store cozy afghans inside. A small, multidrawer stainless-steel cabinet makes a stylish, contemporary end table (head to IKEA) yet can house a host of gear.

- **Entertaining Enlightenment** If the family seems to congregate to your house every Sunday afternoon, keep a set of nesting tables for impromptu dinners or board games.

MAJOR TUNE-UP

You could spend hours daydreaming about what you'd like to do to your living room. Try your hand at redesigning the space by following one of these methods.

■ **Be Graphic** Figure out your new furniture layout on paper. Rather than spending a day lifting and moving the couch in a dozen different directions, carefully measure your room and re-create it on graph paper (use one square for every square foot of floor space). Measure and mark doors, windows (notate their height, too, so that you may decide if you can move a small table underneath one of them), electrical and telephone outlets, light switches, and even heating fixtures, such as radiators. Next, cut out models of your furniture from heavy card stock and start arranging them on the graph paper (start with the largest pieces first). Be creative— try moving furniture at right angles or even in the center of the room.

■ **Software Savvy** These days, technology has a solution for every problem. Punch! offers a variety of home-design software packages for your computer. Just click and design to your heart's content, all in 3-D format.

By the Book

Whether your passions lie in art and antiques or detective thrillers, chances are you have a lot of written proof. I'm talking about books. Paperback or hardcover, most homes have dozens of editions, big and small. And in spite of what computer wizards may proclaim, the Internet won't be taking the place of the written page any time soon. There are few who can curl up on the couch on a chilly, rainy afternoon with a blanket, cup of tea, and a laptop reading the latest from Stephen King. Although you may agree that there's nothing better than the feel of a leather-bound book or the warm look books add to virtually any room they grace, the question remains: where do you put them all?

KEY ORGANIZING TIPS

■ **A Cool, Dry Place** Books need a bit of pampering to last the generations. Store them out of direct sun in a cool, dry environment. Avoid rooms with dramatic swings in temperature and humidity, too (such as a sunny, south-facing room or the basement). Don't push them all the way to the back of the shelf either. Books need about an inch of air circulation behind them.

■ **Dust Bunnies** Dust and dirt can hurt books, too, so they'll need to be cleaned regularly. Gently brush from the spine toward the front using a clean, soft cloth.

Picture-Hanging Perfection

Nothing brings out a home's personality more than the photographs and paintings that grace its walls. Take the time, however, to think about creating the perfect composition—scale, line, balance, and symmetry—before swinging the hammer.

Odd Man Out Using an odd number of paintings when designing a grouping works best (two is the only even number that works well; four if grouped in pairs).

Order, Please Think of a grouping as a unit. The eye requires order, so remember your high school geometry when arranging pictures—create vertical or horizontal lines.

Fascinating Rhythm Bring rhythm to your groupings by varying the sizes (small and large) and shapes (squares and rectangles) of your pictures.

Keep It to Scale A six-inch still life will disappear if placed over a seven-foot sofa. At the same time, a horizontal picture will look out of place over a vertical piece of furniture like a bureau. Remember to keep your artwork in scale to the furnishings they will adorn.

Give Me Space Use the "hand" rule when properly spacing pictures in a group—no more than four inches apart, or the size of a hand. Too much space disrupts the design; too little appears crowded.

The Eyes Have It Most people hang their pictures way too high on the wall. Artwork looks best when hung at eye level—the center of the picture should be about sixty to sixty-seven inches from the floor (about twelve inches above the top of furniture).

Hang Like a Pro Avoid picture-hanging horror by making templates of your grouping. Trace each picture or photograph onto brown butcher paper. (Be sure to identify each picture on its matching template.) Next, carefully mark where the picture hook will meet the wire on each template (don't forget to pull the wire taut for accuracy). Arrange your templates on the wall with low-tack drafting tape, moving them around until you find the look you desire. Finally, install your picture hooks directly onto the templates, carefully rip the paper off, and hang your pictures.

- **Every Room in the House** Break up your collection to accommodate every room in the house. After all, if you're a family of readers, you probably read in nearly every room.
- **Stud Protection** Make sure to anchor freestanding bookcases over four feet tall to wall studs (drywall alone isn't structurally sufficient) to prevent toppling.
- **Long Division** Dividing and cataloging your book collection can take on many forms—arrange books by size (putting large books with smaller ones will cause covers to spread), by subject matter, or even by author.

We have a beautiful collection of California pottery decorating the shelves in the living room. Before Nathaniel and Mia came along, we never touched it; it was just for show. Now that we're more crowded, the pottery had to assume a more functional role. All our spare keys, for instance, sit in a beautiful Bauer bowl that used to sit empty. We put checks that need to be deposited in another bowl, bills to be paid in a third. They've essentially become family in-boxes.

QUICK FIX

Glance through the pages of *Architectural Digest* and you'll see beautiful art books tastefully displayed on well-dusted coffee tables. Yeah, right. Not in this house, with three small boys and thirty curious—and often dirty—fingers. I've had to think of clever ways to get our books out of the way but within easy reach of my husband and myself.

- **Dime-Store Detective** Line up those not-so-pretty paperbacks on the top of a dresser or nightstand in the guest bedroom, enticing overnight visitors to peruse through their own private library.
- **Mantel Magic** Dress up a fireplace mantel with a series of large hardcover books. Be sure to use bookends on either end to help support their spines.
- **A Step Up** If you have a wide, open staircase in your home or apartment, try arranging a series of books between the railings (they'll make perfect bookends as long as you don't pack the books in too tightly).
- **Temporary Contemporary** A large, stainless-steel shelving unit is an inexpensive and contemporary way to house your book collection as well as your electronics. Mix and match stereo components with your hard-

covers. Place small, matching decorative baskets along the bottom shelf to store CDs, videotapes, and other equipment, such as headphones.

W*e have a rule in our house—the TV Guide and the remotes go right on top of the TV in the entertainment center before you close it up. This way, we always know where they are.*

MAJOR TUNE-UP

Building custom bookcases can enhance the look and value of your home. Start by measuring your books (cluster them in groups) to determine how much room you'll need. Short, thick shelves are sturdier than long, thin ones—a one-inch-thick shelf shouldn't be longer than thirty-six inches; a three-quarters-inch shelf, no longer than twenty-four inches. Remember, too, when planning for a big project such as bookshelves to allow for future growth (about 50 percent for a serious book collector).

■ **Sofa Shelf** Install a series of narrow shelves on the wall above the sofa (you can build them out of plywood just as long as you paint them the same color as the wall to make them less obtrusive). Be sure to begin the first row high enough to allow for ample headroom for people sitting.

■ **Close Call** A narrow space between two windows is a perfect spot for a tall and slender bookcase.

■ **Floor to Ceiling** Floor-to-ceiling bookcases make a very dramatic statement. Try building a series along an entire wall in a formal dining room or along the wall of a long hallway. (Be sure not to restrict traffic flow.)

⏰ **TIME-SAVER**—If you have young children, use semigloss paint throughout your living and family rooms rather than flat. It's much easier to sponge off dirt, food stains, and fingerprints.

Lust for Life

The family that plays together stays together, and nothing can be better than hanging out in a well-organized, truly functional room. You don't have to be a professional designer to make the place look great—work with what you have.

Master Bedroom

If you ask most parents what they want from their master bedroom, they'll tell you a private sanctuary, a place to rest and relax after a long day of work or taking care of the family, perhaps a temporary office to finagle the family finances or tinker with other work, and, and if they play their cards right, a cozy nest where they can reconnect with their spouses after days of passing him or her matter-of-factly in the kitchen. For one room to be all those things, it needs to be functional as well as luxurious, and that is one heavy proposition.

Yet for most of us, the master retreat often takes a backseat to the rest of the house. Too many other things take priority, such as reorganizing the kids' bedrooms, remodeling the kitchen, or landscaping the front yard. The typical master bedroom is far from typical at all—it often functions as a secondary laundry room (walk in and you'll see the laundry basket brimming with clean clothes waiting to be sorted and put away), a fast-food joint (how many times have you eaten a late-night dinner in front of the TV because you came home too late?), or a makeshift office (on weekends, the bed is often covered with work-related files or bills that need to get in the mail *today*). And romantic boudoir? Forget about it. The last time those sensuous linen throw pillows made it onto the bed was the night that your daughter was conceived—three years ago!

Don't give up. Your bedroom can be organized, stylish, and restful even in a small amount of square footage. It's all how you approach the space.

Organizing the Space

When you're ready to give your sanctuary a makeover, start by sitting with your significant other and doing some brainstorming. Talk about what works and should remain (you each have your own nightstand and reading lamp, for instance) and what doesn't (the TV and VCR perched on the dresser just take up too much valuable room), and discuss ways to make changes. Think about what would make the room more fulfilling to each of you. For instance, you may both love books and want to create an intimate reading area.

Yet you'll need to be practical, too. Sharing a room with someone else presents a whole host of problems—you'll both need ample space for your clothes and other personal belongings, room for dressing and undressing, and, of course, a bed—all without intruding too much on the other's territory.

Organizing the master bedroom can be fun, though. Unlike other communal rooms in the house—the kitchen, the den, and the living room—the master bedroom is rarely seen by outsiders. Because it's not on display for public view, it can be decorated in a purely personal style.

KEY ORGANIZING TIPS

■ **It's All About the Bed** The largest and most important piece of furniture in the bedroom, the bed can't help but be the focal point of the master bedroom. If you're in the market for a new bed, don't skimp on quality here. Shop around and get a comfortable, well-made mattress. Be sensitive to the dimensions of your bed in comparison to the size of your room, though—a king-sized bed may be a bit too big for many smaller master bedrooms. Placement of the bed is important, too. The best location is where it won't interfere with a door or window, usually on the opposite wall of the main door. Leave as much space as possible around all sides for foot traffic.

■ **Size Matters** Once the bed is out of the way, you'll need to furnish the rest of the room with a dresser, nightstands, and perhaps a reading chair or two. Choose appropriately sized furniture for the room. A four-poster bed or bulky antique armoire would dominate a small master bedroom. Yet before you go out and start buying different furnishings, see if you can make do with what you already have by simply eliminating excess or unused pieces or borrowing or trading from another room.

■ **Choose a Style** Tuscan villa, a night in Morocco, shabby chic—whatever your taste, start with furnishing the bed with coverlets, quilts, and shams and build the rest of your room around it. Use different textures by mixing different types of fabrics to create interest. Choose a soothing color palette for your walls and window treatments, too. Get some ideas by flipping through the pages of *Architectural Digest*, *Better Homes and Gardens*, *Country Living*, or any other decorating magazine.

■ **Let There Be Light** Nothing kills atmosphere quicker than overhead lighting. (Use the overhead socket for an energy-efficient ceiling fan instead.) Set the mood for relaxation by investing in bedside lamps. Use a lower-wattage bulb for softer lighting, or better yet, install dimmer switches so you can vary the brightness depending on your task—soft light when you're talking or relaxing, bright light for reading.

Creating More Space

Unless you live in a newly built or remodeled home, chances are you're anxious for more space in the master bedroom. For many parents, the bed *is* the space, and everything else is packed in wherever it can fit. If two adults share the room, clutter is inevitable. A simple housecleaning will often give the illusion of more space. Not only should you begin the process of weeding out excess clothes and accessories, but you should also move certain tasks out of the bedroom altogether, such as laundry sorting or bill paying and mandate them to another area of the house (set up a laundry prep area in your back porch or turn a corner of the family room into a mini–home office).

QUICK FIX

If you have no plans to remodel any time soon to gain a few more square feet, follow a few quick-fix tricks to open up the room, allowing you to at least walk around your bed without knocking your shins.

■ **Rise and Shine** Raise the bed twelve to fifteen inches off the ground, creating a romantic retreat and increasing valuable storage space below. (Look for Bed Rizer, steel legs that fit directly onto your bed frame, adding height.) Place drawers with wheels or covered boxes underneath to store all types of clothing or extra bedding. Or look for a platform bed with built-in drawers so you can do away with the dresser altogether.

■ **Into the Closet** If space allows, move your dresser into the closet. It cuts down on clutter by keeping the furniture closer to its source. Plus, this simple act adds an enormous amount of floor space to the room.

■ **Move It on Over** Most beds look best when placed on the wall opposite the doorway. Yet you can create a bit more space by moving it completely against the wall or turning it at a right angle (or catercorner). Experiment with placement until you find a combination that affords you a bit more room.

■ **Headboard Heaven** Do away with bulky nightstands on each side of the bed and instead opt for a roomy headboard with built-in shelves. Or, if you don't want to buy a new piece of furniture, improvise by placing a hall table behind the bed. Consider installing a narrow shelf along the back of the bed high enough to clear your head while sitting up. For lighting, install swing-arm lamps directly on the wall.

■ **Double-Duty Furnishings** Look for ways to make your furniture do double duty. Choose nightstands with drawers and shelves to corral reading material and glasses, place a trunk at the end of your bed to store extra bedding (it makes a handy place to sit, too, when dressing in the morning), or search tag sales or secondhand stores for a tall armoire to house the TV and other electronic equipment and accessories. Be inventive: stacked vintage suitcases make an interesting side table with plenty of room to spare inside for storage.

■ **TV Heaven** Get that TV off the dresser or toss that cumbersome media stand and mount the set on the wall (nearly every organizing catalog offers an affordable model—some with room for a VCR, too). Not only will you save valuable floor or dresser space, but also it allows you to watch without craning your neck in bed.

MAJOR TUNE-UP

With a just small budget, you can add additional space, often without the expense of consulting an architect.

■ **Wall Wardrobe Wonder** Build floor-to-ceiling wardrobes on each side of the bed. The covered cabinets will provide storage space. Moving the bed directly between the two provides an intimate sleeping niche. (See

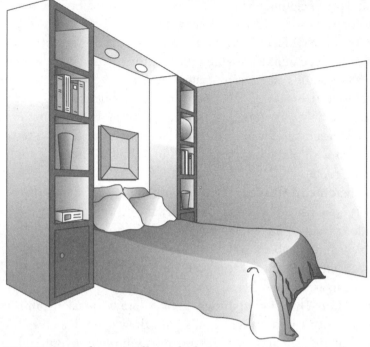

FIGURE 15. Bedroom wall wardrobes

Figure 15.) Or, frame the master bedroom or bathroom doorway with a series of small built-in cabinets. Not only will it open up more storage, but also the architectural feature adds privacy, a buffer zone between master retreat and outside world.

■ **Pop-Out Possibilities** Pushing out an outside wall and installing a cantilevered bay window adds additional leeway to a master bedroom floor plan without changing the roof line or foundation—both expensive propositions.

A Case for Clothes

Do you ever walk into your bedroom only to find a pile of not-quite-dirty, not-quite-clean clothes strewn in the corner? Nothing makes a room messier than a heap of clothes on the floor. Yet if they're not exactly dirty, like those sweatpants you wore for just a few hours while cooking break- fast this morning, it's wasteful to toss them in the wash (not to mention more work). And you can't put them back in your drawer with all your clean clothes, so what other options do you have?

Take a cue from the "Children's Bedrooms" chapter and develop the hook habit. Your options are many.

- Line a short hallway from the master bedroom to the bath with decorative hooks hung all in a neat row.
- Position hooks on the back of the bedroom or closet door (for those sweatpants and T-shirts) and on the back of the master bathroom door (for pajamas and bathrobes).
- Hang an old-fashioned hall rack with pegs next to the closet.
- Place a brass, wood, or wrought-iron hall coatrack (choose a style that fits the décor of your bedroom) in the corner.
- Go British with a formal valet—a wardrobe organizer for men (although practical enough for women, too) with a wide hanger for a suit jacket, a bar for folded pants, and a small bin for your pockets' contents.
- Be creative—drape clothes over a bamboo ladder leaning against your bedroom wall or any other unusual object that you find at a tag sale or antique shop.

Another Case for Clothes

Although men may be guilty of stockpiling clothes on the floor, women are far from innocent. "I have nothing to wear," is the cry of many a female, yet most of us can't close our closet doors and drawers because of the overwhelming mass that is bulging from the inside. With most people wearing only 20 percent of their wardrobes 80 percent of the time, letting go should be easy, but it isn't. You don't mean to be impractical; you're just hopeful. You're patiently waiting, for instance, to lose ten more pounds in the hope that those prepregnancy black tweed pants will zip up once again.

And the shoes! Dozens of them on last count, yet you only wear about six different pairs consistently. Those red patent-leather ones, for instance, may be totally out of style, but there's not a blemish on them and they cost more than $100. You can't get rid of those. Or can you?

Contrary to the feminine point of view, less clothes stuffed in drawers and closets actually opens up more choices. Rather than weeding through old fashion faux pas and misfits every morning and pulling out numerous bad choices before deciding on the outfit for the day, keep only a selection of clothes that have already passed the test. Pull any one of these outfits out, and it looks good. Besides, paring down your wardrobe to only those pieces that look great and work well with each other allows you to clearly see what's missing in your overall wardrobe, like a pair of smartly tailored black pants or a camel-colored wool skirt.

Dive In

It's a "girl thing," so grab a trusted friend who will offer an honest and clear opinion (forget your significant other; you're just setting yourselves up for an argument), and devote an afternoon to the task. Because you'll be spending the day trying on clothes, wear a snug-fitting tank top and shorts. Start with the obvious—clothes in need of repair or a good cleaning. Has time robbed you of taking care of them or have they seen better days? Congratulations—you've just identified your first casualties.

KEY ORGANIZING TIPS

■ **Weed Out the Bad** Clothes with holes or frayed fabric have successfully put in their time, nylon body suits have gone the way of the seventies disco, and "thin clothes" rarely fit again (and just remind you of the weight you so desperately want to lose). Donate or toss them all and move on.

■ **Get Rid of the Mistakes** So what if you paid $100 for a designer blouse that never looked quite right or fit well? It's taking up valuable space. Admit defeat and donate it; perhaps someone else will be delighted with this future thrift-store gem. The same goes for clothing fads (remember khaki utility suits?) that now look just plain silly.

■ **The One-Year Rule** Look at each piece and ask yourself when was the last time you wore it. If you don't remember or it's been at least a year, you know what to do. (If you simply can't let go of some pieces, set them off to the side for six months. At the end of that time, if you still haven't worn them, it's time to move on.)

■ **A Fantastic Fit** Try on your remaining clothes with a careful eye toward the way each piece fits your body (it should enhance rather than exploit your figure), how the color makes you feel when you put it on (I always feel energized when I wear green), and the style (classics are always keepers). Set these off to one side.

- **An Altering Point of View** Some clothes may still fit well but their lines or shape may need a bit of tweaking to make them work well. No need to get rid of these; often a simple and inexpensive alteration, such as raising the hem of a skirt to just below the knee, will do the trick.

- **Fill in the Blanks** After this eye-opening exercise, make a list in your personal notebook (see "Appointments") of noticeable holes in your wardrobe, but make a vow to choose clothes in the future that only flatter your figure and skin tone.

Combating Closet Chaos

Because all of your clothes are now scattered across your bed, take the time to properly organize your closet before putting them back in. This is a perfect opportunity to do a complete closet makeover. (Home Depot offers a ten-foot laminated Mills Pride closet system with a shelf and five rods of various sizes. You can further customize your space by adding more shelves and drawers.)

QUICK FIX

If you haven't the time, money, or inclination to install a new closet system, you can still carve out a bit more space by simply raising the clothes bar you have a few inches higher and adding a second bar half the width from chains. Use the two shorter lengths to organize blouses and skirts; use the longer section for pants and dresses. There are many other quick-fix tricks for creating haute couture bliss.

- **Hang in There** Rule number one: no wire hangers! Invest a few dollars in good-quality wooden hangers as well as a few padded ones. They help keep clothes properly shaped. And while you're at it, come up with a system for organizing your hangers without crowding your closet with them so you can locate one easily. For instance, when you take an article of clothing from your closet, deposit the empty hanger in a small laundry basket placed on the closet floor or install a hanger organizer over the door (available through organizing catalogs).

- **Shelf Life** That one long upper closet shelf has lots of storage possibilities. Invest in a series of clear plastic boxes with lids to store sweaters, place a shoe cubby up there to get your footwear off the floor, or use modular laminated shelves to organize large accessories.

■ **Shoe Bag Alternative** Not necessarily the best place to store your shoes (they often leave behind dirt), a clear plastic or mesh shoe bag is a great place to sort and store accessories such as scarves, belts, pantyhose, and even jewelry. So, what should you do with your shoes? Wardrobe experts suggest shoe cubbies, but if you don't want the expense, try stacking them in their original boxes and either taping a snapshot of each pair on its appropriate box or simply cutting out a three-inch-square window to identify the contents.

■ **Fold, Don't Hang** It's tempting to put everything on a hanger, but it's not always the best for your clothes. Try folding sweaters and T-shirts so they won't stretch. (It also frees up more rod space for other clothes.)

■ **A Nice Arrangement** To see the abundance of wardrobe possibilities, arrange clothes by type—skirts in one section, blouses in another, and so on—and by color and fabric—light cotton fabrics on one end, dark heavy garments at the other.

■ **A Few Essentials** If you lack light in the closet, install a battery-operated one on the ceiling. Keep a stepladder to the side to help retrieve items on the top shelf. To encourage a quick, morning press, install an over-the-door ironing board on the inside of your closet door. And don't forget a clothes hamper, preferably one with several sections to help sort the laundry before you hit the washing machine.

Just Jewelry

Organizing your jewelry shouldn't take too long for most—an hour, tops. Start by untangling necklaces and sorting your jewelry into several piles: pieces you wear every day, sentimental or valuable items, jewelry you like but that needs repair, and, finally, all the other castoffs. Be ruthless in what you discard. You certainly don't need broken costume jewelry (if it can't be easily fixed, give it to your kids for dress up), and toss all single earrings (unless they're valuable; in that case, have a jeweler remove the stone and make it into a pendant).

Take care when storing your jewelry. Pearls and precious stones such as diamonds, rubies, and sapphires, and even precious metal such as gold, should all be stored separately or at least wrapped in soft tissue paper before being placed in a felt-lined box.

How Much Closet Space Do You Need?

Three Dresses
9"

Five Shirts
10"

Three Skirts/Pants
8"

38"

68"

10"

14"   8"   6"

3" Tall

FIGURE 16. Closet makeover, with built-ins

In planning a closet makeover complete with built-ins, whether using wire shelves or wood laminate, first figure out exactly how much space you'll need to create. Before you spend a dime, inventory your clothes. Count the number of shirts, dresses, suits, skirts, and pants, and follow Figure 16 to create a perfect fit. But remember, you're bound to get more clothes, so allow for a little extra room.

QUICK FIX

If diamonds are a girl's best friend, then pearls run a close second. Hey, what the heck—they're all welcome in my house. Now, where am I going to store that new piece I'm expecting for my anniversary?

■ **Clear as Glass** Store large, colorful costume jewelry in glass bowls or inexpensive vases displayed on your dresser or master bathroom countertop.

■ **Jewel-Case Beauty** Don't hide your favorite necklace in your jewelry box; show it off on a felt-clad neck display (find one in thrift stores or antique shops).

■ **Iced Ears** If you have a large collection of small earrings, keep them separated in an ice-cube tray tucked away inside your drawer.

■ **Goes with the Outfit** Pair certain pieces of jewelry directly with the outfits you wear them with by placing the jewelry in plastic Baggies and hanging them from the garment's hanger.

■ **Jewelry's a Shoe In** Hang a mesh shoe bag over the back of your closet door, and organize large pieces of jewelry in each pocket.

■ **I've Been Framed** Take an attractive desktop frame, remove the glass, and add a sheet of wire mesh in place. Hook earrings.

Close the Door and Say Good Night

Forget giving the kids a time-out; grab a glass of wine and a good book and head for your *own* room. A bedroom should be a reflection of your style and provide comfort and solace from a hectic world.

Mealtime

Although I love to dabble in the kitchen almost as much as I love to eat, most times I feel more like a short-order cook rather than a world-class chef. Instead of hearing "My compliments to the chef," I get "More milk, please" or my personal favorite, "This is gross. Can I have a bowl of Cheerios?"

Let's face it—if you've got kids, mealtime often becomes the "whining hour." Too many discriminating palates and impatient tummies to please, all making demands when you're hungry, tired, and just plain worn out from a long day. Although I can't suggest ways to get your children to eat what's in front of them, there are tricks to mellowing the madness and transforming the stress of preparing dinner into a time when you can come together and reconnect as a family.

Meal-Planning Magic

How often do you shop for groceries? Once a month? Once a week? If it's every day, you're wasting time in the supermarket when you could be hanging out with your family. Yet some parents can't help but shop every night after work simply because they haven't a clue what to cook for dinner until the hour approaches.

Take some time once a week or once a month and plan your meals (it can be as simple as scribbling down grilled chicken, baked potato, and salad). It's a huge time-saver. Just by writing down the week's or month's menu, you'll avoid that last-minute dash to a crowded market and the added stress of what to prepare once you get home. Furthermore, if you know what will appear on the table each night, who's home first can get the prep work going, relieving you of the job the second you walk in the door.

*M*eals are always a challenge because we're vegetarians. Most families can throw a piece of meat on the grill, fix a salad, and they're done. Our choices are more limited. By sitting down with the kids and planning two weeks' worth of meals, I can shop more efficiently, and when I come home at night, I don't stare at the stove and wonder what to fix.

KEY ORGANIZING TIPS

■ **All Systems Go** You should choose a menu-planning system based on the way you normally shop for groceries. For instance, if you shop every Monday morning, then plan your meals every Sunday night. But if you prefer to hit the supermarket once a month for a big stock up, with a few quick side trips every week for fresh produce, then you should plan your meals a month at a time.

■ **It's in the News** If you shop at the same supermarket every week, plan your menus around their weekly specials. For instance, if chicken is a deal, center your recipes on different poultry dishes.

■ **Keep It Simple** Rather than preparing an elaborate meal every night of the week, choose simple dishes that you know your family will enjoy—spaghetti and meatballs, pot roast, chicken cutlets and mashed potatoes. But if you love to cook, try designating one night—say, on the weekend—to try a new recipe.

■ **Involve the Kids** Many parents find that planning meals with their children works best. Not only is their input important (if they choose the meals, they're more likely to eat them), but Mom or Dad is also teaching them valuable skills—planning ahead, budgeting, and a bit of mathematics, too.

■ **Plan for Emergencies** Keep a well-stocked pantry with lots of solid staples such as canned tomatoes, mushrooms, beans, a variety of pastas, and so on.

QUICK FIX

If meal planning is a new concept to you, there are plenty of techniques to make it work. Peruse the quick-fix ideas below, and choose the method that's right for you.

■ **Paper and Pen Method** Sit down with paper, pen, and your weekly grocery list. On one sheet of paper, write down what you'll serve— one main, side, and vegetable dish for every day of your cycle. This is your working menu planner and should be placed where it won't get lost in the kitchen shuffle and where you and other family members can refer to it every evening. Next, jot down the ingredients you'll need to prepare your recipes on your grocery list.

■ **Print It Method** Print out a monthly calendar from your computer or photocopy a handwritten one. Fill it in and leave it in a prominent place in the kitchen. Take it with you, along with your grocery list, when you shop.

■ **To-Do List Method** While writing up your daily or weekly to-do lists (see more about to-do lists in the "Appointments" chapter), include a heading at the bottom of each day for the evening meal.

I do a lot of precooking on the weekends. For instance, I'll grill several pounds of chicken breasts. Then I can use the cooked chicken to make chicken salad when I get home. I grill a lot of vegetables and keep them in separate containers in the refrigerator. At night, I can add them into some spaghetti sauce or top a homemade pizza. I have all these healthy, well-prepared, nonoily ingredients that I can add to a host of other dishes. I'm never overwhelmed by too many cooking steps, and we never resort to fast food.

Ready for a Recipe

On occasion, I cut out and file articles from magazines on such subjects as gardening, wine appreciation, antiques, and home renovation, but I have to admit I rarely clip recipes. Why? Because it never ends! Everywhere you look there's a delicious something that you've just got to try. The choices are overwhelming. Chicken recipes alone must number in the tens of thousands. Because I can't possibly manage that much paper, I choose to skip the recipe sections of most newspapers and magazines.

That's not to say I don't have a recipe collection. On the contrary, I do. It just happens to be small and manageable—every recipe in my file has been previously tried and has passed the family taste test. To cut down on the clutter, all blunders and bombs have been weeded out, never to be tried again.

QUICK FIX

This is one area of meal planning that can get out of hand if you let it. When organizing your recipes in the coming weeks, think about this: there are only 365 days in a year. Do you really need a collection numbering in the thousands? Weed out, pare down, and shape up by following a few of these tips.

■ **Banish the Books** Take a long, hard look at your collection of cookbooks. Any that can finally retire, like the 1965 edition of *Fondue Cooking*? If you can't part with a few sentimental volumes, at least move them out of the kitchen, where they're taking up valuable space, and add them to the living room bookcase.

■ **Make a Note of It** Do you have a favorite cheesecake recipe but never can remember which one it is because you have *six* stashed away in your recipe file? Leave room on your recipe cards for notes, such as, "favorite cheesecake."

■ **Copy That** If you're in the habit of cutting out recipes from the newspaper or a magazine, make several photocopies of each. If the recipe gets covered in food splatters while you're cooking you can toss the current copy out and work from a clean one the next time.

I'm not here to do everything for my children; I'm here to teach them how to take care of themselves. So, Tom and Ken were helping with dinner from the time they were little and began cooking it on their own by high school. Tom became an expert at spaghetti sauce. He claims he learned how to do it by watching the movie The Godfather. *It was great to come home from work and have dinner all ready. The table would be set, too. And I knew my sons were engaged in something very wholesome—making dinner!*

■ **To Try** If you clip recipes on a regular basis (and don't plan on curtailing the habit) but never can find them when you're in the mood to try something new, create a folder—"new recipes to try"—and stash it with your other household files. If the family gives the new recipe two thumbs-down, toss it. Two thumbs-up, file it with the rest of your favorites.

■ **The Highlight of Your Day** Use a colored highlighting marker to note an unusual ingredient in your recipe, making it easier to spot while writing up your grocery list.

MAJOR TUNE-UP

If your current filing system isn't working for you, take a look at these three other options. Each has its own distinct advantages. Find one that's right for your appetite.

■ **Recipes Make the Rounds** If you cook from recipes rather than from memory on a regular basis, head to your local office supply store and purchase a round Rolodex file, the kind with plastic sleeves that are normally used to hold business cards. Slip all your recipe cards and newspaper clippings into the sleeves and file under menu headings such as "vegetables," "desserts," and so on (just cover up the A through Z tabs). You can even use the same file to note the location of a favorite recipe in one of your cookbooks (it saves you from rummaging through your cookbook in search of it). For instance, if you love the chili recipe in the *Silver Palate* cookbook, place a note in your Rolodex file under C, for chili, giving the name of the cookbook and the page number.

■ **Box It** If you prefer to keep your recipes tucked away in a traditional file, try using a photo box—it's long enough to hold hundreds, just wide enough to accommodate a four-inch card, has a top to keep things neat, and its rectangular shape makes it easy to store in a cabinet.

■ **Potluck Photo** Get a three-ring notebook and place recipes inside plastic-covered photo-album pages. If you splatter a bit of tomato sauce on a page during cooking, no problem; just wipe it clean. This recipe notebook is easy to store, too, right next to your other cookbooks.

Prep Time Prepared

Dinner at six? Better pull out the cutting board around five if you want to eat on schedule. Preparing the evening meal takes time, often more time than the act of eating itself! Before you start chopping, dicing, and slicing,

The Internet—The Next Small Kitchen Appliance

Imagine a kitchen free of cookbook clutter. Instead of perusing your crowded recipe file, you just flip on your Internet appliance and pull up this evening's recipe on your favorite food website. What is this wave of the future? They go by a number of names like Internet appliances or Internet devices. They let you surf the Web and send and receive E-mail, but because they don't come with an expensive hard drive (which means they can't run software), they're half the cost and size of a regular computer. Most have wireless keyboards, one-touch features, and color screens and can fit right on the kitchen counter; but most require a commitment, usually of one year, from a specific Internet provider. Here are a few to check out:

3Com Ergo Audrey Not only can you surf the Web for dinner, but this little cutie lets you synchronize two Palms with the touch of a stylus and wireless keyboard—great for organizing the family calendar. You can even jot down notes to the family directly on the screen. (Around $500; no long-term Internet service contract required, but won't work with AOL or MSN.)

Gateway Connected TouchPad Although this model works with AOL Internet service only, the monitor can be mounted under a kitchen cabinet and folded back when not in use. Surf the Web with a stylus or built-in keyboard mouse. (Around $600; AOL service contract required.)

Compaq IPaq IA-1 Looks and feels like a real computer but at a fraction of the size. Built-in keyboard mouse and special buttons that link you directly to Microsoft Network (MSN) sites. (Around $600; works only with MSN Internet service.)

Epods ePodsOne Don't let the small size (it's not much bigger than a magazine) fool you. This handheld computer let's you surf the Internet or send and receive E-mail three different ways—with a stylus, on-screen keyboard, or with a simple touch of the screen. (Around $200; Epods Internet service contract required.)

study the following quick-fix solutions. There are lots of shortcuts and cooking tips that can save you time.

QUICK FIX

■ **Deep Freeze** Slice onions, dice jalapenos, chop garlic, or prepare any other cooking ingredient that you use often and freeze in recipe-ready portions (first freeze portions in muffin tins; then transfer to containers once they're frozen). Pull out as much as you need when you need it.

■ **Mr. Potato Head** Love the flavor of baked potatoes more than microwaved but hate the long cooking time? Try sticking a nail (yes, a nail) in the center of a washed and slightly buttered potato and pop in the oven. This unconventional method cooks a spud twenty minutes quicker than one wrapped in foil. (Don't forget to remove the nail before eating!)

■ **Mrs. Potato Head** Double your next mashed potato recipe and turn the extra into duchess potatoes, an elegant treat. Just mix one beaten egg to every two cups of mashed potatoes; then fill a pastry bag and pipe single-portion mounds onto a parchment-lined or waxed-paper–lined baking sheet. Place in the freezer until firm; then store in a plastic bag (they'll keep up to three months). Pull out as many frozen potato portions as needed onto a greased baking sheet and brush with melted butter. Bake at 375 degrees for twenty-five minutes (edges should be golden brown).

■ **Grateful for Garlic** Never mind mashing garlic cloves with the flat edge of a knife to remove the skin—try soaking cloves in cold water for a half hour or steeping in hot water for a mere twenty seconds. Both methods quickly remove the peel without altering the flavor or shape. (The hot water technique works well to remove the skins of tomatoes and peaches, too.)

■ **Hot off the Grill** Build the perfect five-ounce burger (either ground beef or turkey) by lining the lid from a one-gallon pickle jar with a piece of plastic wrap, filling it with meat, and pressing it to form a patty. Remove the burger and plastic together, wrap tightly, and freeze until needed. (You can make a few dozen at a time and pull out as many as you need on a moment's notice.) To reduce its cooking time, poke a few holes in the patty prior to grilling, enabling the heat to circulate freely and speeding up the process.

■ **Double or Nothing** Virtually every recipe that you make can be successfully doubled and frozen to use on another day. Spaghetti sauce, chili, casseroles, stews, soups—you name it. It takes a minimal amount of extra effort to increase the amount, but the payoff is tremendous—a night off from cooking.

■ **Too Much of a Good Thing** Even cooking double the amount of unadorned food such as plain pasta or white rice can save some time. They both make great leftovers! For pasta: dunk the excess in cold water immediately after cooking for just a moment. Drain and freeze. When you need it again, just drop back in boiling water for thirty seconds. For rice: store in tight container in the refrigerator (it will keep up to five days). To reheat, add a tablespoon of water, cover, and microwave for one minute. Or add it directly to soup, or get out the wok and whip up some fried rice.

■ **Ice Cube Creations** Ice-cube trays are a remarkable tool for creating single portions of just about anything. The idea is simple: fill trays with tomato paste or sauce, chicken or beef stock, cookie or brownie dough, pancake batter, pesto, baby food—the possibilities are endless. Freeze until firm; then transfer to plastic containers. Pull out what you need without worrying about waste.

■ **Cluck Like a Chicken** A year-round dinnertime staple, chicken is a great make-ahead meal. For moist barbecued chicken in a snap: wash boneless, skinless chicken breast and toss well with your favorite barbecue sauce. Wrap individual portions in foil and store in freezer bags (don't forget to date the bag to ensure freshness). Cook them directly from the freezer (no need to thaw first) at 325 degrees for about forty minutes. For tender chicken ready to turn into a casserole, taco salad, or pasta dish, try this: place wings, drumsticks, and thighs into a slow cooker overnight (add a bit of water). In the morning, move contents to the refrigerator to cool the meat. Remove the meat from the bones (save them for chicken stock), and store the meat in family-sized portions in freezer bags.

■ **Talking Tacos** When you see ground beef on sale in the supermarket, buy in bulk and cook up the whole package with taco seasonings. After the meat has cooled, divide into family-sized packets and freeze. With tortillas on hand and some fresh chopped vegetables, you can have a delicious taco dinner in no time.

■ **My Main Squeeze** Just about any condiment is more efficient when placed in a squeeze bottle. Try jelly (no more sticky knives), oil and vinegar (easier to measure in a spoon than from a large bottle), Worcestershire or soy sauce (great to squirt in a sauté pan), or even sour cream and

Tools of the Trade

Although too many gadgets can clutter a kitchen, some well-designed tools can cut your prep time in half. Here's a list of must-haves nominated by busy parents.

Lettuce Bag Stop washing just enough lettuce for one salad and invest in a salad bag (about $10 at kitchen stores). This drawstring terry bag keeps two heads of washed lettuce fresh for a week. Just tear off the leaves (don't use a knife; it will turn leaves brown sooner), rinse, and store damp.

Slow Cooker If you grew up during the sixties and seventies, you probably remember your Mom or Dad making a tender stew with a slow cooker. It all but disappeared from the American kitchen in the decades that followed, but it's back and better than ever with more sophisticated recipes. The slow cooker is a great tool for busy parents. Add your ingredients to the pot first thing in the morning, turn it on, and when you come home hungry at six, it's ready.

Over-the-Sink Chopping Board Not only will this little feat of ingenuity save you valuable counter space, but it also eliminates the need to constantly walk over to the trash can to toss out vegetable cuttings. Just discard them in the sink.

Pizza Cutter If you've got kids, you need a pizza cutter! Never mind using a knife to cut through pancakes, omelets, hot dogs, chicken breasts—you name it—a pizza cutter is faster and less messy.

mayonnaise (be sure to label the bottles to ensure freshness). No more big, messy bottles to deal with!

■ **Clear as Glass** Fill empty spice bottles with items that you use often, such as flour or cornmeal (for sprinkling into pans), powdered sugar, cocoa, or even breadcrumbs.

■ **Grating on Your Nerves** Skip the grater and instead look for preshredded semisoft cheese—mozzarella, cheddar, and jack. The time you save is well worth the minor compromise in taste.

■ **Butter Is Better** Save all those butter or margarine wrappers and store in a freezer bag. Pull one out when you need to grease a cake or pan.

Let the Kids Help

If you feel like a slave to your kitchen, try letting your kids lend a hand. Not only is it an enormous help, but it's also a perfect time to bond as a family as you share in conversation. Helping out doesn't have to be anything elaborate—something as simple as retrieving the salt and pepper from the cabinet and giving a shake into the mixing bowl is a help to a busy parent.

⏰ **TIME-SAVER**—Help the kids help themselves by placing healthy snacks front and center in your refrigerator. For instance, whip up a big bowl of fresh fruit salad, spoon out in individual serving containers, and leave at arm's reach.

KEY ORGANIZING TIPS

- **Environmentally Friendly** Avoid the heirloom mixing bowl and stick with stainless steel and plastic equipment. Expect accidents; they will happen.
- **Practically Perfect** Don't expect perfection—or anything near it—in the first few attempts, but if you're patient and continue to let them help, ultimately they will become proficient at any number of simple kitchen tasks.
- **Freedom Fighter** Although most children love to dabble in all areas of the kitchen, let them explore what interests them rather than trying to push them into doing a certain job. Your son rejects washing the lettuce but would rather make the salad dressing? Let him.
- **What a Chore** Not only should children help out with food preparation, they should also learn responsibility by having an evening chore to perform before or after dinner, such as setting the table, getting everyone's dinnertime drink order, or taking out the trash.

What's for Dinner?

Next time you hear that familiar question, "What's for dinner?" don't sigh. You've got it under control. Organizing your pots, pans, and utensils more efficiently; keeping meals simple and nutritious; and assigning mealtime chores to the kids can turn dinnertime into the peaceful gathering you always knew it could be.

Mementos

I admit it: since the birth of my third son, Matthew, a pile of photographs has been building on a shelf in the corner of my office waiting for a home in an album. In my defense, it is an *organized* pile—each envelope is labeled with the date, and all photos are filed with their negatives. I see it as a rainy-day project, but unfortunately for me, rainy days mean bored children who can't go outside to run off their perpetual energy. This fall, however, I vow to take a few hours each week to sort through them.

From photographs to your son's first pair of OshKosh overalls and baseball cap (you *can't* give those away to your cousin's new baby), not to mention the mountains of artwork that your daughter brings through your door on a daily basis, what in the world are you to do with all of this stuff? There are lots of imaginative ways of celebrating your child's creativity as well as plenty of practical solutions to protecting the memories of your life as a family—all you need is the desire and that rainy afternoon.

Wherefore Art Thou?

My mother, God love her, was never very sentimental when it came to saving her children's artistic treasures for prosperity. Although two large folders of hand-drawn pictures and accompanying stories of mine have survived from the second grade, I was the one who recognized their value and dutifully kept them alive, transporting them with me to every new home. Rereading the stories is comforting, amusing, and reminds me of what I was like at the tender age of seven. My mom did, however, save one Mother's Day gift that I made for her in the third grade—a crude clay figure of a woman holding her infant child. I can remember my mom prominently displaying the figurine for years in the living room of the home where I grew up. Every time I passed it I felt proud that she not only thought to save it, but she gave it such a place of honor. Now that my mom is gone, I have the statue (it sits on my desk). I'm so glad it survived.

It's important to show an interest and encourage your child's creativity by displaying her artwork. Showing off her designs tells your child that you're proud, helping to boost her self-esteem. It's a window into her fast-moving development, it documents her likes and dislikes, and in years to come, it will serve as a reminder of what she was like at each stage of her life. With that said, let me caution that it's crucial to edit the good stuff from the everyday scribbles; otherwise, you'll quickly drown in a sea of construction paper.

KEY ORGANIZING TIPS

- **Follow the 3-D System** Display, decide, destroy. As your child brings home her daily masterpieces, find a place of honor for them. At the end of the week, let her choose which is her favorite—this you'll save in a memory box, accordion folder, flat file, or artist's portfolio (all available at art supply stores) of just her artwork—then discard the rest (make sure she's not around for this part).

- **Be Ruthless** When it comes to tossing their art, take no prisoners. You have to be a discerning art critic, saving only the best. My kids, on average, bring home three magnum opuses each nearly every day. Multiply that by the number of days in school, and I could easily wallpaper their room yearly.

- **Review Yearly** At the end of each school year, sit with your child and go through all the pieces that you've saved over the past nine months. Once again, it's time to weed through it all, keeping the best and getting rid of the rest. Save only a few favorites (don't worry—by the end of twelfth grade, your child will still have plenty to show for her creativity). Make sure they're labeled with your child's name and approximate date or grade, and then permanently store them.

Displaying Your Child's Art

Contrary to popular belief, the refrigerator is not the best place to showcase your children's talents—dozens of memos, pictures, postcards, and coupons, in addition to her first self-portrait, all begging for attention. With that much disorder, who could possibly appreciate your daughter's use of color, her attention to detail? Not to mention that over time the door becomes so laden with stuff that every time you close it, half the papers come crashing down. More importantly, though, it looks terribly messy and unkempt.

QUICK FIX

Clean off that refrigerator and consider these quick-fix ideas for properly displaying or turning your budding Michelangelo's masterpieces into something useful.

■ **Hang Dry** String a lightweight clothesline in a corner of the family room or your child's bedroom and display his artwork using clothespins. It's easy to exhibit pictures (no tape or pushpins) and a snap to take them down at the end of the week in anticipation of the new creations to come.

■ **Creative Cork** Buy sheets of corkboard and cover with colorful fabric. Hang the boards on a small wall in the kitchen or family room, and tack pictures there.

■ **Picture This** Designate one entire, out-of-the-way wall, such as in the mudroom, laundry room, or playroom, and assign each child a parcel to showcase his or her work. At the end of each week (or month) before you remove any items and toss them, have each child stand in front of his or her creations and take a picture. (Taking pictures of your child near or holding his artwork is especially helpful when the art is three-dimensional—papier-mâché hats, Popsicle villages—and just too difficult to store.)

■ **Under the Glass Top** Slip several pictures under the sheet of glass covering your coffee table, dining room table, or office desk. They'll stay perfectly preserved as family and friends admire them all week long.

■ **Art Light, Art Bright** Fasten art on the ceiling above your child's bed so that she can critique her own work as she drifts off to sleep each night.

■ **It's a Wrap** Use several colorful drawings to wrap a gift.

■ **Send My Love to You** Faraway family members would love to share in your child's artistic progress. Select a few pieces and have your child write a short note (or have her dictate one to you) explaining the picture. You could also include a recent photo or your child and then send the love.

L illie and Elliott are working on a collage of our trip to the Berkshires. They're cutting out pictures from all the brochures of the museums and arranging them with ticket stubs and little tidbits of things that they found at the lake. Once I get the photos developed, they'll add those, too. It's a great visual reminder of our trip without having to dig through an envelope of memorabilia.

MAJOR TUNE-UP

When something comes through the door that strikes you as genius, seize the picture and give it the special treatment.

■ **Fabulously Framed** During the year, look for interesting or well-made frames on sale. Buy a few of varying sizes and keep them handy for that special creation. When your child brings home a masterpiece that's a keeper, frame it and display it with pride. You can rotate the work inside the frame, taking the last exhibited piece and tucking it away in your child's personal portfolio.

■ **Speaking of Portfolios** Creating an artistic portfolio that stands out from the crowd is easy: at the end of the year take a few chosen pieces to permanently put on view in clear plastic sleeves and then organize in a three-ring notebook. Use subject dividers to separate the art by years, perhaps including vital statistics on a cover sheet (your child's grade, teacher's name, child's favorite food or song, best friend, etc.). You could also make an unusual and colorful portfolio by mounting art on swatches from a wallpaper sample book (visit a wallpaper retail store and ask if they have any old books about to be thrown away). Label the back of each piece with your child's age or grade and the name of the piece.

■ **A New Life** If you're of the practical nature, you can give a new life to your child's favorite art by transforming it into something utilitarian. Laminate larger pieces, for instance, to make placemats. Create stationery by taking smaller pictures to the copy store and reducing them to two-inch designs. Cut them out, place at the top of an eight-and-one-half-by-eleven-inch sheet of paper, and copy onto heavy-stock writing paper. (The computer literate can do this quicker by scanning the creation into one of many design programs.) Artwork can be made into cross-stitch samplers, magnets, rubber stamps, bookmarks—you name it!

■ **Trophy Triumph** Your child's trophy collection is important, but it sure takes up a lot of shelf space! When it's time to weed them out, pull off the faceplates with your child's name and his accomplishments and mount them on a finished piece of wood with either epoxy glue or small finishing nails. The memories are still there, but not the clutter.

I bought each girl a small, eight-drawer cardboard box from the Lillian Vernon catalog. When either Jenna or Cara comes home with artwork or important schoolwork, we put it on the top shelf of the closet; at the end of the year, we weed through it all, and they choose their favorites. These we put in one of the drawers of the cardboard box, along with report cards or favorite birthday cards. Then we label the drawer. When the box is finally full, they'll have memories from first to eighth grade.

Saving the Story of His Life

Just as it's important to save some of your child's artwork, it's equally meaningful to put aside some of his schoolwork—favorite stories, book reports, and term papers. As they come into the house, take a moment and reread them with your child. If your son wants to save it, place it in his art portfolio (otherwise, save until other family members have a chance to take a look; then discreetly place in the recycling bin). At the end of the school year, as the two of you go through his collection, save his favorites by filing them in a three-ring notebook designated just for "Best Schoolwork." Use subject dividers to separate papers by grade.

Clothes Make the Man (or Woman)

Periodically you need to weed through your children's clothes, pulling out the garments that they've outgrown. Some outfits will obviously be so threadbare that it's more humane to toss them in the trash than to pass them on. Other pieces will happily find a new home either at the Salvation Army

or in your neighbor's nursery. Further still, there are always a few special outfits that hold such sentimental value that it's impossible to part with them—
your daughter's baptism gown or a hand-knitted sweater. No need to force
yourself to give them up; these are memories that should be saved.

For Safe Keeping

When it comes to preserving old clothes, you have two choices—store
them or display them. The former is the easiest solution, requiring not
much more than a well-sealing box, but with a bit of creativity the latter
gives you the opportunity to freeze a piece of time in your child's ever-
changing history. Perhaps you're up to doing a bit of both, but remember,
just as in saving your child's art- and schoolwork, you need to be extremely
judicious when deciding what to keep and what to give away. There's no
need to put aside an entire wardrobe, just a piece or two every year or so
will be more than enough to capture your child's young spirit.

Like Moths to a Porch Light

For clothes to last to the next generation, you need to make sure certain
little flying creatures never get near them. I'm talking about moths, of
course, and if you don't prepare and pack the clothes properly, chances are
that that finely knitted sweater will resemble a loosely crocheted pot holder
in a couple of years.

Resist the urge to smother the garments in mothballs, however.
Although in concentrated amounts mothballs do kill moths, their eggs, and
larvae, a recent study by the National Toxicology Program concluded that
naphthalene, the main ingredient in mothballs, caused cancer in rats when
the chemical was inhaled at similar doses to what most people experience
in the typical home. Two other ingredients in mothballs—camphor and
paradichlorobenzene—are also toxic to humans. Besides, mothballs stink!

So, what should you do? First, inspect each garment inside and out,
looking for stains. Moth larvae—the hole-making culprits—feed on food,
sweat, and even dandruff and urine for up to two and one half years before
turning into full-grown moths (the often accused but actually innocent
bystanders in all of this). Don't give them the chance to feed—thoroughly
wash or dry-clean each garment according to the manufacturer's instructions before storing.

Because moth larvae can fit through a space less than the diameter of a piece of thread, store freshly laundered outfits in tight-sealing containers. If you use a cedar chest, be sure to line the bottom with an old sheet (the acidic oils of cedar can stain fabric). But remember, cedar is only somewhat effective in repelling *small* larvae for just a few years until it loses its scent. Clean clothes stored in airtight containers are your best defense against these pesky eaters.

Only the Shadow Knows for Sure

If you're looking for a rainy-day project (aka "Major Tune-Up"), try creating a tableau of your child's favorite memorabilia and display it in a deep, glass-covered frame called a *shadow box*. (For an interesting selection, check out Exposures, an archival photography catalog, at exposuresonline.com.)

Start by choosing a theme, such as "Jackie's First Year," or "Claire's Baptism," and include an article of clothing that best represents your subject. Add a photograph—perhaps of your little muffin dressed in said article of clothing—a favorite small stuffed animal, a hair ribbon, you name it. Then experiment with various layouts before securing them all to the frame's backing (you can do this with either small Velcro circles, which often come with the box, or with pushpins). Then spotlight your work of art on a hallway wall with other childhood montages for an interesting family retrospective.

Everyone Say "Cheese"

I know I'm not the only one with piles of photographs accumulating in my home. Remember the initial few months following the birth of your first child? No doubt flashbulbs were exploding nearly every minute. Pictures are fun to take, a joy to look at, but a chore to catalog. Unfortunately, the alternative is not to take any, and you don't want to do that. Children love to look at old family photos. It gives them a sense of self, a feeling of belonging. You can't give that up.

There are several ways to organize your photographs—each has its advantages and disadvantages. For instance, arranging pictures in an album beautifully displays your family's life chronologically, yet each album (and if you like pictures, chances are you'll have a lot) takes up shelf space.

Although filing pictures in a card box may be quicker to assemble, it doesn't make for a cozy evening with the kids the way turning the pages of a family album does. Perhaps implementing both strategies is the key.

⏰ **TIME-SAVER**—When considering your next camera, think about a digital model. Digital technology has vastly improved, and so has the price. They're great for documenting your growing garden or home renovations (continue using a 35 mm camera for important events such as vacations, weddings, etc.). With a digital camera, you can quickly download the pictures to your computer and easily send them to friends and family.

■ **Double Jeopardy** Although it's tempting, don't automatically order double prints unless you routinely send photos to family and friends. Otherwise, you'll just end up with a double pile of pictures to organize.

■ **Edit** As soon as you get your pictures back from the lab, go through them and edit out and toss the ones that will *never* make it to an album—out of focus, no heads, the accidental shot of the inside of your backpack.

■ **Don't Forget to Label** With so much going on in your life, do you really think that you'll remember where each picture was taken two years from now when you finally get around to putting them in an album? Probably not. Put your mind at ease by labeling the back of your photos *before* you put the packet away. (If you don't have the patience to label each photo, just label the envelope.)

■ **It's a Sticky Situation** When shopping for a photo album, look for a high-quality book that uses archival paper (to keep the photos from deteriorating) and photo corners instead of glue-back paper (your photos will stick and you'll undoubtedly destroy them if you try to take them off the page).

■ **It's Not Negative** Many people never know what to do with their negatives. Make sure they survive the generations by storing them in negative sleeves—eight-and-one-half-by-eleven-inch plastic sheets with individual slots for each negative strip—and filing them in a three-ring notebook. Label the top of the sheet with the subject. Pay special attention to important negatives—weddings, the birth of your children—and keep them in a safe-deposit box.

🖉 **STYLE TIP**—At the end of your next family vacation, have the kids create a *memory bag*. Take a quart-sized Baggie and cut a piece of construction paper to fit inside. Let the kids jot down where you went, what they saw, and what they liked best. Next, have them fill the bag with poignant reminders of the trip—a seashell from the beach, a colorful leaf from a hike, a ticket stub from an amusement park. They can even add a few photos, too.

QUICK FIX

Even if you have thousands of photographs just begging for a spot in an album, you can make quick work of them all. Don't approach your pictures as one whole unit. Instead, focus on them in stages.

■ **From This Day Forward** Digging all the way back to the beginning of your photo collection to arrange them in an album is a bit tricky—you're bound to find just one or two more photos that should have gone in. Instead, start assembling an album with your most recent photographs and work forward. (As time allows, you can dig back and make additional family albums.)

■ **Photo Wall** Arranging photos takes an enormous time commitment that you just may not be in the mood for, yet you'd love to enjoy looking at some old family photos now. Try making a photo wall: randomly choose enough pictures to fill a two-foot-by-two-foot section of wall and attach your images with a removable, low-tack tape. The best part is—you can change the photos at any time.

■ **Box It** By far the easiest way to organize your photographs is by filing them in a photo box (available at photo supply stores; or use a shoe box covered in wrapping paper). Use index cards to divide the box into categories—birthday parties, family vacations, school photos—because it's easier to locate a picture by subject than it is by year. No need to put them in chronological order (but try to note the back of each photograph with approximate date and place).

■ **My Favorite Subject** Highlight important family events and milestones by choosing images from one subject, such as your vacation to Yellowstone National Park or your wedding, and arranging them in a special album of their own.

MAJOR TUNE-UP

Personally, I like the look and feel of photo albums. Yes, it takes an enormous amount of time to create a special chronology of your family through pictures, but when complete, it's there for everyone to enjoy for years to come. You can combat the time commitment by working on your albums in small chunks of time—say, one hour every Wednesday while watching your favorite TV show—and breaking down the task—sorting, arranging chronologically, and finally displaying.

Don't be afraid to crop out half the picture if you feel it's useless to the meaning of the photo. Add some props in the background to help tell the story, such as a ticket stub, a brochure, or even a map. Type subject captions to place at the top of each page.

Thanks for the Memories

Just because you've made the commitment to organize and unclutter your family's life doesn't mean you'll have to get rid of your son's first portrait of the dog. To the contrary! Frame that colorful depiction of man's best friend in the joyful knowledge that you've not only captured a moment of history, but were also able to let go of his art that had far less meaning.

Memorabilia is an important aspect of living. Embrace it, but make sure it's organized in a proper home.

Moving

Let's face it—no one likes to move. It's a major disruption of family life, what with boxes everywhere, hundreds of little details to be worked out (such as when to turn off the gas), and filling out all those change-of-address cards. Your life is basically on hold until you establish yourself in your new digs. There is good news, however. Moving is a great opportunity to get organized. Moving forces you to finally sort through and discard all those dead files sequestered in boxes at the back of your closet, donate the plethora of old clothes that you keep hoping will come back in style, and toss out stray objects.

Moving Yourself

Moving yourself by renting a truck or van is a cheaper option to hiring a professional company, but it's obviously an enormous amount of work—you'll be doing lots of heavy lifting, it's tricky to organize the boxes to fit just right in the truck, and you may have to hire someone to help you unload once you get to your new home.

When inquiring about a van, look for a model with a tailgate lift rather than a ramp, and always overestimate the size of van you'll need (a twenty-four-foot van can hold the belongings to approximately a three-bedroom home). If you have large appliances, be sure to rent a dolly, too. Choose a company with no return charges and easy driving features on their fleet of vans, such as power steering and automatic transmission.

Just like a professional moving company, you'll need to know how far you'll be traveling to estimate your costs because most truck rental agencies charge by the mile. But you'll also need to add in the cost of gas, food, and lodging (if you're traveling any distance).

Packing Perfection

The most dreaded part of moving yourself, packing tops everyone's list of the *Ten Ways You'd Least Like to Spend Your Saturday Afternoon*. Yet, it's got to get done. Packing can be fun if you make it a family night—pizza, soda, a little music, and reminiscing until your heart's content. You can all work together in the same room (this way you can carefully supervise the kids), or break up into smaller groups and each tackle a different room. Or try hosting a packing party, an intimate gathering with your closest friends who'd lovingly volunteer to help you in exchange for a nachos and beer buffet.

Let the Packing Begin

Armed with boxes, tape, a marker, six months' worth of newspapers, and some bubble wrap, you're ready to roll. The best ways to start are with cluttered closets and the dreaded "junk drawers." Set up a workstation on a card table that can be easily moved from room to room. Have a trash bag on hand for all those things that haven't a chance of making it to your new home, a large box for items that will find a new home at your garage sale (we'll talk about that later), another large box for donated items, and finally, your packing box. Keep a roll of paper towels and a spray bottle of window cleaner by your side. You should clean or dust everything before packing it—you don't want to spend your first days in your new place scrubbing grime off your books and knickknacks.

KEY ORGANIZING TIPS

■ **Start Early** Once the decision has been made to move, start packing. Even if you haven't found that perfect house or apartment yet, it pays to start plowing through your belongings ASAP so you won't feel overwhelmed the days just before the big move. Begin with nonessential items, such as out-of-favor toys, out-of-season clothes, artwork, and knick-knacks—items that won't be missed if boxed for a few weeks or even months.

■ **Be Merciless** Now is the time to get rid of stuff! Think carefully about whether you really want to have that old cuckoo clock hanging on the wall in your new place. Sell it in a garage sale or donate it to charity along with anything else that doesn't make the grade. If you haven't used it, worn it, or thought about it in a year, out it goes.

■ **Room by Room** When packing boxes, work room by room mixing items together rather than putting all books or all framed photos in one box. It's much easier to unpack that way—no wasted steps.

■ **The Perfect Box** Start with a layer of crumpled newspaper for cushioning; then add heavy, bulky items first. Layer with more crumpled paper and then perhaps add a cardboard liner to create a flat surface. Unless you want a pile of broken glass, never mix large, weighty items with fragile breakables. Pack books flat as not to ruin their spines.

■ **He Ain't Heavy** Keep boxes small and manageable—never more than forty pounds (use your bathroom scale). Large, heavy boxes are much more difficult to move and may even burst during transport.

■ **What's in the Box?** Always label all four sides and the top of each box, stating the room where it belongs and briefly listing the contents to avoiding guessing later on.

■ **Color Code It** In addition to labeling, assign each room a color (e.g., green for the kitchen, blue for your son's room) and apply a large colored circle on top of each box to help others see where each one goes.

■ **What's Your Name?** If you're using a moving company, it's a good idea to put your name and new address on the top of each box.

Fragile Items

Breakables, like crystal and china, need a section all their own. First, start with lots of small boxes rather than one large box. When it comes to packing breakables, the less in the box the better (fewer cracks, chips, and breakage). For china, wrap each plate or bowl individually with bubble wrap; then stack four to five and wrap again, creating a small package.

After wrapping, place plates inside the box vertically rather than horizontally to distribute weight more evenly. When packing teacups, wrap separately and place rim-side down on the top layer of the box (don't pack anything on top). Crystal goblets should be wrapped individually, too, and placed on top.

Fill the open spaces and air pockets of the box with crumpled newspaper or Styrofoam peanuts. Mark the box "fragile" and "this side up" in *red* to ensure gentle moving hands.

⏰ **Time-Saver**—Think about leaving or selling both your window treatments and large appliances to the next owner of your house or apartment. Because they rarely fit in your new space anyway, or if you're thinking of a new look to go with the new house, it makes sense to include them in your negotiations. Less packing, less moving, less setting up, and maybe even a buck or two in the process.

QUICK FIX

Packing seems like a straightforward proposition, but there are a few tricks that make it even more organized and safer.

- **Rubberize Me** Keep a supply of thick rubber bands on hand to corral electrical cords and group small, like items together, such as stationery supplies.

- **Proper Padding** No need to rent dozens of moving blankets— employ your own less-than-perfect blankets. Sleeping bags work well also. When the move is complete, add the old blankets to your rag pile or donate to charity. Wrap clean bed linen around fragile items.

- **Know Your ABCs** Most people don't unpack all their boxes for several months after they move. Help distinguish the significant from the unimportant by marking boxes that contain first-week essentials with an *A*, somewhat vital cartons (items such as hardcover books) with the letter *B*, and once-a-year stuff (such as Christmas decorations) with a *C*.

- **Does Not Compute** If you've long thrown away the original boxes to your computer and printer, fear not. Head to your local computer store and ask if they have any discarded boxes you can take off their hands.

- **Out of the Closet** When packing clothes in cardboard wardrobe boxes, be sure to use the empty space at the bottom to stow other clothing, such as underwear, socks, and lingerie. Or group several clothes on hangers together and secure the top with tape and cover with a plastic bag to keep clean.

- **All for One** Instead of unpacking dresser drawers, keep the contents of each drawer intact, and slide the drawer into a labeled plastic bag, taping it tightly shut so that the contents won't shift during the move.
- **Liquor License** Head to your local liquor store and start collecting boxes with cardboard dividers—they're great for packing glasses, vases, and crystal.

⏰ **TIME-SAVER**—If you think next year's the year that you're going to move out of your apartment and into the mansion of your dreams, start collecting boxes now. Save and store sturdy, medium-sized packages that you receive in the mail during the holidays or birthdays in your garage or attic. When you do make the decision to go, you'll be ready to start packing immediately. Keep all the Styrofoam peanuts and bubble wrap, too. Not only will you be helping the environment by recycling, you'll also save money—packing materials are expensive!

One weekend, Dan, Nathaniel, and I went to two estate sales in our neighborhood. Big, beautiful Spanish homes where the owners had died of old age. I can't tell you the horror of seeing what someone had kept with him until the end. It was morose, really. Why would someone, for instance, keep a large box of envelopes that were all stuck together? So, we went home and had our own yard sale. You have to ask yourself, "What's the worst thing that's going to happen if I throw this out?"

Handling All the Details

If you thought finding a new home was difficult, just wait until two months before you must move out of your old house. There's so much to do, from calling all utility companies both at your old place and your new one to transferring medical and school records. How will you ever keep it all straight? That's right; write it down. Use a small notebook divided by task—packing, moving, dealing with employers—or by week—eight weeks before the big move, seven weeks, right up to the big day. Or, head to an office supply store and purchase a large, laminated wall calendar and fill in each appropriate date. Then hang it in a prominent spot for all family members to see. Either method you choose, remember to check off each task when it's completed.

Countdown to Moving Day

Every move is different. Even if you've changed addresses a dozen times in the past ten years, each time something new crops up. On your last move, you may have had to worry about navigating your furniture up two flights of stairs; this time, your attention has been on enrolling the kids in a good school. Whatever your situation, take time to run down the following list (you may want to photocopy it and use it as a checklist).

Two Months Before the Move

- ☐ Set up moving calendar or notebook; jot down notes.
- ☐ Set up moving folder for estimates, receipts, and service contracts. Staple business cards inside. (Keep all your receipts for moving-related expenses. If they meet certain criteria, say, you moved because of a job promotion, you could deduct the expenses from your federal income taxes. For more information, ask the IRS for "Publication 521, Moving Expenses.")
- ☐ Finalize new housing—enter escrow or pay deposit for apartment.
- ☐ If moving yourself, call two to three van-rental companies for quotes.
- ☐ If using a professional mover, call three to four companies for estimates.
- ☐ Start collecting boxes and packaging material.
- ☐ Call for pickup on large, donated items, such as an old refrigerator or table.
- ☐ Take a personal property inventory (videotape or photograph your home's contents).
- ☐ Begin evening packing of closets and junk drawers.
- ☐ Set up doctor, dental, and vet appointments for entire family and pets (one less thing to worry about once in your new neighborhood). Make sure immunization records are up-to-date. Ask doctors for referrals in your new town.
- ☐ Enroll children in new school. Call old school to forward their transcripts.

One Month Before the Move

- ☐ Keep tabs on escrow or check in with new landlord.
- ☐ Decide on moving day.

It's Time for a Garage Sale

Two years ago, right after we moved to our current home, I held a garage sale and cleared more than $400 in less than three hours. Not bad for a morning's work. Organizing and running a garage sale is not for everyone, though—it takes lots of planning and hard work. (I certainly didn't sit for one moment that morning, and I had a headache that afternoon to prove it.) Yet holding a garage sale is an excellent way of clearing out your home and making a tidy little profit in the process. Here are a few tips to help make yours a lucrative event.

Before or After First, decide whether you'd like to hold your sale before your move or after. If you hold it before you leave town, you'll have less to pack and less to cart with you. The benefit of holding the sale after you move, however, is that you'll find tons more stuff to sell as you unpack in your new home. Some savvy families hold *two* garage sales—before *and* after they move.

Location, Location, Location Just like the old real estate axiom, the location of the sale will either make or break it. If you live in an isolated neighborhood, your home isn't easily accessible, or you can't see your yard from the street, team up with a friend who has a home where there's lots of foot traffic or lives on a street that's heavily traveled.

Tag It As you pack up your house and decide which items to sell, assign a price and tag it (a piece of masking tape will do) immediately before you place it in your garage-sale box. This way, on the morning of the sale, you won't have to think about how much to charge.

Prepare for Early Birds At my sale, I made $300 by 10 A.M. How did that happen when the sale officially started at 9 A.M.? We were barraged with early birds starting at 7 A.M. as we were setting up. (Good thing I had all my pieces tagged with a price.)

Get Help You can't bargain with one customer, answer a question of another, and make change for a third all at the same time. Recruit your kids and use them as roving salesclerks.

Have Lots of Change People always pay for a $1 item with a big bill. Be prepared with a minimum of thirty singles, six fives, and four tens. Quarters, dimes, and nickels help, too, for that ten-cent box of old paperbacks.

Advertise Wisely It's not enough to place an ad in your local paper—on any given weekend there could be dozens of similar garage sales. Make yours stand out by mentioning what's unique, such as kitchen collectibles, old LPs, hardcover books, and so forth. In addition, on the day of the sale, hang large, clearly written signs within a one-mile radius of the sale and use arrows pointing in the direction of the sale. (Don't forget to remove the signs when the sale is over.)

Be Realistic Don't expect big bucks for furniture (you'd be better off selling good-quality pieces by placing a separate ad in your local paper), never price clothing for more than $1 per item, and remember that people like to bargain, so leave room in your price for negotiating.

- [ ] Decide on moving company. Sign necessary papers. Or reserve a van.
- [ ] Set up moving budget.
- [ ] If moving far away, decide on route and overnight destinations. Visit the auto club for necessary maps. Make hotel reservations.
- [ ] Subscribe to newspaper in your new town. (Make it a temporary subscription or tell them when to forward to your new address.)
- [ ] Pick up change-of-address cards at local post office.
- [ ] Contact Department of Motor Vehicles in new state and have them send forms for new drivers' licenses and vehicle registration.
- [ ] Arrange for new carpet installation, painters, or cleaning service for new home.
- [ ] Choose garage-sale date. Secure location. Place ad in local paper.
- [ ] Continue evening packing. Tackle attic, garage, and basement.
- [ ] Arrange for child care and pet care on day of the move.
- [ ] If moving yourself, call in a few favors from some muscular friends who will help load the truck. Arrange for a few bodies to be at the other end of the trip, too, to help unload. (If it's too far

away for your friends to help, contact a local moving company in your new city and ask for some referrals.)

Two Weeks Before the Move

- ☐ Continue keeping tabs on escrow proceedings.
- ☐ Contact all utility companies to discontinue service the day after you leave, and begin service at your new home the day before you arrive. (Look through your files of old monthly statements to ensure that everyone is contacted, such as Internet provider and cell-phone company.)
- ☐ Fill out and mail change-of-address cards for credit card companies and all other creditors, magazine and newspaper subscriptions, and trade associations.
- ☐ Notify friends and family of new address and phone number by picking up cards at the stationery store. Fill a few out each night.
- ☐ Call insurance company to cancel old policies and write up new ones. Ask about coverage of your belongings during transport.
- ☐ If you'll be staying with the same employer, contact your human resources department and make necessary changes to insurance, 401(k), and W-2 forms.
- ☐ If moving to a high-rise building, reserve elevator time.
- ☐ Properly dispose of hazardous liquids that can't be moved, such as paint.
- ☐ Continue evening packing. Remove art from walls and mantle tops and carefully wrap.

One Week Before the Move

- ☐ Confirm moving van arrival time.
- ☐ Contact new landlord to verify move-in day and time and key exchange.
- ☐ Set up appointment to sign escrow papers and exchange keys.
- ☐ Open up checking account in new location. Cancel old account. Close safe-deposit box.

☐ Make a sketch of new home or apartment and decide where each piece of furniture will go. Make several photocopies of the final design (you'll use them on moving-in day).

☐ Get travelers' checks for your trip.

☐ Continue evening packing—it should be nearly complete. Take advantage of paper plates, plastic cups, and takeout! Set aside items that will travel with you, such as important papers, toolbox, or anything of value, such as jewelry.

☐ Pack First-Night Survival Box. (See sidebar.) Have each family member set aside his or her own survival bag.

The Day Before the Move

☐ Clean and empty freezer and refrigerator.

☐ Unplug all major appliances and secure them for moving.

☐ If moving yourself, pick up rented moving van.

☐ If moving yourself, pick up sandwiches, sodas, snacks, and plenty of ice for your muscular friends who've volunteered to help.

☐ Dismantle all beds.

☐ Make a few important good-bye calls. Say farewell to a few of your neighbors.

The Big Day

☐ Take small children and pets to sitter. Give plenty of reassurance that you'll return that afternoon or evening.

☐ If using a moving company, make sure you or another adult is at the old home to answer questions and to read the bill of lading and inventory sheet before signing.

☐ Sponge down countertops. Vacuum rugs.

☐ Pack any extraneous belongings.

☐ Make a note of all utility meter readings.

☐ Carefully walk through your home opening all cabinets and built-ins for any missed items. Look through garage, attic, and basement. Take a walk around the yard.

☐ Hit the road!

First-Night Survival Box

A corkscrew, bottle opener, or even a roll of paper towels never seems more important than when you can't find them on your first night in a new home. To make your transition as stress free as possible, you need certain creature comforts, such as coffee in the morning. Not only should each person have a survival bag, but also you should have a household survival box, too, filled with essentials that you'll need in the first twenty-four hours in your home. Here are a few suggestions.

- Liquid hand soap
- Paper towels
- Toilet paper
- A set of bath towels for each family member
- Toiletries (shampoo, toothpaste, toothbrush)
- A set of bedsheets for each family member
- Blankets and pillows
- Coffeemaker and toaster
- A cooler of basic foodstuff: milk, bread, coffee, juice, and snacks
- Paper plates and cups and plastic silverware
- Corkscrew and can opener
- Matches
- Flashlight and batteries
- Fire extinguisher
- Toolbox
- Cleaning supplies, bucket, vacuum, mop, and broom
- Phone books and important phone numbers

Moving In

- ☐ Hang a photocopy of furniture floor plan on each door to help movers see what goes where.
- ☐ Quickly vacuum rugs before moving furniture into place. Place plastic or paper runner on floor to prevent movers from tracking in dirt and mud.

- ☐ Clean bathrooms and stock with toilet paper, soap, and towels.
- ☐ Install new front- and rear-door locks.
- ☐ Childproof cabinets, outlets, and any other trouble spots.
- ☐ Unpack First-Night Survival Box.
- ☐ Set up and make beds.
- ☐ Set up kitchen.
- ☐ Help organize kids' rooms.
- ☐ Call for takeout.
- ☐ Sometime during the first week, unpack fragile items and check for breakage.

Surviving the Move

Let's face it—when you move, stuff gets lost for days. No parent wants to be hunting through a pile of boxes searching for Junior's favorite stuffed animal the first night in a new place. With this in mind, have everyone, kids included, pack their own survival bag—a satchel filled with must-have books, blankets, cosmetics, sweatshirt, whatever is valuable in the owner's eyes. Having comfort and essential items (such as your eyeglasses) at your fingertips will ease the stress of the first night in a new place.

Keep a toolbox in the car—you may need it when you arrive in your new home. Keep both your old and new phone books handy. Some boxes should travel with you, too, such as your most prized art, photographs, and jewelry.

Packing the Van

Take time to evaluate what will go where before you start packing your rented van. Remember, balance is the key—a van packed too loosely will ultimately end in disaster. Boxes will fall, objects will break or damage furniture, and you may even lose control of the vehicle. So, pack tightly, putting more weight toward the front (driver's end) of the van. To help, appliances and furniture should go in first—fill the space around them with additional boxes. Make a foundation of heavy boxes and add lighter boxes on top. (Never place a heavy item on top of a lightweight box.)

Mentally divide your van into sections, working on one at a time. When one area is done, strap it together with a furniture wrap to prevent movement, and then move on to your next section. Have one person stay in the van coordinating where things should go while the others carry boxes and appliances. Don't let a square foot of space go to waste—place boxes under chairs, use sleeping bags for padding between pieces of furniture, place flat artwork under dresser legs, and fill dresser drawers with lightweight items. Load your First-Night Survival Box last. It will be the first off the truck and should be unpacked immediately.

Before you hit the road, it's a good idea to take the van for a test spin. See what it can do and what it can't. Adjust all mirrors and use them. If you must back up, use an assistant to guide you. Go slowly, and if you're traveling a long distance, take frequent breaks.

But What About the Children?

Children under the age of ten should be left with a relative or someone they feel close to on moving day. Although preteens and teenagers can be an enormous help, the younger set simply impedes progress. Not only will they undoubtedly get in everyone's way, but also, with no one watching them, they can quickly get into trouble or wander off into their new, but unknown, neighborhood. Remember, though—moving is scary to young children; assure them as you say good-bye for the day at the sitter's that you'll be back for them as soon as the van is loaded and set to go, or if you're moving locally, as soon as it's unloaded at your new home.

Settling In

It took us more than a year to unpack all our boxes from our last move, yet I've known people who can host an elegant party in their homes the weekend they arrive. The advantage to the latter way of living is that you know immediately what survived the trip and what didn't. For us, however, I'm still puzzled as to what happened to several boxes. After two years, we may never know.

So many boxes, so many rooms. It's hard to know where to begin. Don't just dive in, however. Take the time to prioritize what needs to be organized first, such as the kids' rooms and, of course, the kitchen. The books for the bookshelf and the framed photos of the family for the mantel can wait. Although you've probably seen the house or apartment many times before, take a walk through and get a feel for the place and start to visualize your furniture and belongings in their proper places. Yes, I know, you've already made a furniture floor plan, but this is your last chance to easily make any changes. Remember, now's a great opportunity to organize your home in an efficient manner. Make your decisions carefully.

Setting Up the Children's Rooms

Moving is especially hard on children. They don't understand that within no time they'll meet plenty of new friends and discover new hiding places in the backyard. All they know is that they left their old rooms, comfortable and familiar, and they're now sleeping in some strange place that Mom and Dad are insisting is home. With that in mind, plan with your child before the move how his new room will look. Have him help pick out which colors to paint the walls and which curtains to hang. (If it's only a crosstown move, perhaps you can have his new room decorated before moving day.)

When you arrive at your new home, spend some time with your child to help him unpack his room. The sooner it feels like home, the better. Making his room feel special will help ease his fears of being in a new place.

During the first few days after your move, take your kids for a tour of their new neighborhood. Visit some local parks, drive past their school, and take a tour of the library. Knock on a few of your neighbors' doors and introduce yourselves. If they have children, invite them over to see your new home (and maybe the great backyard fort that you've set up).

Setting Up the Kitchen

If you were never truly thrilled with the design and layout of your old kitchen, now is a perfect opportunity to make changes. Before unpacking, take a moment and analyze your current cabinet and counter space and think about the best location for dishes, pots, silverware, small appliances, and the pantry. If time permits, hit the local supermarket and stock up on staples and condiments.

Thoroughly clean and dry each cabinet before adding your stuff. (To learn more about arranging your kitchen, turn to the "Kitchen" chapter.)

There's No Place Like Home

There's nothing like the smell of new shelving paper to make a house feel like a home! And the look of newly organized closets is enough to make me smile. Your new home is a fresh opportunity to swear off bad house-keeping habits by adjusting your old way of life, so please take off all shoes before entering the house. Yes, moving is stressful, but the rewards once you're unpacked are enough to make it all worth the effort.

Paperwork

Even with the advent of E-mail replacing good old-fashioned letter writing, electronic bill paying, and the plethora of online stores, the influx of paper on our lives is still overwhelming. The paper parade that travels to our homes on a daily basis—the newspaper, school newsletters, the catalogs, the supermarket circulars, junk mail, and brokerage statements—just keeps coming. If you turn your back for a moment, it multiplies at an alarming rate (just take a vacation for a week and return home to see what I mean). Although technology promises to reduce the quantity in the future through electronic invoicing, we live in the here and now. And paper is everywhere!

KEY ORGANIZING TIPS

- **Simply Simplify** Cut down on the amount of paper coming into your home by canceling subscriptions to seldom-read magazines and newspapers, doing more research of products on the Internet rather than having companies send brochures to your home (if you don't have a computer, most public libraries offer free Internet access), and making a gallant effort to get your name off direct-mail marketing lists (more on this topic later in the chapter).

- **Act on It** If you've got kids, you've got school flyers coming in constantly—the bake sale, the school play, the class trip. Don't save them! Read them, mark your family calendar with all the pertinent information, and then put them in the recycling bin.

■ **Contain It** Even after ebbing the paper flow, there will still be monthly statements and dozens of documents that will need a home. Choose one permanent spot in your house or apartment to store your files, such as a corner of your home office or bedroom, and a container to hold everything neatly. A simple, two-drawer filing cabinet is usually enough space for the typical family's personal papers, but even labeled cardboard boxes with lids stored under the bed will do the trick.

■ **Persistency Is Key** Take ten minutes each day to sort, file, or toss papers, including mail, flyers, and outdated documents. Even a small daily commitment will tame the paper tiger.

🔖 **STYLE TIP**—If space is tight in your home, many mail-order companies offer compact filing systems on wheels that you can keep in an unused corner or closet and pull out when needed. Holdeverything, for instance, offers a letter center, a fifteen-inch-square rolling desk complete with a pull-out writing surface, file drawer, divided niches, two shelves, and a drawer. Solutions catalog (solutionscatalog.com) sells a similar product on wheels but with two file drawers, a side in-box, a flip-top writing desk, and plenty of cubbies for sorting bills and supplies.

Mail Call

We get a stack of stuff in our mailbox every day. Yet, once I sit down and start to plow through it, within minutes I've whittled it down to just a mere two to three pieces. The rest is just junk.

And therein lies another key to controlling the paper flow—*never let your mail sit around until the weekend to open; sort through it the day it arrives.* Immediately tear up credit card offers and solicitations from mortgage brokers. Look over your bills to make sure they're accurate, discard all promotional material tucked inside the envelope, write the due date on the outside of the original envelope, and file immediately with other bills to be paid. Browse through catalogs briefly. If something catches your eye, dog-ear the page and file it with other catalogs, being sure to recycle the last one sent. If nothing is of interest, toss it in your recycling bin immediately.

🍶 **STYLE TIP**—Display several decorative recycling bins around your home to catch the paper as it falls. For instance, keep a wicker basket near your favorite reading chair to toss the newspaper in once it's read. Place another where you open the mail so that you can drop in the supermarket circular and other promotional material as you sort through it.

Moneymakers, Money Takers

The majority of mail contains bills, or money takers, and for some lucky (and disciplined) folks, statements from savings and brokerage accounts, or moneymakers. Although these guys produce a wealth of paper, you've got to keep careful tabs on them for the lights in your house to remain on and for your plans of retirement to stay on track.

QUICK FIX

Once again, simplifying goes a long way toward paper peace.

■ **Less Is More** Six or seven credit cards peeking from your wallet? Cancel all but two—a low-interest-rate-card and a perk card. Fewer cards equal fewer monthly statements and that translates to less paper and confusion. (To read more, turn to "Bill Paying" in the "Finances" chapter.)

■ **The Urge to Merge** Consolidate bills by paying for certain services (such as newspaper delivery, Internet use, long-distance provider, etc.) on the same credit card. You'll write one check at the end of the month instead of several.

■ **Picture This** Instead of receiving a pile of canceled checks each month, ask your bank if they offer photoimaging, copies of your canceled checks complete with reference numbers. You'll have only one or two sheets of paper to file with your statement instead of a stack.

■ **All in the Family** You and your spouse both have IRA accounts at the same financial institution, yet you each receive a separate quarterly statement. How wasteful is that? Call customer service and request a "family statement," one combined statement but with separate entries for each account.

■ **Internet Savvy** Need an application to open a new IRA? Forget calling customer service; not only will they send you the application (and in many cases, the wrong one!), but the information packet will contain a plethora of unnecessary brochures. Instead, log on to the investment company's website and download the application of your choice, or open an account online and wire transfer the money from your bank account. Fast, easy, and no mail or paper forms involved. And forget about receiving your monthly or quarterly statements in the mail—many brokerage houses, investment companies, and even mortgage companies are now offering statements online. More and more utility companies are offering the service, too. Call the individual companies for more details.

Catalogs

Although it seems I recycle a pile of paper nearly every day, I have one paper fetish—I love catalogs. And rather than pitch them in the trash the day they arrive—as many organizational experts recommend—I hoard them. To me, catalogs provide a valuable time-saving service: I can pick out a gift and send it in a flash without wandering aimlessly through a novelty boutique; I can shop for Christmas toys without dealing with holiday shoppers; and best of all, I can browse and purchase merchandise at my convenience day or night.

> I save catalogs, and when I have free time, say, waiting at the doctor's office or sitting by the pool, I scan them. If I find something interesting, I rip out the page and the order form and then toss out the remaining catalog. It keeps the clutter under control. I leave the sheet listing the item on my desk for a day or two. Sometimes in that time I have second thoughts, and I end up throwing that out too.

Admittedly, too much of a good thing is rarely good, and nowhere is that more true than with catalogs. Once you get on "the list," it seems everyone—from the nut growers in the South to the maple syrup makers in the North—tries to hawk wares to you through the mail. But if you love catalogs as much as I do, you have to be ruthless in thinning them out on a regular basis; otherwise, they'll just end up as another unpleasant stack of printed matter. Call customer service immediately if you're getting duplicate catalogs or if they seem to send you one a week! Also ask that they *not* share your name and address with other companies.

Junk Mail

Do you get two to three credit card offers in the mail a week? Ed McMahon tempting you with a million bucks? Junk mail comes in all sorts of interesting disguises to entice you to tear open the envelope. Don't get duped by such wording on the envelope as "Time-dated material enclosed; open immediately." It's all the same stuff—junk. It's easier than you think to get your name off direct-marketing mailing lists. Just ask to have your name removed by writing to Mail Preference Service, Direct Marketing Association, P.O. Box 9008, Farmingdale, NY 11735-9008. (If you order from catalogs frequently, however, you'll need to write to get your name off lists on a regular basis—about once a year.)

Newspapers and Magazines

When I entered college, my mom thought it would be nice to have the local newspaper sent to me. Every day I'd find our little journal waiting for me in my mailbox. But as soon as I'd enter my room, I'd toss it in the corner with the dozens of others that I hadn't had time to read. My growing pile of newspapers soon became a dormwide joke. I felt too guilty to throw them away, and I swore that I'd get to them soon, but those papers kept mounting up until it became a downright fire hazard. Eventually, I came to my senses and canceled the paper. Whew! What a relief!

QUICK FIX

If you have time to read the paper every day and feel it's an important part of your world, more power to you; but if you let the papers stack up day after day and then recycle them with your bottles and cans every Tuesday, read on.

■ **Simply Sunday** Cancel your Monday through Saturday newspaper subscription and get only the Sunday edition. (It's the best edition of the week, anyway!)

■ **Extra! Extra! Read Your E-mail!** To stay informed, sign up to get the headlines E-mailed to you daily. Many major newspapers offer this free service and have links directly to dozens of articles. No paper involved!

■ **The Mad World of Magazines** We used to subscribe to six different magazines, but the madness drove us to cancel all but three. Here

All the News That's Fit for the Internet

Most newspapers seem to contain more advertisements than feature articles. Instead of spending half your time combing through the ads In search of an Interesting piece to read, log on to your favorite periodical's website and read on.

Arizona Republic—azcentral.com

Chicago Tribune—chicagotribune.com

Detroit Free Press—freep.com

Houston Chronicle—chron.com

Los Angeles Times—latimes.com

Miami Herald—herald.com

New York Times—nytimes.com

Philadelphia Daily News—phillynews.com

San Francisco Examiner—examiner.com

Washington Post—washingtonpost.com

are a few alternatives: log on to your favorite magazine website, read them at the library (or browse the headlines while waiting in line at the supermarket), swap with friends or neighbors, or alternate subscriptions—one per year.

M*y local library has a website where I can browse the card catalog and reserve books from any one of their local branches. When the books come in, they notify me by phone and I go pick them up. It's so convenient.*

Creating Household Files

You've canceled, cut back, and simplified. It's helped, you say, but you still have a pile of important papers that must stay. We all have vital documents, sentimental papers, and articles of interest that we want to keep for future reference. You can't toss it all! But you can contain it by setting up a personal filing system. Before you begin organizing, head to your local office supply store and pick up a few essentials—colored hanging folders, manila folders, a three-hole punch, a stapler, paper clips, labels. This small invest-ment now will help in the long run by setting up a process that will never fail you.

Next, gather up the goods—those stacks of papers piled high on your desk and on the kitchen table that never seem to find a permanent home—and begin to sort through them. Toss out scraps of paper that no longer have any meaning or value to you—stray envelopes, old ATM deposit slips, grocery receipts, and expired coupons and warranties. Finally, it's time to divide and conquer—separate what remains into logical categories, and give each one an appropriate home, making it easy to find what you're look-ing for when you need it.

Irreplaceable Papers

Important papers such as birth certificates, marriage licenses, adoption papers, automobile titles, stock and bond certificates, wills, deeds, divorce decrees, and anything else that has significant value should be stored at a safe-deposit box at a bank (though you can keep copies of each of these documents in your home files). If a safe-deposit box isn't convenient (there's nothing more frustrating than wanting to retrieve a document on a Sun-day, when the banks are closed), consider buying a fire safe for your home, available at most office supply stores. Don't skimp on quality here; look for a safe that's UL classified for two hours of fire protection.

Active Papers

Topping the active paper file are bills to be paid, letters to be answered, permission slips to be signed, and forms to be filled out. In the front of your household filing cabinet, create a hanging *active file*, and then break it down further according to your needs. For instance, set up two file fold-ers—one marked "bills due first through the fifteenth," the second labeled "bills due the sixteenth through the thirty-first." Other ideas include school-related forms, calls to be made, and so on. Or keep them visible by sort-ing your files in a vertical wire organizer. Whatever system you choose, because you'll be referring to these files often, it's best to keep them in a consistent, convenient location.

Inactive Papers

The majority of household files fall under the inactive paper category—files that you'll refer to only from time to time but are important enough to keep around in an easy-to-reach spot. The list includes invoices from bills paid during the year, tax receipts for the current year, credit card information, insurance policies, brokerage statements, checking and savings account statements, canceled checks, employment-related material, personal folders for each family member, health-care information, appliance warranties, and manuals.

QUICK FIX

Although you should never let an important piece of paper go without a home, some household records can quickly become too large for a typical two-drawer filing cabinet. Therefore, it's important to weed through on occasion and pitch out appliance manuals to equipment that you no longer own, health-care booklets to HMOs that you no longer belong to, employment information to a job that you left two years ago. You get the idea.

■ **Filing the Moneymakers** Organize monthly brokerage statements, quarterly IRA or 401(k) statements, and savings and CD statements into a three-ring notebook. Use subject dividers to separate each group, putting the most recent statement first. Label the spine "Finances."

■ **Appliance Science** Every time you purchase a new TV, stereo, or even small kitchen appliance, staple the sales receipt to the inside cover of the owner's manual and file in another three-ring notebook. Label the spine "Appliance Manuals."

■ **Filing Paid Bills** Some folks set up twelve folders for this category, one for each month, and file each bill in the appropriate month once it's been paid and notated on the invoice. At the end of the year, they remove all tax-related or important invoices, toss the rest, and begin the process all over again. Some parents choose to use an expandable, accordion-style folder each year, sorting everything from insurance and medical receipts to car and household maintenance—one subject per individual file. Again, at the end of the year, all tax-related information is removed and the remainder tossed. Others choose a third system by creating just two folders: tax-related receipts and invoices and non-tax-related receipts and invoices. At the end of the year, all tax-related receipts are stapled to a copy of federal and state returns and filed away. (Although this is the easiest method of the three, the files can get stuffed by December, and sifting through the pile to find a specific invoice is time-consuming.)

■ **Checking Around** When your checking account statement arrives in the mail, and you don't have the time to reconcile your account right away (and who does?), file it in your *active file* so it won't get lost in the day-to-day shuffle. When you finally do reconcile your account, move it to a banking file.

■ **Family First** Keep a separate file on each family member, too, and fill it with personal information and forms that pertain to that individual, such as education transcripts, scouting information, and so on.

■ **Project Files** If you're like me, you're always thinking about the next project. Whether it's a household one (such as adding an addition to your home) or a personal one (like writing the Great American Novel), create a file for it, fill it with interesting and informative tidbits, and watch your idea grow until it becomes a full-fledged plan. Set up a colored hanging file for each subject—gardening, home improvement, travel, and so forth. Within each main subject heading, break it down even further using manila folders.

Dead (but Shouldn't Be Forgotten) Paper

The dead file is a small tomb of important papers that, for whatever reason, the U.S. government would prefer you hold on to for a time. I'm talking, of course, about copies of your past taxes and supporting documentation, bank statements, and canceled checks. Cardboard boxes with lids, contents neatly labeled on top and sides, stored high on a shelf for safekeeping in the basement or garage will do the trick.

Paper Pusher No More

It may seem overwhelming now, but once you simplify, purge, and then set up a comfortable filing system, the rest is just a-minute-a-day maintenance. Paper is not only comforting, but also has an important role in our lives—we can gain information, prove a point, or live a dream, all on paper.

Parties

Now that your home functions flawlessly because of your newly acquired organizational skills, you find yourself with an abundance of free time. Hey, you should throw a party!

To some, there's nothing more frightening than hosting a get-together of any size. We've all had our share of party nightmares, from our son's sixth birthday, where his entire kindergarten class ran amuck through the house, to the adult cocktail party where the guests quietly stared at one another, glancing every other minute at their watches. Let's face it—putting together a great bash takes a bit of imagination, finesse, and lots of planning.

This chapter will help you tap into your creativity and give you some tips and ideas on organizing three types of parties: a child's birthday party, adult evening parties, and a family get-together. Although I suggest party themes, decorations, games, favors, entertainment, and a few menu ideas, recipes are not included. If you need some help with your menu, however, try a few great books on the subject: *Martha Stewart's Menus for Entertaining*, by Martha Stewart (New York: Random House, 1994); *Entertaining*, by Malcolm Hillier (New York: DK Publishing, 1997); and *Bon Appétit Weekend Entertaining*, by the editors of Bon Appétit (New York: Condé Nast Publications, 1998).

Child's Birthday Party

Although I'd rather forget my own birthday, to a child there's nothing more important. Not only is his birthday proof that he is indeed one step closer to being an adult, it's also a day that he can call his own, where everything and everyone centers on him. (Hey, isn't that every day?)

KEY ORGANIZING TIPS

■ **Involve the Birthday Boy or Girl** You may be thinking cowboy party, but your child sees pirates, complete with buried treasure. Not only will he be disappointed when the big day arrives, but ultimately it's *his* party and should reflect his current boyhood passions. He *should* have a say in the proceedings, so plan the event together. If the requests are too great (no one expects you to build a six-foot ship adorned with working cannons), try compromising (you can make a smaller version by painting a few appliance boxes). Besides, planning a party together is an investment in your child—the memories he'll carry will last long into adulthood.

■ **Start Early** Start by making to-do lists with your child at least four weeks ahead of the party, leaving you with plenty of time for last-minute details. Make four separate lists: guest list, party theme and decorations, games and prizes, and menu (don't forget food for the adults if your little guests will be accompanied by a mom or dad). As you complete each task, check it off your list.

■ **Don't Outdo or Overdo** The party doesn't have to be big or expensive, especially if your child is young. If you host a western party complete with pony, hayrides, and barnyard animals for your three-year-old, what will you possibly do to top it next year, short of flying your young guests to Hawaii for a luau? Your child doesn't need (or want) fancy entertainment or props, just a festive day with friends.

■ **Limit the Number Invited** The general rule of thumb is one child invited for number of years old—fifth birthday, five guests. Although my twins think that number is way too small, you need to set a limit on the number of guests. First, smaller groups are easier to control, allowing the host parents to give each guest individual attention. Smaller parties are easier to clean up after as well. And if you can keep the number of kids down, you can keep the cost of the party down, too.

■ **Child Proof** Before party day arrives, go through the house and put away breakables. Your child may know to stay away from the antique lamp in the hallway, but will ten of his friends? And if your daughter simply can't bear the thought of her classmates playing with her prized doll collection, tuck it inside the closet until after everyone has gone. Although it's important to teach her to share, it's OK to hide a few special toys.

■ **Keep Things Moving** Don't let the party just drift; you need to play the emcee and move the event along by telling the kids what they'll be doing next. Allow about an hour or so for the main party activity or game, a half hour for food and birthday cake, and fifteen minutes each for breaking the piñata (if you plan to have one) and opening presents (if you plan to make it a part of the festivities). Finally, start handing out the party favors, a subtle signal to parents that the gala is coming to a close. All in all, an average birthday party should last about two to two and one-half hours.

■ **Plan for the Unexpected** Be prepared with a few extra party favors and food for those who show up with a sibling or didn't RSVP. Quickly switch gears with a few bonus games or activities in case some of the ones you planned are not popular. Make a contingency plan in case of bad weather—nearly every party can be adapted for indoors. And if you can, hire extra help (we often hire our baby-sitter for the day) to pick up the slack or take care of a younger family member.

Toddler Parties (Under Three Years Old)

It's tempting to throw your little tyke a big party for his first, second, and even third birthday, but chances are you'll remember the day better than he in years to come. If you do decide to celebrate his birthday, though, *keep it simple*—just a few friends with an easy-to-prepare theme. A few suggestions: Pirate Party (complete with a treasure hunt), Firefighter Party (many local fire companies will send a truck and real firefighters to your house for a demonstration), Transportation Party (anything that moves), and Dress-Up Party (clean out your closet and add lots of costume jewelry).

Arts and Crafts Party (Three to Ten Years Old)

■ **The Theme** Encourage your budding Rembrandts with a total sensory experience! Set up art stations: painting and drawing; sculpting with clay (Play-Doh works well); collage making using screws, rocks, seashells, and so forth; or any other craft that your child enjoys.

■ **The Decorations** Fill the room with posters of famous artists' paintings, and encourage the kids to try and imitate their work. Rent or borrow easels, and don't forget to cover the walls with sheets of butcher paper taped for stability and let the kids color away.

■ **The Food** Set up food at each art station so that kids can eat as they create. Try small peanut butter and jelly sandwiches at one, chicken fingers at another, sliced vegetables and dip at a third, and so forth.

■ **The Games** Award a "Certificate of Merit" to each child for Most Creative Artwork, Most Colorful Artwork, Most Humorous Artwork, and so forth (make sure each child gets one). If you'd like to introduce the techniques of famous artists, try the creative activities listed in the sidebar on the next page.

■ **The Favors** Paint sets, jewelry kits, paintbrushes, or anything to do with art.

I *actually liked it when the boys got older and we'd celebrate birthdays by going out to dinner and a movie just as a family. Or I'd let them each bring a friend or two, depending on the place. I'd give them a choice of places that were fun and memorable, with singing waiters dressed in costume, for instance.*

Carnival Party (Four to Twelve Years Old)

■ **The Theme** Remember summer evenings spent on the boardwalk playing arcade games? Re-create a festive midway in your driveway, backyard, or even your basement. It's a real hands-on party where everyone can participate.

■ **The Decorations** Streamers and balloons. Paint colorful signs with clown faces describing each game. Award tickets (buy a roll from an office supply store) to each child as he tries his hand at each game (he can cash them in later at the prize booth).

If You Have More Time . . .

Creating Matisse Collages

French artist Henri Matisse, one of the greatest colorists of the twentieth century, began creating boldly colored paper cutouts late in his career when illness forced him to stay in bed. In what he called "drawing with scissors," the artist cut out various shapes—geometric and free-form—from colored paper and intuitively arranged them on sheets of either black or white paper, creating vibrant abstract designs.

Your young party guests can make their own versions of Matisse's collages. Start by showing them pictures of his cutouts and explaining his technique; for ideas, check out *Matisse* (Famous Artists series), by Anthony Mason (Hauppage, N.Y.: Barron's, 1995). Then set them free with brightly colored paper, scissors (younger party guests will need parental help), glue, and large sheets of white or black paper for the collage background.

Drawing Seurat Dot Pictures

In the late nineteenth century, French artist Georges Seurat developed a painting technique called pointillism, or divisionism. Rather than blending colors in the traditional impressionistic style, Seurat juxtaposed tiny dots of contrasting color on his canvas, believing that the viewer's eye would optically blend the hues together, forming subtle differences in color. His painstaking technique paid off beautifully!

Eager partygoers can use a paintbrush and paint, colored pencils, markers, or pens to re-create Seurat's pointillism. Start with an example of the artist's work before the kids begin. For ideas, look for *Seurat: Drawings and Paintings*, by Robert L. Herbert (New Haven, Conn.: Yale University Press, 2001). You can show by example, too, by putting blue and yellow dots on paper in very close proximity, and then have the kids stand back. From far away, the dots appear to be one color—green!

Building a Pie-Throwing Booth

OK, so it's not really pies the kids will be throwing, just sponges. But they'll love hurling something at an adult face just the same. Start with a thin piece of plywood (about one-quarter-inch thick, three feet by five feet in size), sketch an image of a "muscle man" on one side, and then paint him. Cut a hole for the head large enough for an adult's head to fit through. Next, attach plywood wings on each side with hinges so that the booth can stand on its own. Round up several large, soft sponges. Find a willing victim, and turn the kids on him!

- **The Food** Hot dogs, corn dogs, french fries, popcorn, ice cream.
- **The Games** Beanbag Toss is easy to make (paint large computer boxes, cut geometric holes in each, and stack in a pyramid) and challenging as kids try to get a beanbag in one of the holes. For Balloon Burst, attach inflated balloons to a large piece of plywood; then have the kids try to burst one by throwing darts (a parent must supervise this one). Other ideas include a Face Painting booth, Ring Toss (try to land a plastic ring around a large soda bottle), and Water Works (use squirt guns to try and knock down a pyramid of soda cans). But if you really want to impress your guests, create a Pie-Throwing booth by following the instruction in the sidebar above.
- **The Favors** Set up a prize booth where kids can cash their winning tickets in for small stuffed animals, beaded necklaces and bracelets, whistles, and other carnival trinkets.

Little Chefs Party (Four to Twelve Years Old)

- **The Theme** What child doesn't like to play around in the kitchen? Depending on the time of year, guide your little guests in the art of cooking or baking. If the party is near Christmas, for example, have the kids make (or just decorate) Christmas cookies using prepared dough. But whatever you choose, remember to gear it to your child's age group—four-year-olds have a shorter attention span and therefore require a faster recipe than, say, twelve-year-olds.

■ **The Decorations** Decorate the kitchen and dining room with photos and magazine cutouts of food, and have a large supply of metal bowls, measuring cups and spoons, and wooden utensils at the ready.

■ **The Food** Let them eat what they create! Pizza works great, as do tacos or sloppy joes.

■ **The Games** While the food is cooking or baking, have party guests decorate plain white aprons (available at craft stores) with colored markers, fabric paint, or glitter (try tie-dye if you don't mind the mess). Play a Food-Tasting game by blindfolding guests and having them sample treats and guess what they are.

■ **The Favors** Cookie cutters, small wooden utensils, even kids' cookbooks.

Detective Party (Six to Twelve Years Old)

■ **The Theme** You set the clues, and the kids play detective and solve a murder mystery. But remember: keep the game simple and give lots of clues or the kids won't be able to solve it.

■ **The Decorations** Set up a crime scene: tape construction-paper footsteps throughout the house, add a chalk outline of a body on the floor, or even overturn some furniture. As guests arrive, give each one a fedora, a magnifying glass, and a pad and pencil.

■ **The Food** A fun favorite to try: Mystery Soup. Take the labels off of various canned vegetables and have each child add the contents to a large, simmering pot.

■ **The Games** For the main event, stage a Whodunit: tell your young guests that a murder has occurred and whichever team finds the ten clues (a bloodied plastic knife, a noose, a finger-printed glass, etc.) hidden throughout the house solves the case. Set up teams of two and hand out a sheet of riddles, each answer leading to a clue.

For an additional game, wrap a variety of small, inexpensive toys for a few rounds of Mystery Toy. Pass each package around the circle of children and have them guess what it is. Whoever guesses the toy correctly gets to keep it. Or try Dusting for Fingerprints: have each detective hold a glass in his or her hand for a moment. Carefully place the glass on its side and lightly sprinkle baby powder (don't use talc) on the glass. Blow the powder away and gently brush off the residue to reveal an official fingerprint!

■ **The Favors** Spy books, like *Harriet the Spy*; detective-type comic books, such as *Dick Tracy*; jigsaw puzzles; or even walkie-talkies.

Sleep-Over Party (Eight to Twelve Years Old)

■ **The Theme** If you have the patience to host a group of energetic kids, a sleep-over party is always a favorite. Have guests come dressed in their pajamas and slippers, and tell them to bring their sleeping bags and pillows.

■ **The Decorations** Buy or borrow lots of pillows, and cover the sleep-over room from wall to wall. After all, what's a sleep over without a pillow fight? Attach glow-in-the-dark stars to the ceiling for a great effect once the kids turn out the lights.

■ **The Food** Sinful midnight snacks are the way to go: make-your-own sundaes, pizza, made-to-order omelets, or even waffles with whipped cream.

■ **The Games** To play Truth or Dare, write politely probing questions on slips of paper. (Did you ever cut a class? Who's your worst teacher and why?) Those who decline to answer pick from the "dare" slips of paper and face the consequences (stand on one foot for five minutes). If your birthday girl wants to add an art project to the evening's festivities, try the one listed in the sidebar on the next page.

■ **The Favors** A favorite stuffed animal, ghost stories (the *Goosebumps* series is popular), or fun hair accessories such as scrunchies or barrettes.

Camp Out Party (Eight to Twelve Years Old)

■ **The Theme** Re-create a wilderness oasis and take your young guests on an overnight camp out. Kids love the great outdoors, even if it is just your backyard. Have your little campers come dressed in their outdoor gear—long pants and boots—and tell them to bring a sleeping bag and bedroll.

■ **The Decorations** Let nature be the decoration, and just set up tents around a large campfire pit.

Personalized Pillowcases

Let the kids clothe their favorite pillows with personalized pillow-cases. Just have a supply of noncotton (synthetic blend) pillowcases on hand, fabric crayons, and eleven-by-fourteen-inch sheets of plain white paper (nonglossy).

Have each guest draw a design with the fabric crayons onto a sheet of paper (all letters must be written in mirror image, or back-ward). Next, slip the pillowcase onto an ironing board (cover the surface of the ironing board with a thin sheet of cardboard to pre-vent any transfer of the fabric crayon), place the paper—design side down—onto the pillowcase, and press a medium-hot iron over the paper for a second or two; then remove. Repeat the process until the entire design has been transferred to the pillowcase.

■ **The Food** Serve campfire stew or chili, or barbecue some hot dogs and hamburgers. For a midnight snack, have plenty of trail mix on hand. But no camp out would be complete without S'mores—toasted marsh-mallows sandwiched between two graham crackers and bits of chocolate.

■ **The Games** Three-legged and sack races are great fun. If you have the room in your backyard, set up a horseshoe pit. But when the sun goes down, nothing beats telling ghost stories by the campfire.

■ **The Favors** Flashlights, compasses, butterfly nets, binoculars, or other inexpensive camping gear.

Sixties Party (Nine to Twelve Years Old)

■ **The Theme** Peace, love, and Bobby Sherman. Well, maybe not, but hosting a sixties party is like, groovy, man. Guests will love re-creating the days of the Beatles, Motown, and flower power.

■ **The Decorations** Plug in your lava lamps and hang beaded cur-tains. Decorate the room with paisley pillows and period posters that you've either unearthed in the attic or that you make yourself: rock concerts, peace symbols, and smiley faces. Hang old album covers or string 45s from the ceiling.

■ **The Food** Fondue was all the rage forty years ago (has it been that long?). Or remember pigs-in-a-blanket? It's all kid-friendly food and easy to make, too.

■ **The Games** Tie-dyed T-shirts and shoelaces are easy to make and so radical, man (but can be a bit messy). Start by knotting shoelaces about one-inch apart. If using T-shirts (all cotton), knot sections tightly together using wide rubber bands. Next, set up a variety of colored dyes (Rit is a good brand and available at most supermarkets) in large bowls, one color per bowl, on top of large plastic sheets to contain spills. Have the kids dip the T-shirts in their favorite color (it's best to choose one color for one section of the T-shirt). Shoelaces can be dipped in many colors by dipping each section in a different bowl. Set laces or shirts out to dry on plastic tarps in a warm, dry spot, but do not untie until nearly dry.

■ **The Favors** Love beads, mood rings, psychedelic headbands, or any other retro item you can find.

Adult Evening Parties

In my postcollege, prehusband days, my roommate Gina and I loved to throw parties. Our philosophy for a successful bash was simple: invite everyone you know, and make sure there's plenty of cheap wine and good food. (Being two nice Italian girls, we always made homemade meatballs served with fresh, crusty bread—a hit every time.)

Even after I married, I entertained often. Although I thought I was a pro at throwing together a sit-down dinner for twelve, looking back there were many food faux pas (like the first time I made tiramisu—don't ask) and dining disasters. Fortunately, I was too naive to be embarrassed. Even now, after more than twenty years of entertaining, I still make mistakes, but I've learned that it's the overall sentiment of the evening and how special you make your guests feel that matters most, not whether your risotto is al dente.

As a parent, your life centers on your children, but it's important to make time for just the adults. Entertaining at home offers a chance to spread your creative wings and express your individuality, show off your home, and spend time with friends you may not see as often any more. Besides, when you throw a party in your own home, you're not the one who needs to find a baby-sitter!

KEY ORGANIZING TIPS

■ **Choose a Theme** Not unlike planning a child's birthday party, choosing a theme anchors an adult party and helps bring it into focus. It's also easier to decide on decorations, table settings, and menu when you have an idea to work around.

■ **Number Crunching** Limit the number of guests to six to eight (twelve for a cocktail party). Especially if you're new to entertaining, a smaller number is much more manageable.

■ **Set the Stage** Think of your living and dining room as a stage or a bare canvas waiting for your sense of artistry. Add color and texture with candles and flowers, lighting and music, table linens and food. A vase overflowing with bright yellow sunflowers, for example, sets the tone for a Tuscan country buffet; a dining room chandelier adorned in streamers and a table dusted with colorful confetti make the perfect backdrop for a New Year's Eve gala.

■ **Menu Magic** You'll want to choose food to suit the occasion, but if you're constantly in the kitchen with last-minute preparations for an elaborate meal, leaving your guests to fend for themselves, then perhaps you should rethink your menu. Select items that can be made ahead of time or ones that are effortless and can be thrown together in just a few moments. This way both you and your guests can enjoy the evening together.

■ **Relax** Fortunately, the days of rigid social conduct of the nineteenth century are gone. You don't need to fret over which wine to serve with vichyssoise or whether you have the proper bar glasses for a vodka gimlet (although throwing a formal dinner party is fun, too, so be sure to check out the sidebar on "Setting a Formal Dining Table"). Use your own sense of style to guide you through any gathering of your choosing, whether an elegant cocktail party or a potluck buffet.

■ **Be Inventive** Dining room not big enough for a sit-down dinner? How about filling the basement with candlelight, draping beautiful fabric across the walls, and infusing the air with fresh flowers? Now you've created a baronial dining room fit for a grand celebration. Have a cocktail party in the garden, or set up a wet bar in the coat closet (minus the coats and rubber boots, of course). Using space creatively adds newness and life to any celebration. Stretch your inventiveness to all your decorative decisions: quilts and rugs make for interesting table linen, mix and match your china and glassware, or use items from your garden to adorn the inside of your home, such as a watering can as a vase for a garden-themed baby shower.

Setup

Thursday: Choose and iron linen
           Gather and clean serving
           bowls, platter, etc.

Friday:
    A.M.   Set table
    P.M.   Clean and vacuum
           living room

Saturday:
    A.M.   Clean and stock guest
           bathroom
           Arrange flowers
    P.M.   Choose music and stock
           CD player

Menu and Food Prep

Thursday: Make and refrigerate
           miniquiche

Friday:
    A.M.   Prepare and refrigerate
           dessert
    P.M.   Buy and refrigerate
           perishables

Saturday:
    A.M.   Wash lettuce, cover
           Choose and chill wine
  4 P.M.   Put roast in oven at
           350 degrees
  5 P.M.   Add vegetables to roast
  6 P.M.   Shower and dress
  7 P.M.   Set out appetizers

FIGURE 17. Party planning lists

■ **Make Copious Lists** In addition to your guest list, menu, and list of party supplies to buy (food, drinks, flowers, candles, etc.), write out two side-by-side time schedules—one for food preparation, the other for non-cooking responsibilities. Cross off each task as completed. (See Figure 17.)

A Night at the Academy Awards

■ **The Theme** If you and your circle of friends love the movies, then throw an Academy Awards Party. It's an informal evening filled with plenty of party gossip as you watch the couture and the ridiculous of Hollywood's rich and famous as they make their way down the red carpet during the Sunday-night broadcast.

■ **The Decorations** Set up padded folding chairs—theater style—in front of your TV (if you don't have a large TV, you may want to rent one for the night). Get copies of *Variety* (if you don't live in a large city, call your local newsstand and ask if they can order it), and leave them on guests' chairs. Hang movie posters. Have plenty of bowls of popcorn on hand.

■ **The Food** With a three-hour-plus broadcast, there's no time for a sit-down dinner. A four-star buffet is the only way to go.

■ **The Entertainment** Pass out Oscar ballots (pick up *Variety* the Friday before the Sunday broadcast for an official copy, or log on to oscar.org), and have your guests vote before the show. The person who votes closest with the Academy wins a door prize, say, a video of a classic movie. Try a Movie Trivia game during commercials—the Oscar website has dozens of suggestions.

⏰ **TIME-SAVER**—Before the meal, it's easier to have one drink type— a pitcher of margaritas, martinis, or champagne punch—than an open bar, where you'll be running back and forth filling each person's individual order. (But always also have a nonalcoholic alternative.)

I find recipes that can be frozen. I make as much as I can ahead of time and freeze them. On the day of the party, I just heat them up. The first thing in the morning of a party, I make my salads, cover them with paper towels, and stick them in the refrigerator; or I'll prepare a dish, say, mashed potatoes, and put it directly in its serving dish, cover it with plastic wrap, and put in the fridge. When it's time to eat, I just zap it in the microwave.

Wine-Tasting Party

■ **The Theme** In case you haven't noticed, wine is hot. Hosting a wine-tasting party is not only easy to pull together, but a fun way to educate your friends (and yourself) on the nectar of the gods. Try a horizontal, or cross-varietal, tasting—the easiest type of wine tasting—where each guest brings a bottle of the same type of grape, such as Chardonnay, Pinot Noir, or Chenin Blanc, or from the same region, such as Napa Valley, for instance. Set a price cap at $15 a bottle.

■ **The Decorations** Hang maps of Bordeaux, Napa Valley, Tuscany, and the Rhine region in Germany. Anchor your wine-tasting table with a large basket filled with fresh, juicy grapes. Set out tasting placemats (sheets of white paper will do fine) for each bottle and number them to correspond with each guest's tasting notes (small writing pads where guests can jot down their impressions of each wine). Place each bottle in a corresponding numbered bag for a blind taste test (fancy labels have a tendency to sway some people) and place on the appropriate mat.

Setting a Formal Dining Table

Although throwing together an informal buffet dinner or afternoon barbecue is more in line with today's casual living, sometimes it's fun to pull out the cocktail-length dress, dust off the leaded crystal, and host a formal dinner party for twelve (OK, so six is an easier number to work with). But does the salad plate go on the right or the left? Follow Figure 18 to help clear up any confusion.

Charger Plate An optional large, decorative plate that remains on the table throughout the meal, a charger plate frames each course as it's served.

Side Plate Placed to the left of the first-course fork, the side plate functions as either a bread or salad dish. A cloth napkin is usually placed on top.

Cutlery Forks on left, knives and spoons on right. Guests work their way in from the outside. On the right, starting from the outside: bread knife, soupspoon, first-course knife, larger entrée knife, and, finally, teaspoon closest to the plate. On the left: first-course fork, larger entrée fork, and dessert fork.

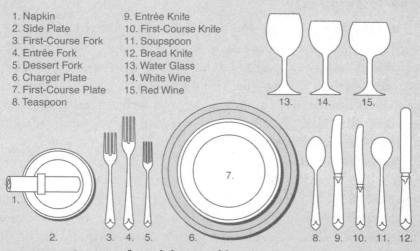

1. Napkin
2. Side Plate
3. First-Course Fork
4. Entrée Fork
5. Dessert Fork
6. Charger Plate
7. First-Course Plate
8. Teaspoon

9. Entrée Knife
10. First-Course Knife
11. Soupspoon
12. Bread Knife
13. Water Glass
14. White Wine
15. Red Wine

FIGURE 18. Setting a formal dining table

Glassware The water glass sits directly above the knives. If more than one type of wine will be served, the glass closest to the plate is used first—usually white wine.

Accoutrements One set of salt and pepper shakers per six guests. Keep centerpieces, such as candles and floral arrangements, low so they won't interfere as guests converse across the table.

■ **The Food** French bread and cheese during the wine tasting. A country-style buffet set up on a kitchen island or breakfast bar for after the tasting.

■ **The Entertainment** Let the wine be your entertainment. Have a maximum of six to eight bottles (lest it turns into a college kegger where guests end up sobbing, "I love you, man") and twelve guests. Have plenty of long-stemmed glasses on hand and a pitcher of drinking water. Remember, there are no right or wrong answers either—have fun and don't turn the event into a snobfest.

To taste each wine:

1. Pour a small amount of the first wine into everyone's glasses, and observe its color by placing it at a forty-five-degree angle against the white tasting mat. Write down what you see.
2. Sample the aroma by swirling the glass on a flat surface and quickly raising it to your nose. Fruity like berries? Earthy like mushrooms? Make a note of it.
3. Next, taste it and write down the flavors you detect—butter, nuts, apples, and pears for Chardonnay, for instance. Encourage your guests to do the same, and share their comments with the group.
4. Repeat the process with the remaining bottles. (You can rinse out everyone's glasses with a bit of water from a pitcher kept on the table.)

🍾 **STYLE TIP**—It's all in the details. When searching for ways to reinforce your party theme, look to uncommon yet curious objects for help: small seashells filled with table salt for a Hawaiian luau, for instance, or a sombrero filled with tortilla chips for a Cinco de Mayo party.

If I choose a menu item that requires a lot of fussiness, I make sure every-thing else is easy; otherwise, I get worn out and then I don't care. I'm not afraid to ask guests to bring things like salads. Most are happy to participate.

Around-the-World Party

- **The Theme** We all have a bit of wanderlust inside of us. If you long to visit a far-off land, but have to wait until the kids leave for college, host an Around-the-World Party—an evening of exotic food, story swapping, and big dreams.

- **The Decorations** Hang maps of different countries and travel posters. Cover your dinner table with foreign coins (you can buy some at many banks). Have your fellow travelers bring their passports (current or expired, it doesn't matter—the official country stamps and the corny photos are the real conversation starters), and use them as place cards at your table. Select your music to fit your menu.

- **The Food** You can choose your menu based on one particular country, a region of the world—say, Mediterranean, Asian, or South American—or you can have hors d'oeuvres from one country, a main course from another, and dessert from a third.

- **The Entertainment** After dinner, hold a short slide show. Let each guest present ten to fifteen of his favorite travel slides to the other guests (don't let it drag on for hours; most guests will get bored). Arrange all the slides in a single carousel as the guests arrive, and write down the order in which they will introduce their minitravelogues.

In the past I would make everything from the hors d'oeuvres to the dessert for a party. Now I've learned to simplify. There are some beautiful frozen desserts out there. Go to Sam's Club and buy a few frozen items instead of making them. That is a big time-saver. At first I felt guilty, but I've gotten over it.

Family Parties

I was talking with a friend the other day who recently had a baby. She con-fided that now that kids have come onto the scene, she hasn't had much time to see some of her old gang. "Because I work during the day, I want to spend as much of my free time as I can with my kids," she explained. "If a party doesn't include children, sorry, I can't attend."

Her point is well-taken. But the solution is simple—throw a party that spans the generations. Family parties can be a great opportunity for both young and old to enjoy the day together.

KEY ORGANIZING TIPS

■ **Tempting Time** Families with small children may not be able to attend a party starting around noon (too close to nap time), yet households with school-age children may opt out of a Sunday-evening bash (the kids need to get ready for school the following morning). Saturday afternoon is usually a good time for most family events.

■ **Kid-Friendly Food** Some savvy moms and dads always travel with food that they know their children will eat, but unfortunately, others don't. So, although your kids may love barbecued London broil, many small-fry visitors would prefer a hot dog or hamburger. Try to include kid-friendly treats on your menu (it avoids lots of whining at dinnertime), and don't forget plenty of juice boxes (less messy than bottled juice).

I always plan for kids by making treat bags—small Baggies filled with pretzels, granola, Cheerios—and leaving them in a big bowl on the table. When the kids are hungry, they know where to find them rather than interrupting their parents. When the kids are happy, the parents are happy, and everyone can have a great afternoon.

■ **Have Kid-Friendly Activities** Most kids won't be content hanging out watching their parents catch up with old friends. Plan some activities—rent a video, arrange an arts-and-crafts table, set up a volleyball or badminton net—or hire entertainment (magicians, storytellers, etc.) to entertain the underage masses. Try to include inexpensive party favors that the kids can take home.

■ **Give Plenty of Notice** If you're planning an anniversary party or a family reunion where folks will fly in from various parts of the country, give substantial notice—about four months—so that relatives have a chance to ask for time off from work or shop around for competitive airfare.

Backyard Clambake

▪ **The Theme** You don't have to have a house on Martha's Vineyard to throw an upper-crust New England clambake. Even an eager hostess with a home in the Dakotas can transform her own backyard into a sleepy sand dune. Can't you just smell the salt air?

▪ **The Decorations** Picnic tables with gingham tablecloths festooned with baskets of seashells; streamers of nautical flags draped across the backyard; beach chairs and umbrellas; and big beach balls for the kids. If you're up to it, haul in some sand from your local home improvement store (you can always mix it into your garden after the party), and add some inexpensive sand toys. Kids, and kids at heart, will love burying their toes or building a castle.

▪ **The Food** A pit-dug clambake takes a bit of sweat, but, oh, when you pull that fragrant pot from the dirt, suddenly all your hard work has paid off.

1. Start early in the day by digging a pit two feet deep and two feet wide—maybe in the garden or back by the garage—to accommodate a galvanized tub (available at hardware stores). Fill the pit with large stones and top with either charcoal or firewood and cover with chicken wire to support the tub. (The fire needs to keep its gusto for two hours—long enough to heat the stones.)

2. Meanwhile, fill individual cheesecloth packets with fresh, well-scrubbed clams, crab claws, mussels, and scallops. Tie closed with string.

3. Layer the seafood packets with well-washed seaweed in galvanized tub. (Rockweed is best. It has water pockets that help in the steaming process. You'll need about a bushel.) Add about one gallon of water. Cover tub tightly. (For a simpler approach—wrap seaweed with seafood tightly in foil packets and toss directly on the fire.)

4. When the fire embers are bright red, lower the tub into the pit and cover with water-soaked canvas tarp. Steam until clams shells open, about one hour.

(For those who'd love the taste but not the work, try wrapping seafood and seaweed in foil packets and toast over an outdoor grill.)

Other dishes to offer include barbecued chicken, corn on the cob, grilled vegetables, toasted garlic bread, and, of course, good old-fashioned fruit pies for dessert.

■ **The Entertainment** Lots of lazy backyard games where parents and kids can team up together: boccie, horseshoes, croquet, and backgammon. Leave decks of cards on the tables for card playing.

Family Reunion

■ **The Theme** If it's been a while since you've seen your favorite aunt, or your cousin just had a baby, maybe it's time to assemble the generations and throw a reunion. A bit tricky to organize, a reunion is worth the effort by reconnecting family members, establishing new bonds, and introducing your kids to their heritage. Yet it doesn't have to be big to be successful—an afternoon picnic with just a few family members can be just as memorable.

■ **The Decorations** If you're expecting a large crowd, and if weather permits, reserve space at a local or regional park. Bring along all your family albums and scrapbooks and tell your relatives to do the same (be sure the owner's name is written on the inside cover). Set aside one table for the family tree—a large poster board where visitors fill in their own branches.

■ **The Food** Lots of old family favorites, such as Grandma's potato salad or Uncle Bill's Boston baked beans. (Photocopy these precious recipes and leave copies by the buffet table to encourage family members to carry on the tradition.) Make it a potluck where every local family member brings a dish (you can assign each guest a category, such as salad or dessert).

■ **The Entertainment** There are lots of ways to make a reunion memorable, especially for the younger members of the family who may drag their feet at the thought of attending. As your younger guests arrive, give each a task: hand out disposable cameras and set them free to document the day's festivities with candid shots (you may want to also give them a notepad to write down who they photographed). Or, assign two children to interview family members—one videotapes while the other asks questions from a list that you prepared. (Show the minidocumentary at the end of the party.)

For the adults: to break the ice for relatives who may not be well acquainted with one another, play a family quiz game. Ask each to write a memorable story about growing up in the family and then share it with the group during cocktails. Save the collection of stories in a book. The highlight of the day, of course, is the family portrait—ask a neighbor or hire a professional to document this monumental occasion. (And don't forget to send a copy to all who attended.)

Anniversary Party

■ **The Theme** It seems like just yesterday, doesn't it? Whether it's been ten, twenty-five, or even fifty years, celebrating an anniversary is a great excuse (rather than a wedding or a funeral) to gather faraway family and friends.

■ **The Decorations** Start with the number of years married and build your theme around that. If it's a fifty-fifth, or emerald, anniversary, for instance, think green—a garden theme perhaps or maybe even an Irish theme if the duo hails from the Emerald Isle. Play the music of their day, whether big band or disco (maybe start the evening off with their wedding song). Adorn your home with photographs of the happy couple, particularly of their wedding day.

■ **The Food** The menu should be elegant, befitting such a jubilant occasion. Champagne and caviar for appetizers, a sit-down dinner of beef tenderloin with sautéed mushrooms and new potatoes. For dessert, try to re-create their wedding cake (if they remember what it was).

■ **The Entertainment** Have the couple renew their vows. After dinner, stage some sort of tribute for your guests of honor. Create a photographic family tree, for instance, or have everyone write a letter to the couple on fine stationery and display in a scrapbook. Have each person read his or her letter aloud; then present the album to guests of honor as a keepsake. A friend once told me that she and her siblings performed a humorous "This Is Your Life" for their parents' fiftieth anniversary, much to the guests' delight.

And Now a Toast

Entertaining is one of the great pleasures of life. Although some may really throw themselves into creating an unforgettable experience for all, a party doesn't have to be elaborate to be fun. As a wise, old friend once said to me, "If you have a good heart and are thoughtful in what you do, your friends will travel from nearly anywhere just to eat hot dogs out on your fire escape."

Shopping

Whether you stay at home and take your kids with you to the store or you work full-time and must stop in the supermarket at the end of a long day, shopping is a chore many of us would rather do without. Yet I've learned a few tricks over the years about shopping with kids (and without), mostly through trial and error. Yes, shopping can be done quickly and efficiently, but you'll need to strategize first!

KEY ORGANIZING TIPS

■ **List It** Keep a running list of things you need from every store that you patronize frequently, from the hardware store to the supermarket. For instance, I stop by Target about once every other month. When something I need occurs to me, I jot down the item in my personal notebook so I won't forget (see more about creating a personal notebook in the "Appointments" chapter). I also keep a running list for Home Depot and a few other stores. I even divide my list into sections based on the store's design (I'm in and out of the store quicker this way, and there's less chance of my overlooking something). After my shopping spree, I toss the list and start a fresh one.

■ **Keep It Visual** Place your weekly grocery list in a prominent spot (such as on the refrigerator door or on the kitchen desk) where everyone from family members to baby-sitters can easily note when something is low.

■ **Got Kids? Bring Distractions** Even my six-year-olds appreciate a toy to fiddle with while I'm perusing the sale racks. Pad and pen, calculator, car keys, or any other grown-up accessory holds their interest long enough to get the job done. Take along a bag of popcorn, Cheerios, or crackers, and hand it out at an appropriate time. Busy hands and full mouths have little time to interrupt or touch everything in sight.

■ **Be Prepared** Like the old Girl Scout motto, it's best to be prepared before you head out shopping. It saves time! That means have your list ready (don't rely on memory), coupons sorted, a calculator to compare unit pricing, and if you're headed to the bank, have all your checks and forms filled out so you won't need to do it when you get there.

■ **Call Ahead** To grab and run with just a specific item, always call ahead to make sure it's in stock. Most places will hold it at the register for you so all you'll need to do is pay and go. (This works great if you want to rent a specific video, for instance.)

Grocery Shopping Made Simple

You may be able to avoid the mall for a better part of the year, but you've got to eat! Although saving money tops everyone's list when it comes to food shopping, don't overlook the importance of choosing a well-stocked store where you feel comfortable shopping.

QUICK FIX

There's nothing more frustrating than returning home after a big food buy only to have forgotten to get ketchup and you're having hamburgers tonight! Make your trips to the market more efficient by following a few of these quick-fix tips.

■ **The Early Bird** Shop on the off-hours—early in the morning on a weekday is best. It's less crowded, and you'll get in and out quickly. Avoid peak times—weekdays from 4 to 7 P.M. and Saturdays.

■ **By the Aisle** To make your trip more efficient, arrange your grocery list by aisle (you can make a master shopping list using a copy of the store's floor plan, usually located at the entrance to the store). You're less likely to forget something and have to backtrack.

■ **Coupon Capers** Arrange your coupons aisle by aisle in a plastic expandable organizer. (You can buy one at most stationery stores.)

■ **Envelop It** Make your shopping list on the front of an envelope and stick the coupons you'll need directly inside.

■ **Buy in Bulk** Whenever your favorite cereal, shampoo, paper towel, or whatever is on sale, stock up. (I always cruise each aisle to see if my favorite brands or frequently used items are on sale that week, or I check the store circular.) Store your surplus goodies in your secondary pantry location and pull them out as needed. You'll save money and time because there's no need to buy these items again for a while.

■ **Let Them Help** If your child is a bit older, let him help you shop. Hand him a coupon with a picture of a food product on it and tell him to find it. (It's easier if you lead him to the right aisle.) After a few tries, he'll get pretty good at the game and you'll be able to shop in half the time.

MAJOR TUNE-UP

Because most of us grocery shop at least once a week, it makes sense to create a system that in the long run will save time. For those who feel time is money, however, the last tip is for you.

■ **The Master of All Lists** Create a customized master shopping list based on what you buy regularly. Save a month or two's worth of your grocery receipts to see your shopping habits; then prepare your own list of products on the computer (or write it up by hand) and sort items either by aisle, alphabetically, or by category. Leave a few blanks spots for new or overlooked products. Print up a copy each week and check off those items that you need. Take it with you when you grocery shop, and you'll be sure to get everything on your list.

■ **Pay the Perfect Price** Enhance your customized master list by adding a grocery price column. Having prices close at hand helps you identify a good bargain in the store. List separate prices from each of your favorite supermarkets to help make an informed decision. Include the everyday price and the unit price (how much per ounce, how much per roll, etc.). When a particular dish liquid goes on sale, for instance, you can check your price column to see what you usually pay for brand X and then you can decide if the sale item is a good buy or not.

■ **Online Is Fine** Although the online supermarket giant, Web Van, closed its cyberdoors a while back because of overwhelming fixed costs, many smaller, independent chains are actually thriving in the online grocery business. With online food shopping, you can place your order at any time of the day or night, and delivery, depending on the company, is usually within twenty-four hours. Besides the time factor, many reviewers of online grocery stores claim the quality meets or exceeds expectations. Yes, you will pay for delivery, but when you shop online, there's little chance you'll impulse spend—a true money saver. To find a cybergrocer in your area, ask your local supermarket if they're affiliated with one. Here are a few that I checked out. Peapod.com serves the Chicago and Northeast area; PeachTree.com is big in Canada but also delivers to New York State and Washington, D.C.; Egrocer.com covers Minnesota, Texas, Oregon, and California; and GroceryWorks.com is based in Texas. NetGrocer.com delivers to the lower forty-eight but doesn't deal with perishable goods; however, GrocerOnLine.com covers the entire country and does deliver perishables packed in dry ice.

All of my local stores are on Randell Road, but instead of going from one place to another, I start at the farthest end and work my way back to my street. It saves time by driving through the parking lots rather than trying to get back on that busy road.

Clothes Shopping Made Simple

Some people say they are born to shop and never tire of it; others enjoy the twice-yearly ritual to update their wardrobes and then move on to other things; and then, of course, there are those who loathe shopping altogether and put it off as long as possible. I'm going to assume that you fall in one of the last two groups. As a busy parent, you barely have enough time to lounge with the paper and a cup of coffee, never mind window-shop at the local mall.

KEY ORGANIZING TIPS

■ **Know Before You Go** There are two ways to shop for clothes: wander aimlessly until something strikes your fancy (aka impulse buying) or go with a specific list of those items that you need. The latter is much more time efficient, not to mention cost effective. Always keep a running list in your personal notebook of the clothing that you need to update your wardrobe—tailored black pants, white wool cardigan sweater, and so on—

and your current size. This helps in two ways. First, if you have a list when you visit the mall, you're less likely to buy something that you don't want, need, or even like. Second, if you happen to pass your favorite store and they're having a big sale, stop in for a moment to see if they have any of your items.

■ **Take Aim** Target the stores you want to visit by knowing where they're located in the mall (you can get a map of virtually any mall off the Web or call the center's customer service number and ask that they send you one). Avoid all other shops, where you'll just waste time and be tempted to splurge on something that you probably don't need.

■ **Dress for Comfort** Wear slip-on shoes, comfortable pants or skirt, and a neutral-colored shirt.

■ **Feelin' Good** Shop only when you're fully rested and fed. Don't shop to improve your mood—it will usually make you feel worse.

■ **Mail's In** Get on mailing lists (or E-mailing lists) to notify you of seasonal sales only if you truly love the store; otherwise, you'll just be bombarded with more useless paper.

■ **When in the Neighborhood** If you have a store that you truly like, stop by occasionally when you're in the neighborhood. Quickly peruse the sale rack and see if anything matches your clothing wish list. Frequent short visits rather than one long marathon shopping spree is a better use of your time.

■ **I'm Lovin' It** Only buy an article of clothing if you absolutely love it. If you're ambivalent (it's a bit tight or maybe the color isn't right), chances are it will only sit in your closet no matter what price you paid.

Clothes and Kids

My boys haven't quite reached the point where they are fashion conscious, so I haven't dealt with the daily wardrobe hassles or the "I've-gotta-have-these-$150-gym-shoes" battle, but I've been a careful observer of friends' older children and my own nieces and nephews. What have I learned? To kids, "in" clothes count—they can make the difference between having a good school year, fitting in with peers, or an uncomfortable one filled with teasing and humiliation. Although you want to be careful not to indulge your child's every fashion fantasy, when it's time to purchase back-to-school clothes, choose your battles carefully. Style is the number-one concern of kids, and they'll feel more comfortable at school if they like what they're wearing.

Because most clothing purchases for children are made in the month before and following the start of the new school year, that's where we'll concentrate our attention.

KEY ORGANIZING TIPS

- **Do You Have an Appointment?** Make an appointment to visit your child's closet with the clothes-conscious child herself. Ask her if there's anything that she no longer wants to wear (you've changed your mind about last year's fashions, too) and either donate them, hand them down, or move them to the back of the closet (she may change her mind in a month). Clothes that are stretched or worn out should be removed as well. Have her try on the remaining outfits to make sure they still fit. If not, donate or hand down.
- **Clothes Cruising** Browse through fall clothing catalogs, department store circulars, or surf the Web together to get a feel for the current looks. Have an informal discussion about fashion and what the difference is between clothing fads and clothing classics, and then talk about what's age appropriate. Give her some pointers on how to pull a wardrobe together by mixing and matching a few central pieces.
- **Wish List** Together, come up with a fashion plan in the form of a list before you head to the mall. Have your child write down what she'd like to buy, and then pare it down until it's reasonable and within the family budget. Make sure that your child understands what it means to stick to a budget and how if you go over this time, she may not be able to buy what she wants come next season.
- **Let the Buying Begin** Shop for clothes over several weeks rather than one long, exhausting day where the two of you will undoubtedly end up arguing. Besides, once school starts and she sees what the other kids are wearing, she may just change her mind about the clothes she likes and dislikes.

Holiday Shopping Made Simple

Although I love Christmas, sometimes getting ready for the holiday can be overwhelming, especially if I take on too many projects like hosting a holiday party, making cookies *and* gingerbread houses, or going to town on decorations inside the house and out. But shopping for presents can be the worst stress builder of all—too many kids, too many tastes, and not enough money. In recent years, however, I've come up with a system that has made it all more manageable—don't wait until the last minute to do everything and do only those holiday rituals that I really love (like building gingerbread houses) and forget the others (I'll get my fill of holiday cookies from everyone else out there baking).

KEY ORGANIZING TIPS

■ **Start Early** Don't wait until the last minute to Christmas shop. If you start shortly after the Season of Candy begins—Halloween—you're more likely to get the toys your kids want without paying an arm and a leg.

■ **Always Write** Make a list of everyone you need to buy a present for, including teachers, work colleagues, baby-sitters, the paperboy, your spouse or current companion, nieces and nephews, and, of course, your own kids. Specifically list what you'll purchase for each, or if you haven't a clue, jot down their interests.

■ **Budget Basics** Allocate a specific dollar amount for your gift buying based on your current annual budget, and then break it down for each person—$10 for each niece and nephew, $5 to $7 for work colleagues and teachers, $25 for the baby-sitter, $75 for each child, and so on. If you don't set up a Christmas budget and stick to it, you'll certainly be in trouble after the New Year when the credit card bills come in and you can't pay them.

■ **Receive a Receipt** Always get a receipt for all your purchases, no matter how small. It's the only way to ensure a full refund in case you need to return the product (ask the store to explain their return policy). To avoid confusion, write the name and model number of the item directly on the receipt. Many stores will supply gift receipts for your purchases, too, allowing the gift recipient to make an exchange if he chooses to do so. Don't worry—the price is left off the gift receipt, but the original purchase price is retained in the store's computer.

■ **The Way to Pay** Before you leave for the mall, pare down your wallet to only two credit cards—one card that must be paid off in full and a low-interest card for purchases that you'll pay off over time. Record all purchases in your checkbook, even if you don't write a check. This way, when the bill comes, you'll have the money to pay it off in full.

That's a Wrap:
Organizing a Gift-Wrapping Center

Just a twenty-four-inch-long space in your utility porch or laundry room is all you'll need to create a wrapping station. Mount curtain rods horizontally on the walls, six inches between each, just above your counter, and hang rolls of wrapping paper. Use a smaller rod to add spools of ribbon. Hang a basket to hold scissors and tape. Designate the cabinet directly below to act as a holding bin for all the goodies waiting to be decorated.

Or attach curtain rods for paper and ribbon and a basket for supplies on the inside of a closet door. Add a small, fold-down table to act as a counter, and use the inside top shelf of the closet to house unwrapped gifts. If space is tight, check out wrapping organizers—plastic containers that house wrapping paper, bows, and ribbons—available at a number of catalogs, including Lillian Vernon and Solutions. Just tuck it under the bed or in a spare closet.

■ **It's an Age Thing** When buying toys, always pay attention to the age recommendations on the package. Toys recommended for older children may pose a safety hazard to younger children through small or sharp parts.

■ **Safety First** Use common sense when shopping in crowded malls. Always keep a close eye on your children; never leave your purse, wallet, or credit card on the counter; take along a friend to run interference for you; and park in a well-lighted area as close to the mall entrance as possible.

The Early Bird Special

If you can drag yourself out of bed before dawn the day after Thanksgiving, you can save a bundle. The busiest shopping day of the year, that Friday is when most stores roll out the sales signs. But be prepared to deal with throngs of other budget-minded folks who are out for the best deals, too.

I like to start Christmas shopping around June. It's just little things, really. I'll be at the checkout stand at the drugstore, for instance, and pick up a videotape. Once a month I try to buy something, even if it's just one thing. I'll put it on my weekly grocery list so I won't forget.

QUICK FIX

Get to bed early (it's best if you don't cook the Thanksgiving dinner) if you want to catch the worm, and follow a few of these quick-fix ideas to make the most of your shopping spree.

■ **Plan of Action** No time for ambivalence when you're shopping with thousands of other pros—have a list of exactly what you're going to buy at which store. Have store circulars handy with products and prices circled and coupons clipped.

■ **Dress for Success** Don't be distracted or dragged down by your winter coat or bulky purse—leave them at home or in the car. Malls are hot and stuffy, anyway.

■ **The Blue-Light Special** Head for the "hot" toy first; otherwise, you may not get it. Then hit the remaining items on your list.

■ **The Boys in Green** Avoid long lines by paying in cash. Cash-only lines move much quicker.

■ **Time for a Test** Examine all electronics before you buy them to make sure they work. The last thing you want to do is head back to the store to exchange an item that malfunctions.

I have a big plastic bin that's a running gift box. Anytime I see something nice on sale that would be a great hostess gift, I buy it and put it in the box. If my husband comes home from the office and says, "So-and-so's birthday is tomorrow. Do you have anything I can give her?" I say, "Sure; let's go through the gift box." I've got stuff for everybody.

Catalog Convenience

Catalog shopping? Now you're talking. It's my preferred way to shop for Christmas and birthday gifts, household gadgets and home furnishings, and, on occasion, even clothing. What's the appeal? First, I save time. With three kids, a husband, a house to run—blah, blah, blah—time is precious. Yes, I like to head to the mall or window-shop down Main Street every now and then, but I'd much prefer to browse through a catalog at my leisure, day or night. No need to get in the car or battle for the perfect parking spot at the mall. And now that nearly every large chain puts out a mail-order catalog, why bother visiting the store in person? Also, I can see products such as home furnishings in a real setting. Instead of looking at a lamp simply hanging from a ceiling with dozens of others, I see it dressing up a real room. I get many decorating ideas perusing the pages of Pottery Barn, Crate & Barrel, Spiegel, and Frontgate.

> I do 95 percent of my Christmas shopping the first two weeks after Christmas. I go to all the sales and I stock up on tons of stuff. I'd rather deal with the crowds after Christmas than before the holiday. By shopping early, I have a relatively stress-free few weeks before Christmas. I save a ton of money, too—I usually get things for 50 to 75 percent off the regular price. Because I get the wrapping paper on sale too, after I bring the gifts home, I immediately wrap them. I don't put on the bows because they just get crushed. Then I put a Post-It note on the front of every gift saying who it's for and what the gift is—because I like to know what I got someone and I never remember eleven months later. Then I put them in large plastic bins with lids, and Dan puts them up in the attic. And it's done!

Clothes are a bit trickier. Because every manufacturer has different sizing standards, it's often hard to find the perfect fit. More often than not, I end up sending the garment back simply because it doesn't fit. Yet if you know the styles and colors that look good on you and you consistently shop with the same catalogs, you eventually get it right. Even true bargain hunters like me can save on catalog clothes shopping as more and more companies are adding clearance pages at the back of their catalogs offering tons of out-of-season bargains (selection and sizes are limited on catalog sales, so act quickly).

Yet my favorite is to shop by catalog for toys. It's the best way to avoid the holiday mall madness and save your sanity. Starting in October, toy catalogs begin to arrive in the mail fast and furious. Their colorful displays can entertain my boys for hours as they scan the pages and dog-ear nearly everything in sight. After a few weeks, I sit down with them and formulate their letters to Santa (but I do explain that Santa can't possibly bring them everything they ask for and he puts a limit of three things). Next, I go through the choices with my husband, and together we pick the items that we think fit each child's personality, interests, and our budget. I get on the phone after they're in bed, and in minutes, it's done.

T om wears a size fifteen shoe and it's really hard to find king-size socks to fit him. Now I get three catalogs that sell them—Repp, King Size, and JCPenney. It's much easier because it's nearly impossible to pop into a men's store and find them on display.

The Downside to Catalog Shopping

Obviously there are a few problems with shopping by catalog. My number-one complaint is when an item is on back order. All excited about finding the perfect comforter for your bed, you call the company, and the sales associate explains that it's out of stock—on back order—and won't be in until XYZ. Sometimes the wait can be just a few days; other times it turns into a few weeks or even months. When you shop in a store, on the other hand, and you see that perfect comforter, you pick it up, buy it, and take it home that day.

On occasion, I've received damaged goods—a broken lampshade, a cracked chair leg. Most catalogs have excellent customer service departments, and after a brief phone call explaining the problem, a new item is in the mail directly. Nonetheless, it's a disappointment and an inconvenience, for now you have to repackage the damaged product to send back to the company.

And, of course, when you catalog shop, you take the chance that you simply won't like what you've ordered once you get it out of the package. You run that risk when you buy something in a store as well, but at least you have the chance to examine the color, texture, and style closely before buying it.

If you do take the catalog plunge, pay attention to shipping costs, which can add a substantial amount to your order. Sometimes the amount is offset if you order from a catalog in a different state and you aren't required to pay sales tax on your purchases, but in other instances you'll have to pay both shipping and sales tax.

Shopping on the Internet

Recently, we renovated my sons' bathroom. And where did I shop for the bathroom sink, faucet, tile, and tub? The Internet, of course. Not only can you find just about anything on the World Wide Web, but I've found many sites to be competitively priced. And just like catalog shopping, I can save an enormous amount of time browsing through dozens of virtual stores any time of the day or night, for five minutes or five hours. Yet if you're not comfortable using your credit card online, not to worry. Most sites include a toll-free number. Simply find what you like online, and then call the company directly to order what you want.

INTERNET SHOPPING TIPS

■ **Order Only on Secure Sites** Protect yourself by ordering from a secure server—check for an unbroken key or padlock in your browser window usually located at the bottom of your screen.

■ **Protect Your Privacy** Read up on a company's online privacy policy where it discloses how they use your personal information. Only give out your personal information if you know why they're collecting it and how it's used. Never give out your social security number or personal bank account number (paying by credit card offers the best consumer protection). And if you're required to form an account with a password, never use your Internet password, and use a different one for each account.

When I'm shopping and I'm confronted with a possible purchase, I don't ask "Is this a good bargain?" or "Could I use this?" Instead I ask "Where am I going to put it?" and "What's the worst thing that will happen if I don't buy this today?" It's very helpful. What's the worst thing that could happen, for instance, if I don't buy the nifty little chip-and-dip combo plate? I'll have to serve the guacamole and chips in two separate dishes.

My Favorite Places

Now, I'm no shopping guru by any means (although it does seem that way after rereading this section), but I have been around the consumer block a few times, so here's a list of my favorite catalog and Internet sites. For a more complete inventory, call to request a catalog, but be sure to check out each company's website for Internet discounts. (And yes, I get each and every one of these catalogs in the mail regularly. Actually more, but these are my favorites.)

Toys

Lillian Vernon Pages of kid's favorites, all within the average family's budget. Great customer service. 800-545-5426; lillian vernon.com

Young Explorers For scientific minds. 888-239-7577; young explorers.com

Back to Basics Toys Great old-fashioned wood toys; plenty of other well-made games, too. 800-356-5360

Everything for the Home

Pottery Barn/Pottery Barn Bed + Bath/Pottery Barn Kids Three different catalogs, three different companies, yet you can order from any one of their toll-free numbers (it gets confusing). Stylish home furnishings with great customer service. Great deals on clearance items, if you can get to them in time! Pottery Barn, 800-922-5507; Pottery Barn Bed + Bath, 888-779-4044; Pottery Barn Kids, 800-430-7373; potterybarn.com

Martha by Mail Martha Stewart is the queen of style and organization. Need I say more? Her catalog is filled with high-end household goodies. 800-950-7130; marthabymail.com

Sundance Robert Redford's nonprofit institute puts out a fabulous catalog filled with home furnishings, accessories, women's fashions, and jewelry, all with a Southwest touch. A real page-turner, but no bargains here. 800-422-2770; sundancecatalog.com

Rue de France Luscious French country furnishings and accessories. Lots of one-of-a-kind items, but no deals here. 800-777-0998; ruedefrance.com

French Country Living Colorful home furnishings with a European flair; provincial china, cookery, and table linen. 800-485-1302

Ballard Designs Lots of wrought-iron and slightly distressed furniture in an opulent European style. 800-367-2775; ballard designs.com

Home Decorators Collection Huge selection of midrange furniture, lighting, rugs, and accessories. 800-245-2217; home decorators.com

Ross-Simons Pages of crystal stemware, flatware and china, jewelry, gifts for the house, and home furnishings—all at very attractive prices. 800-458-4545; ross-simons.com

Lillian Vernon Neat Ideas Affordable gadgets and gifts for the home. Daily phone specials. 800-545-5426; lillianvernon.com

Solutions Lots of storage ideas and gadgets for the home; seasonal items, too. 800-342-9988; solutionscatalog.com

Holdeverything The answer to all your storage needs lies within these pricey pages (but they do offer decent sales on discontinued items). 800-421-2264; williams-sonoma.com, then click on the Holdeverything icon

Sur La Table Everything an aspiring cook could dream of, but pricey. 800-243-0852; surlatable.com

Williams-Sonoma Another cooking giant with equally high prices. 800-541-2233; williams-sonoma.com

Ceramica Gorgeous Italian pottery and tableware in more than sixteen traditional patterns made by master craftsmen. 800-270-0900; ceramicadirect.com

Smith & Hawken High-quality products for your garden—tools, accessories, apparel, and patio furniture. Look for 20 percent savings on end-of-the-season items. 800-776-3336; smithand hawken.com

Gardener's Supply Company Offers more nuts-and-bolts gardening supplies than Smith & Hawken, such as compost bins, fertilizers, bird feeders, and so on. 800-427-3363; gardeners.com

Home Improvement

Home Portfolio Log on and choose a room, a fixture, a style, a price range, and click—you can browse through dozens of products and choose a dealer near you. Love this site. homeportfolio.com

Kohler The kitchen and bath giant has an excellent website. Narrow your search on dozens of products such as faucets, sinks, tubs, and shower doors. Great selection, well-written descriptions, and, for the budget-conscious consumer, manufacturers' suggested list prices. kohlerco.com

Women's Fashions

J. Jill Comfortable, casual women's fashions, shoes, and accessories. Great clearance deals online. Sometimes offers free shipping on minimum orders. 800-642-9989; jjill.com

Coldwater Creek Classic women's clothing (lovely costume jewelry, too) with a bit of Southwest appeal. Check out their online site for great clearance deals. 800-262-0040; coldwatercreek.com

Hanna Andersson Darling kids apparel. A little pricey. 800-222-0544; hannaandersson.com

Aerosoles The most comfortable woman's shoe known to humankind. Excellent deals on end-of-the-season styles. Customer service can be questionable, so choose carefully. 800-798-9478; aerosoles.com

■ **Always Comparison Shop** There are a few great sites out there that will compare online shopping sites for you: CNET (cnet.com) and Price Grabber (pricegrabber.com) both are excellent sources for comparing electronics. For a wider span of products, try My Simon (my simon.com), Gomez (gomez.com), or Biz Rate (bizrate.com).

■ **Deal with Reputable Companies** If you've never heard of a particular online company, check with the Better Business Bureau (bbbon line.org) or the state attorney general's office.

■ **Keep Tabs on Your Purchases** Print a copy of your confirmation sheet listing the details of your transaction and file it in a safe place.

■ **Check Shipping Costs** Choose the delivery option that best suits your needs, and remember to add the cost—sometimes substantial—to your overall purchase.

Shop till You Drop

We've all got to shop. Whichever method you choose—in person, by catalog, or online—think twice before you make that purchase. Remember, it's more to store!

Vacations

ast March, my husband and I took our three young boys to Disneyland for the first time. Although we live only an hour from the mega-theme park, we booked two adjoining rooms at the brand-spanking-new Grand California Hotel (a great place, by the way), where we were to rendezvous with my sister, brother-in-law, and my two nieces. The plan was that we'd get there in the afternoon, making sure we got a couple of choice rooms, just in time for my sister and her family to arrive on a 5 P.M. flight from Chicago. But no sooner had we unpacked than the whining began.

"Why can't we go to Disneyland *now*?" asked our number-two son, Michael.

"This is the worst vacation ever," cried Joseph. (That one hurt, considering the cost of this little getaway.)

"I want to go swimming," lamented little Matthew. (It was close to 5 P.M. and quite chilly.)

My husband and I just threw up our hands in frustration. But this little scenario is pretty typical. Kids want what they want when they want it, and expecting them to act any differently while on vacation, no matter how much money you're spending, is futile. Fortunately, we got a handle on the situation quickly (we let them go swimming), and the rest of the weekend went down in the memory books as a great time.

Sometimes traveling with kids seems more trouble than it's worth— think of the stress just to get to your destination (you try installing *three* car seats in an airplane with 200 disgruntled passengers breathing down your neck to pass), temper tantrums in public places, impossible sleeping accommodations (five people in *one* room), a cranky toddler who missed his nap (so we could take in one more museum). So, why do we do it? Why do we go through all the trouble, time, and expense of organizing a family vacation? Because somewhere along the way your kids win your heart, and you actually begin to talk *to them* instead of just *at them*. Maybe it's the look of pure excitement and joy as they ride Dumbo for the first time that tugs at you. Or they actually play quietly at the restaurant table and let you truly enjoy your meal (that someone else cooked, by the way). Perhaps they snuggle up next to you on the beach blanket, their hair fragrant with salt air, and tell you that this is the best vacation in the whole world. And you agree. Then you think, yes, that's why I went through all the trouble.

So, what's the secret to success? How do ensure that every trip will be one for the memory books? You can't; but it helps to try. When you're traveling as a pack, I've learned you hope for the best but expect the worst. Planning ahead for all sorts of situations and approaching the experience with a sense of humor can make the difference between having a good time and a bad one.

Plan of Action

Whether you're a real hands-on person who loves investigating and orchestrating your family's trip down to the last detail or you prefer to let a professional travel agent handle all the fine points and you just sign the check, planning is the most important aspect of traveling anywhere. When you take the time to do the legwork, you'll make the best decisions based on your family's interests and passions on where to go and what to do.

KEY ORGANIZING TIPS

- **Choose a Family-Friendly Destination** When deciding where to take your clan, make sure both the destination and the accommodations cater to families. These days, that's not hard to do as more and more hotels vie for your family's hard-earned cash, but some places still aren't used to accommodating parents and their kids. Even cities can be fun for young children, providing it's the right city (New York, Chicago, and Los Angeles are all good choices). Before booking a room, ask yourself a few important questions: are there enough activities at your chosen destination to please every member of the family, not just the parents? Does the hotel have amenities such as cribs and free in-room movies? Does the dining room offer a kids' menu? And what about a pool? Nothing's better after a long day of sightseeing than returning to your hotel and heading for the pool.

■ **The Early Bird . . .** A good rule of thumb for any major vacation (a week or more) is to give yourself ten months to plan it (of course, there are many last-minute deals out there waiting for a spur-of-the-moment family). When you start early, you get the best choice in airline and hotel reservations, you're better able to investigate many different vacation options (whether to go to an oceanfront resort or stay at a lodge in a national park), and when you have time on your side, you can compare prices from various sources, making sure that you get the best deal.

■ **Children Rule** Although it may be tempting to plan your trip around the things you used to do before you had kids, such as antique hunting, that may not jive with your youngest household members. Instead, try to organize a trip around at least some of their interests. It's much easier for you to enjoy the trip through your children's eyes than expecting them to "act adult" as you plead with them to take in one more historic site.

■ **Compromise** Your oldest wants to go sledding, your youngest wants to go skiing, and you'd just as soon sit by a big, roaring fire in the lodge. Although it's impossible to please everyone all of the time, try to plan your trip so that each person gets to do something they value. (Yes, even Mom and Dad deserve to do something they want to do, too.)

■ **Don't Obsess** The best trips are the ones that have been carefully planned, but realize that anything can happen—a toddler suddenly gets a stomachache, a teenager's mood grows sullen. Leave room in your day for unstructured play, and always have a contingency plan in case something is closed or doesn't deliver what was promised in the guidebook. Most importantly, have a sense of adventure. Be ready to throw out the "schedule" in favor of spontaneity.

■ **A Need to Read** Whether you're heading to Paris, Texas, or Paris, France, read up on your chosen destination. Brushing up on the local history and culture prior to departure will enhance your trip by giving what you see and experience depth and meaning. And make it a family affair—

perhaps spend ten minutes after dinner letting everyone share what he or she has just learned on the Internet or read in a book from the library.

I like family road trips. There's an excitement about it, and there's a feeling of closeness—you have to be together in a small space for a long time. We always take a relaxed approach. When we have to stop, we stop. And we're always prepared with enough food and drinks for the kids to snack on and enough things to do, from toys and road games to books and music.

Where Should We Go?

The first order of business is deciding where to go. For some, this is a no-brainer—they rent a cabin in the mountains or a cottage near the beach and off they go. For others, however, the decision is much harder.

To help you decide where to take the family, take your cues from past holidays. What worked and what didn't? On your last vacation, did you do too much driving and every minute in the car seemed relentless? Consider your family's lifestyle and current interests, too. Do they like to be on the go, hopping from the aquarium to the zoo, or do they prefer to hang out on a beach or by a pool?

When narrowing down your destination possibilities, consider your children's ages, too. If your kids are old enough, you may want to ask them for their ideas, but, ultimately, it's the folks who pay the bills who decide where to spend the vacation buck, so consider these age-appropriate guidelines.

AGE-APPROPRIATE DESTINATIONS

- **Infants and Babies** Little ones are adaptable travelers, falling asleep in even the strangest environments, such as noisy restaurants. Unfortunately, they require lots of equipment, from cribs to diapers. It's often tough to stick to baby's routine while in a new place—if you don't, he's bound to get fussy. So, where do you go? Beach and lake vacations are not a good choice (the sun is too intense for young skin) and neither are theme parks (one parent will hang back as the other enjoys all the rides). Yet sightseeing vacations in large cities are a good bet as long as you pick a centrally located hotel where you can pop back and forth as needed. Camping is a good choice, too, as long as she enjoys seeing the scenery from a backpack.

■ **Preschoolers** Three- to five-year-olds are an easy group to please. They find excitement in just about all new things, from the hotel ice machine to the room key. Yet you never know when disaster will strike (aka tantrums). Their short attention span is also a challenge—they'll be ready to move on to something new after ten minutes. Resort vacations are great at this age (make sure they have a child-care program to allow for some adult time) and so is any spot with water—lakes, oceans, rivers—as long as the kids are supervised properly. City vacations are good, too, provided you schedule lots of short, entertaining activities such as a quick visit to the natural history museum to look at dinosaurs and lots of downtime at neighborhood parks.

■ **School-Age Children** More independent, less labor intensive than their younger siblings, school-age children are a bit more reasonable. Yet these guys are an opinionated bunch and can develop a poor attitude in a minute ("This is boring"). It's best to be on the go with this group. Try a visit to theme parks or a resort or cruise with lots of activities for kids. You may even want to think about heading to Europe right about now. (Remember, a young adult overseas airline ticket is 25 percent less than an adult ticket—it goes to full fare after age twelve.)

■ **Teenagers** Teens need to feel included, so let them have a say in the planning on where to go and what to do. With their burgeoning independence, they also crave time alone, so pick a destination where you'll feel comfortable allowing them some freedom to come and go as they please. Resorts, cruises, and many adventure-type trips (skiing, river rafting, mountain biking) are ones to consider. If you choose a destination that is a bit remote and the chances of your teen meeting someone his or her own age are slim, consider allowing your teen to bring a friend along. Although it's an added expense and a loss of some family privacy, a content teen is worth its weight in gold.

■ **One of Each** Infant, toddler, school-age child, and teenager—you have one of each. Now what? Consider the opinions of the older siblings as a starting point, but your best bet is to stick with a spot that offers lots of activities for all ages (all-inclusive resorts and cruises are a perfect match).

QUICK FIX

If the thought of finding a dozen kid-friendly restaurants and a host of entertaining daytime venues seems a bit daunting, give yourself a break and try one of these quick-fix destination ideas.

■ **All-Inclusive Resorts** Whether you're looking for a mountain retreat or a seaside paradise, lots of resorts these days are all-inclusive—room, meals, activities, and even airfare are included in the price. What could be simpler?

1. **Club Med** Not just for swinging singles any longer, Club Med has several first-class resorts worldwide that cater solely to families. Their children's programs are broken down into age groups—Petit, Mini Clubs, and Kids Clubs; plus several locations offer Baby Clubs, Circus Workshops, and Kids' Tennis Programs. Call 800-CLUB MED; or log on to clubmed.com.

2. **Beaches** Owned by the Sandals family, this organization offers three deluxe resorts in the Caribbean. Nursery facilities for babies (with Ultra Nannies), Kids' Kamp, and Teen Disco. Call 888-BEACHES; or log on to beaches.com.

■ **Cruising** A floating resort with more food and activities than you could ever imagine, cruising is a great choice for any sea-loving family.

1. **Disney Cruise Line** Disney offers separate activity areas, all fully supervised, for kids ages three to twelve and a special hangout just for teens, complete with photography and movie-making classes, on all its cruises to the Caribbean. Call 800-951-3532; or log on to disney.go.com/disneycruise/index .html.

2. **Carnival Cruise Lines** With more than fifteen "Fun Ships" with ports of call in Alaska, Hawaii, the Mexican Riviera, the Caribbean, and the Bahamas, Carnival has a destination for every family. Camp Carnival operates on all ships with age-appropriate programs for kids two to fifteen. Call 800-327-9501; or log on to carnival.com.

3. **Windjammer Barefoot Cruises** Sail to the Caribbean aboard one of five tall-masted ships. Supervised programs include Junior Jammers' Club and Cadet Programs for the teen who wants to learn how to sail. Call 800-327-2601; or log on to windjammer.com.

The Disney Cruise had excellent service. There were so many people to take care of you. And the ship was very clean—the accommodations were meticulous. But I felt that the kids' camp was lacking—I didn't think there was anything exceptional. Olivia didn't even look forward to it, which is very unlike her. For the adults—I couldn't even get near the pool until 11 P.M. because it was so packed with people.

■ **Dude Ranch** Up with the sun riding the range or hanging out by the pool after a midmorning hike—a dude ranch vacation isn't just about rounding up the cattle (although on some working ranches guests are encouraged to come along and lend a hand). With more than 450 ranches throughout the West, you'll find the perfect match, be it a rustic lodge with family-style meals or an opulent cabin complete with breathtaking mountain views. Many offer children's programs. Log on to duderanches.com for a complete list including amenities (fishing, biking, tennis, etc.). Or call the Dude Ranchers Association for a list of properties throughout the West and Canada at 970-223-8440.

■ **Family Travel Agent** Believe it or not, there are travel agents out there who specialize in arranging trips just for families. Whether a weekend in New York or a month on the French Riviera, these seasoned veterans of family travel will not only steer you in the right direction, but handle all the details as well. Log on to Family Travel Forum (familytravelforum.com) or Family Travel Guides (familytravelguides.com) for a list of family friendly agents. Or contact Rascals in Paradise, based in San Francisco (800-U-RASCAL; rascalsinparadise.com) or Vacation Kids Travel Agent (610-681-7360; vacationkids.com).

MAJOR TUNE-UP

If the idea of a custom-made journey gets your heart pumping, you'll still need a bit of help putting it all together. There are lots of options out there, so take your time and ask around for recommendations.

■ **Log On** Cyberspace is exploding with websites offering everything you'll need to plan and book a vacation. However, with so many to choose from, you could spend months just surfing the Internet and never making any concrete plans. It's best to approach the Internet with an idea of where you want to go—the Caribbean, a national park, Europe, Australia—and the type of accommodations (rustic or five star) that interest you, and then log on to specific sites to help put your plan into action. But how do you know if you're getting a good deal? Travel experts advise comparing several sites before making a commitment.

1. **Fodors.com** Create a city miniguide (there are dozens of cities to select from) by downloading your own personal list of restaurants, shops, attractions and sites, and even maps. Don't miss the Family Travel Center, an excellent resource for traveling tips and bargains, plus great links to theme parks and resorts.

2. **Frommers.com** The king of budget travel, Arthur Frommers' site lets you do a fast hotel, restaurant, nightlife, or shopping search in dozens of cities around the world. The site also has full content of its print guides online. Still don't know where to go? Try browsing Vacation Ideas—road trips, skiing, tropical, offbeat—for inspiration.

3. **Expedia.com and Travelocity.com** Two powerhouse sites where you can book a hotel room, make a plane reservation, or rent a car. Also reserve tour packages on a cruise ship. Or try **Orbitz.com** for some great deals on airfare.

■ **Condo and Apartment Rentals and Home Exchange** An average hotel room can be confining for a family traveling with young children. And where do you warm Junior's bottle at night? Because the cost of most hotel suites with kitchenettes is prohibitive, a better alternative is to rent a condo or apartment. Not only do they offer scads more space, the price is comparable to one night in a hotel. Plus, you get a kitchen so you can save more by preparing some of your meals in your home-away-from-home. Check out Vacation Condos (call 800-932-6658; or log on to vacationcondos.com) for a large selection throughout the United States (with lots to choose from in Hawaii), Mexico, Canada, and the Caribbean. Villas International Realty rents high-end properties throughout the Caribbean, New York, Florida, and several European locations (call 561-835-8200; or log on to villasinternational.com); or there's Resort Quest International, which rents condos in all corners of the globe (call 877-588-5800; or log on to resortquest.com). If you really want to travel on a shoestring yet live royally, consider a home exchange—swap your three-bedroom home just outside of Miami for a three-bedroom home right outside of London. Sounds good to me. Intervac, the largest home-exchange agency in the United States, has subscribers in more than fifty countries (call 800-756-HOME; or log on to intervac.com).

■ **State or Foreign Tourist Board** The first stop for all vacation planners should be the state or foreign department of tourism. For the price of a phone call (or a stamp), they will send you a plethora of helpful maps, brochures on local attractions, and lots of travel tips on local customs, weather, types of available transportation, and road conditions.

■ **Book It** Check out the travel section of your local bookstore or library for titles on family travel, or write to *Carousel Press* (carousel press.com) and ask for their *Family Travel Guides Catalogue*, a comprehensive listing of family travel books, activity books, and audiocassettes: P.O. Box 6061, Albany, CA 94706-0061 (include a self-addressed stamped envelope); or call 510-527-5849.

⏰ **TIME-SAVER**—Make all restaurant reservations *before* you leave home, allowing you more time to concentrate on relaxing with your family. Most restaurants will take reservations up to two months ahead of time (longer if they're in a resort setting, for example, Disneyworld). Don't know where to go? Pick up one of the many different Zagat or Michelin "red guides" for comprehensive reviews, or log on to their respective websites—Zagat.com and Michelin.com.

Making It a Family Affair

Although you will ultimately decide where the family will spend your vacation, try planning at least part of the trip together with your kids. Not only will it allow everyone to share in the excitement and anticipation of your upcoming adventure, but working together as a team also builds family trust and love. It's educational, too, as you all study maps of foreign countries spread across the kitchen table and read aloud about interesting and unusual customs. Finally, being a part of the planning makes children invested in a favorable outcome.

In the early stages of your planning, hold a family meeting to fill the kids in on your various vacation ideas. Next, divide up tasks such as writing away for further information, searching the attic for luggage, or even heading to the library for interesting books on your destination. Obviously,

Packing the Perfect Suitcase

Heading to a Caribbean resort or Disneyworld in Florida for a week this spring and want to pack "light"? Compare your list against this one, and let's see who's the lightest. Resist packing your couture collection—this is a vacation, after all, a time of casual relaxation. And remember—most hotels have coin-operated laundry rooms on the premises if you do run out of clean clothes.

For older female family members:

- Four pairs of socks, panties, and bras (wash in the sink as you go)
- Swimsuit (plus lightweight cover-up)
- Four T-shirts
- One nightgown (or use a T-shirt)
- One long-sleeved shirt
- Two dressy shirts (sleeveless blouse or polo type)
- Two pairs of shorts
- One pair dress pants
- Two skirts or one skirt and one sundress
- Two pair of shoes—comfortable for sightseeing; dressy for dinner
- Flip-flops (for walking to and from the pool)
- One lightweight sweater

For older male family members:

- Four pairs of socks and underwear (wash in the sink as you go)
- Swim trunks
- Four T-shirts
- Two pairs of shorts
- One pair of pajamas (or use T-shirt)
- One long-sleeved shirt
- Two pairs dress pants
- One sport coat
- Two dress shirts (polo type or short-sleeve dress shirt)
- Two pair of shoes—comfortable and dressy
- Flip-flops
- One lightweight sweater

For kids:
- Four pairs of socks and underwear (wash in the sink as you go)
- Swimsuit
- Six T-shirts (use one for pajamas)
- Three pairs of shorts
- One long-sleeved shirt
- Two pairs of dress pants for boys; one pair for girls
- Two skirts or one skirt and one sundress for girls
- Two dressy shirts
- Two pairs of shoes—comfortable and dressy
- Flip-flops
- One lightweight sweater

the more complicated responsibilities (checking airfares on the Web or E-mailing a resort for their latest brochure) should go to the older members of the household. But little guys can help, too. Let your preschooler be in charge of the travel folder, and let her file incoming travel literature. Have her pick out a travel journal at the stationery store, or when you head to the automobile club for trip information, have her ask the attendant for the maps (with your coaching, of course). Even these simple assignments help make a youngster feel important and needed, not to mention build self-reliance.

Packing Pointers

Your reservations are set and you're ready to go. Well, not quite. Now comes the often-arduous task of what to take and what to leave behind.

Once your plans are under way, jot down packing notes—what you'll need, what you should buy, what you can borrow, and so forth. Set aside an out-of-the-way spot in the house where you can begin to compile your goodies—maybe on a bed in a spare room or even an empty shelf in your pantry. Check off each item as you locate or buy it.

As your kids get older and gain more experience traveling, you can let them pack their own bags, but be sure to do a spot check of the contents; otherwise, you might be in for a few unexpected surprises. (When I was in the fourth grade, my mom let me do my own packing for a family trip in April to Quebec. We were all a bit surprised when it snowed the first night we were there, but she was shocked to find that I had only packed shorts and T-shirts for the trip. Hey, aren't all spring vacations to someplace warm? Needless to say, we had to visit the local department store for a pair of pants and a sweater.)

KEY ORGANIZING TIPS

■ **Less Is Best** Be honest—did you really wear all the clothes you packed on your last vacation? Do you really need to pack a long dress or suit and tie "just in case"? If you've ever tried to hurry through an airport terminal only to be slowed by a pair of cumbersome bags, you know that having an outfit for every evening is truly overrated. When it comes to packing, less is definitely best. Before organizing your suitcase, lay everything out on your bed and force yourself to pare it down. Chances are you'll have enough (if not, most of the world has washing machines).

■ **Double Duty** To cut down on your packing even more, think of items that can work double duty—one item that can do the job of two. Shoes are especially vulnerable in this area. Rather than packing a pair for every mood, limit yourself to two—a comfortable walking shoe and a dressier pair for evening. Pack clothing that's versatile—garments that can be worn sightseeing during the day but can be dressed up for dinner at night.

■ **Clothing Savvy** When traveling with young kids, pack dark-colored and striped clothing. They hide dirt and stains much better than tennis whites, so you won't be changing your little messy eaters twice a day. For adults, pack separates in one or two neutral colors so that you can mix and match your outfits. Choose fabrics that wear well and wrinkle less, such as knits and blends. (Stay away from linen!)

■ **Every Man for Himself (or Every Woman for Herself)** Either way, the message is the same—every person is responsible for his or her own bag. Even children as young as two can wheel their own suitcases (provided they're a kid-friendly size). I bought my boys child-sized bags with wheels, pop-up handles, and lots of outside pockets (Target has some). They love rolling them through the airport (honestly, no complaining). The best part is, the bags are small enough to store under an airline seat yet roomy enough to include "blankies," toys, and snacks for the trip.

■ **How Do You Say** *Diapers* **in French?** Although it's tempting to pack *everything* you'll need for a two-week trip, it's often a waste of time and space. No need to pack ten-dozen disposable diapers; these days nearly every country in the world sells them. (Some families, however, devote an entire suitcase to diapers and then fill the emptied luggage with souvenirs.) Besides, some of the most memorable vacations are the ones where you shop at a local mom-and-pop establishment for something as simple as shampoo.

I use mousse for my hair, but I hate packing the big bottle it comes in because it sometimes leaks. Instead, I squeeze the amount I need for my trip into a small freezer bag; when I get to the hotel, I snip the corner of it and squeeze out what I need. I just toss the bag when it's time to go home.

QUICK FIX

No need to rush out and buy the latest lightweight suitcase complete with two dozen zippered compartments and a sturdy set of wheels (although if it's time to invest in a new piece, that is the way to go). There are lots of little packing tips that not only save space, but help you to properly organize so that you can find anything you need in a snap.

■ **Bag It** Roll up clothes and store in large, resealable freezer bags—T-shirts in one bag, underwear and socks in another, shorts in a third, and so forth. It keeps clothes neat, and it's a breeze to search for what you need on the road without disturbing the entire contents of your bag.

■ **Bag It Two** Save all those little cosmetic bags that you get as give-aways when you buy department store cosmetics. Use one to stash all dental supplies, another for a first-aid kit, a third for hair-care products, and so on. By separating toiletries into smaller, more manageable totes rather than one large bag, you'll be able to find what you need quickly. To avoid confusion, label each one on the outside. Always keep them stocked with travel-sized toiletries so that you can pack them each time without having to check their contents.

■ **Roll It** The verdict is in—when it comes to saving valuable suitcase space, rolling your clothes beats folding. Small rolled bundles fit in a variety of different crevices better than bulky folded garments. Besides, rolled clothes stay wrinkle free longer.

■ **Toss It** We all buy something new for an upcoming getaway, whether it's clothing or toiletries, but be sure to unwrap the new item from its packaging—it'll be easier to stash in your suitcase.

⏰ **TIME-SAVER**—Don't spend too much time perfectly pressing your outfits before you pack them. Most likely you'll have to touch up a few with an iron before you wear them anyway. Most hotels now have an iron and ironing board in every room (with the exception of cruise-ship cabins—it's a fire hazard) or one available at the front desk.

MAJOR TUNE-UP

If you're a family on the go, it pays to spend the money to buy each member of the clan a high-quality, soft-sided piece of luggage (two-wheel models with retractable handles are easier to navigate than four-wheel types). Test-drive several models from a reputable luggage dealer before setting down the big bucks (expect to pay anywhere from $200 to $500 per piece, although you can find several good deals online or on sale). In addition, try these tips to ease your packing frenzies.

■ **List Logic** Years ago, my husband and I camped every summer in the national parks in the West. Packing was always a major undertaking because we needed cooking equipment, sleeping paraphernalia, and hiking gear, in addition to clothing and toiletries. It helped, however, once we established a permanent packing list that we drew up and kept on file. Broken down into several categories—clothing, toiletries, cook gear, camp gear, and so forth—it was much easier to gather up our equipment. Nothing was ever left behind, either, because as we packed it into a box, bag, or suitcase, we simply checked the item off our photocopied list. Committed families on the go can take the packing list concept and develop it even further by making a variety of travel lists to suit specific destinations. If you head to the beach house in the summer, for instance, establish a beach packing list. Like the mountains in the winter? Make one up for that, too. Do the first list by hand because you'll be adding and subtracting items up until the last minute, and even on your trip you'll discover a few omissions or gratuitous items. Edit as you go. Once home, however, hit the computer and type up your final revision. Make several copies (you'll toss one after each trip), and file them in your travel folder.

Top Ten Travel Gadgets

If you're like me, you love all the little travel gadgets that you get to use only when you travel. As simple as most of them are, they can truly make a trip more pleasant. In the following list of favorite travel goodies, not all will pertain to your type of trip (obviously you won't need a travel alarm clock at a four-star resort, where a clock radio is sure to grace your nightstand, but it sure comes in handy in a small European inn); just pick and choose for your particular circumstances. Most products are sold through travel stores or online: try Easy Going Travel Shop (easygoing.com) or The Travel Store (travelitems.com).

1. **Swiss Army Knife** Never mind just traveling, you should never leave home without one of these babies—about four inches long and only an inch thick, a Swiss Army knife can do just about anything except pack your suitcase. About $25. (You can no longer carry pocketknives onboard an aircraft; you can, however, pack them in your checked luggage.)

2. **Fanny Pack** Less cumbersome than a purse, a fanny pack rests on your hips, putting no weight on your back like a backpack. It's a perfect hands-free bag. About $20.

3. **Luggage Cart with Bungee Cord** If you insist on bringing your car seats for your kids on the airplane, and you certainly should, then you need a collapsible luggage cart. We've amazed fellow passengers and crewmembers alike by fitting *three* car seats on one cart. They're also great at carrying everyone's luggage so another adult is free to watch the kids as the other carts the bags. About $40 for a sturdy model.

4. **Travel Light** Why is it that most hotels have just one nightstand with one bedside lamp when there's usually two of you sharing the bed? No need to argue who gets the side with the nightstand (or disturb

sleeping children with a glaring light); try a small travel light that clips directly onto your book or magazine. It has a strong, focused beam that illuminates the whole page, yet it won't disturb the person sleeping next to you. About $25.

5. **Calculator** Not just for converting foreign currency, a calculator can help with the restaurant tip and is a constant help in ensuring that your trip stays on budget. About $10.

6. **Night-Light** If you've got kids, you've got to travel with two night-lights—one for the hallway near an exit and one in the bathroom. About $3 each.

7. **Compact Bag** There's never enough room in your suitcase for all those wonderful souvenirs that you unearth while traveling. To be sure that they don't get left behind in the hotel, bring a lightweight nylon gym bag, fold it up tight, and store it in the bottom of your suitcase. About $20.

8. **Coffee Coil** Whether you crave a cup of tea at the end of the day or want to make the kids a quick bowl of oatmeal in the morning, a coffee coil will boil a cup of water in minutes (to prevent a scalding accident, be sure to use it away from little hands). About $11.

9. **Earplugs and Eyeshades** A room with a view can sometimes mean a room with an awful amount of outside noise, whether it's the traffic from a busy piazza or boat horns on that pristine lake. Neither is charming at 1 A.M., when you're trying to sleep. Between $5 and $10.

10. **Menu Translator** Tricky little eaters will be relieved to know that *amurghese alla tirolese* is actually a hamburger and onion rings (at least in Italy). Paperback menu translators take up just inches in your fanny pack and can mean the difference between a dining disaster and a fantastic feast. About $10.

■ **One Outfit per Bag** Some families with small children find that arranging a complete outfit—top, bottom, and underwear—in a resealable plastic bag saves on time and confusion. The child simply pulls out a bag and gets dressed. (Light packers will consider this overkill.)

■ **Stop Stepping on Me** Did you ever wonder how to pack your shoes so that they won't dirty your clothes? One quick fix is to pack them in plastic grocery store bags, but a neater alternative is to tuck each shoe inside a cloth wine bag (available at gift and houseware stores), pull the drawstrings, and place in your bag.

■ **Packing Systems** Peruse any travel store, either online or at the mall, and you'll find several interesting packing systems. Pack-It envelopes and cubes from Eagle Creek come in a variety of different sizes and are color coded to help organize your clothes wrinkle free. Their smallest envelope, for example, can hold seven dress shirts neatly; their largest holds dresses and jackets. There are even Pack-It containers for shoes, Spillproof Neat-Pac Sacks (lined to keep messes to a minimum), and Wet-Dry Pack-It Cubes for transporting damp laundry or bathing suits. (To view the complete line, log on to eaglecreek.com.)

Pack-Mate bags boast that you can create 75 percent more space in your suitcase when you use one of their triple-laminated plastic bags. How do they do it? As you roll your clothes in one of their resealable bags, air escapes through a one-way valve, reducing the content's volume. (Available at travel stores, or try Solutions' catalog.)

⏰ **TIME-SAVER**—Before leaving for your vacation, either make or buy a favorite quick meal such as a chicken potpie or homemade tomato sauce and freeze it. The last thing you'll want to do on the day you return is think about cooking dinner. Just open up the freezer, thaw, heat, and dinner is ready.

Almost out the Door

In the weeks and days prior to leaving, there's much on your mind—from remembering to stop the newspaper and mail delivery to asking the teen next door to mow your lawn. How do you keep it all straight? Write it down, of course. Call it *Countdown to Vacation* and model it after the packing list described above. It may help to divide your list into time slots, such as *Two to Three Months Ahead* (get passports, assess equipment, etc.); *One Month Ahead* (get airline seat assignments; make sure auto club membership is current; gather all prescriptions, including eyeglasses; etc.); *Two Weeks Ahead* (get traveler's checks, arrange for airport shuttle, etc.); *One Week Ahead* (pay all bills, etc.); *Twenty-Four Hours Ahead* (set light and sprinkler timers, pack the car, empty refrigerator, etc.); and *Out the Door* (throw out trash, unplug major appliances, etc.).

KEY ORGANIZING TIPS

■ **Document It** If you're planning to travel abroad, make sure you have the proper documentation, such as passports and visas (and a current driver's license). Give yourself plenty of time to process the paperwork—a minimum of six weeks for a passport, an additional month for a visa—government bureaucracies such as the U.S. Passport Agency get swamped during peak travel times like summer.

■ **Test Drive It** Haven't gone camping in a long time? Set up that tent in your backyard ahead of time. Better to find out it's ripped before you leave than when you're in the midst of Mother Nature with nowhere to sleep.

■ **Confirm It** Regardless of the plane tickets or hotel confirmation in your hand, always call a day ahead to confirm all reservations. Not only does this provide peace of mind, but you can also check on special instructions, such as airline kids' meals or adjoining rooms.

■ **Leave a Paper Trail** Type up your itinerary, including hotel phone numbers, and either E-mail to several family members or photocopy and send in the mail. You might also want to include a list of your traveler's check serial numbers, a copy of your birth certificate, driver's license, credit card numbers, and airline tickets, just in case they get lost or stolen.

■ **Take the Day Off** The day before any major vacation, one adult should take the day off of work to check all the last-minute details, from packing the suitcases and the car to confirming all reservations. So, on the morning that you're scheduled to leave, there's little stress as you head out the door.

QUICK FIX

All the last-minute details can weigh you down, both physically and mentally. Try these easy tricks to lighten the load.

■ **Paper or Plastic?** Consider using a major credit card on the road rather than purchasing traveler's checks (although you should always carry some traveler's checks in case of emergency). Not only will you sidestep the hassle of buying and signing the checks, but you'll save in other ways, too. First, with a credit card there's no guessing how much money you should take with you; you pay as you go. Don't worry if you're traveling abroad either; Visa and MasterCard are widely accepted throughout Europe and much of Asia. And the exchange rate is more competitive when you use your credit card than when you transfer traveler's checks over to local currency. (But call your credit card company prior to departure to check for any hidden fees abroad.) ATM and debit cards using the Cirrus or Plus system are a good option when withdrawing cash—not only do you get a better exchange rate than traveler's checks, but there's no transaction fee (unlike withdrawing money from your credit card). Both Cirrus and Plus systems have more than 200,000 outlets in sixty countries, so you're never far from your money.

■ **What Number Please?** Leave your phone book at home and put your cell phone to use by keying in important phone numbers in the address book section; include numbers for your pediatrician, family members who have your itinerary, and, if you're traveling abroad, even the U.S. State Department or your state senator.

■ **Who's Looking After the House?** Forget finding someone to water the roses. Don't worry about stopping the mail and the newspaper delivery. Toss those light timers. Hire a house sitter to take care of it all. Ask a local college student or single adult seeking a little privacy from his or her roommates for the week. Having someone in the house while you're gone is a perfect solution—he or she can handle all those little annoying details ("Did you leave the iron on?") so that you can concentrate on having a good time.

Getting There Is Half the Fun

Sometimes stressful, more often, I hope, enjoyable, traveling to your destination is always an adventure in itself. Preparation is the key to tranquility (or at least a moment of it). In thinking about making the journey comfortable for all, take into account each person's needs—does your toddler have to have his blanket to take a nap? Make sure you have it with you on the plane or in the car. Make sure everyone has a pillow for the car and all toys are *quiet* (put a piece of tape over the speaker). And always plan for "just in case." Be sure to pack more snacks, juice, diapers, and fun activities than you think you'll need—planes and trains are notoriously late, and cars sometimes break down in the middle of nowhere. But most of all remember to take a deep breath before piling everyone in the car; this is supposed to be a vacation.

KEY ORGANIZING TIPS

■ **Time Waits for No One** There's always traffic when you need to get to the airport quickly. (Leave an hour earlier and window-shop in the terminal before boarding.) The kids inevitably start backseat fighting halfway to Grandma's house. (Stop at a rest stop and toss the Frisbee for fifteen minutes.) When you make getting there part of the adventure, you'll take the pressure off and start having fun sooner.

■ **Feed Me** Be prepared with a multitude of snacks. Go for healthy munchies that don't drip, leak, or stain, such as cheese sticks, cereal (Cheerios is always a favorite), dried fruit, and crackers. Prepare goodie bags in resealable plastic bags and have the kids stash one in their carry-on suitcases; or if you're traveling by car, have a small cooler filled and ready. Have plenty of water on hand, too. Give each family member his or her own bottle with a screw top (flip-tops leak).

⏰ **TIME-SAVER**—These days it seems nearly everyone has a brown or black canvas suitcase with wheels. To avoid grabbing at each one at the airport luggage terminal, mark your bag distinctively. It can be with something as simple as a brightly colored ribbon tied to the handle. Whatever you choose, it will save you time and the muscles in your back!

That's Entertainment

If travel time exceeds an hour by plane, or two hours by car, you've got to entertain your young troops or prepare for mutiny. To kids, contemplating the beauty of the scenery just doesn't cut it. First, encourage them to pack their own day packs (or leave room in their carry-on suitcases) with favorite toys, books, or art supplies. Unfortunately, the magic of things familiar may only last a short time. The rest is up to you. From travel games such as License Plate Bingo and Twenty Questions to comic books and music, be prepared with a plethora of activities.

*B*elieve it or not, toy catalogs—Lilly's Kids, Sensational Beginnings—are *great reading material for toddlers and preschoolers during long car rides. John and Jackie can spend an hour scouring the pages, discussing each item. They don't need to read, either; the pictures are enough to tell the story.*

QUICK FIX

■ **Surprise!** Although it's a good idea to buy a supply of inexpensive toys to slowly dole out to each child during a long car or plane ride, it's often simple pleasures that kids get into more. My boys, for instance, snubbed a set of miniature building blocks during a cross-country flight and instead spent an hour building a contraption using none other than tape and paper. Go figure.

■ **Headphone Heaven** Purchase an inexpensive cassette player and headset. Buy or borrow books on tape, or record your own voice reading your child's favorite stories (take the books with you and have her follow along). And don't forget extra batteries!

■ **Seat Rotation** Every hour or so (depending on whether you're in a car, plane, or train) have everyone switch seats. It's amazing what a new face will do to sagging morale.

■ **Map Your Way** If you're traveling by car, get a duplicate road map and laminate it. Let the kids play navigator as they use a washable marker to highlight the route.

■ **Document It** Give your children disposable cameras, a small tape recorder, or a journal and pen, and instruct them to document the trip, from the sights and sounds of the airport to the family's impressions of roadside food!

■ **Treats Rock!** Never underestimate the quiet pleasure that a sugar-free lollipop affords.

*J*ohn and I always say the best money we ever spend on a vacation is when *we let the kids buy Slurpees. They sit by the pool for a good half hour— totally quiet—crunching away on the flavored ice. It's pure relaxation.*

We're Here! Now What?

You made it! Rather than rushing out the door the moment you set foot in your hotel room to hit the first site, hang out for a while, and let everyone unwind and check out your new digs. The biggest mistake that most families make while on vacation is scheduling too many events. It's understandable—there are so many wonderful things to do and never enough time to do them. But the point of a vacation is to relax and reconnect with family members, not to play beat the vacation clock. It's OK to skip an attraction or two in favor of just relaxing by the pool.

W*hen Marty and I take the kids on a road trip, we usually rent a van; this way the vacation starts the moment we leave the driveway. It's fun, different, and there is so much more room inside than our sedan.*

Before you left home you (hopefully) did enough research to know what's worthwhile seeing. Knowing approximately what you want to do before you hit the road is a better plan of action than deciding (and often arguing) once you reach your destination. If your kids are old enough, you may want to try letting each one pick the agenda for the day—it encourages all members to actively participate in a positive vacation experience, it takes the pressure off parents to be the perfect tour guides, and who knows, you just may see or learn something new. The key to a great time is flexibility.

KEY ORGANIZING TIPS

■ **Obey Nature** Unless your kids are extremely adaptable, try to obey their natural time clocks. If you're still roaming the theme park at two in the afternoon with your lethargic toddler, someone should head back to the hotel to let him have his afternoon nap. Try to keep meal- and bedtime close to what they are at home. You may be able to get away with a late dinner or two, but if you keep pushing the envelope, the consequences are often unpleasant. Cranky, whining children are real vacation busters.

■ **Prioritize** Decide with family members which activities are a "must see" or "must do," which ones are a "maybe," and which ones a "no go." Try to hit the top of your list first. If not, you'll run the risk of never getting to the choice spots. If you visit a dozen or so run-of-the-mill cathedrals in France, for instance, it may be difficult to rouse excitement in the kids when it comes time to visit Notre Dame.

■ **Ask the Locals** Still unsure about a few sites listed in your guidebook? Enlist the help of a local or two—your hotel concierge, front-desk attendant, or even your innkeeper. They always know which ones are hidden treasures and those that are a tourist bust.

■ **Schedule Downtime** Some families prefer to hit the tourist track first thing in the morning, take a late lunch, and then kick back at the beach or pool in the afternoon. Others find that having one full day followed by a laid-back day works better for their family. Either way, find some downtime for relaxing and just soaking up the local color.

■ **Be Realistic** Don't expect perfect behavior simply because you're on vacation—kids will be kids, no matter where they are.

Bon Voyage!

Traveling as a family can be a wonderful bonding experience—a time to devote totally to your children. Without the constant interruptions of phone calls and the hectic after-school activity schedule, being together on the road is the way to go.

Index